MW00377783

15 Generations of
American Stories:
Notable Descendants of
Immigrant Job Tyler

Norman Tyler

Copyright © 2019, Norman Raymond Tyler
  Ann Arbor, Michigan
All rights reserved

First Edition
For permission to reproduce selections from this book,
contact the author at ntyler@emich.edu

ISBN: 9781713277712

Contents

Acknowledgments

Special recognition is given to Willard I. Tyler Brigham, who over one hundred years ago spent many years documenting the family of immigrant Job Tyler, resulting in the 1912 publication of two volumes extensively documenting thousands of names and hundreds of brief biographies. Also especially recognized are Charles and Norma Tyler, who spent years supplementing Brigham's seminal work, resulting in a third volume of the Job Tyler family lineage. These volumes were the starting point for information included in this manuscript. With only minor exceptions, the material in these three volumes is not duplicated in this narrative but is intended to supplement it.

Many individuals offered assistance and support during the period of research and while developing the narrative for this book. Appreciation is given to individuals who were readers for this book during its evolution over three years. They included Kess Eldridge, Phil Gibbs, Alicia LaFrance, Mike Sadecki, David Sitomer, Natalie Tyler, Paul Tyler, Tory Tyler-Millar, Susan VanAllen, and Kim Vancor.

Special appreciation is due to my spouse and partner-in-life, Ilene Tyler. She patiently listened to many of my stories about Tyler family members from earlier generations discovered during research for this manuscript. As a dedicated editor, she also read the manuscript through its many iterations. Without her support, the effort would not have been as complete as is now presented to you as a reader.

Sources for photographs and graphics included are either footnoted or, if not footnoted, are available in the public domain.

It should be noted that with the exception of quoted material, the work included in this narrative is that of the author only. Any errors are mine alone.

Author Biography

Norman Tyler is a historian, architect, and city planner with a special interest in historic preservation. For many years he served as president of the national Job Tyler Family Association. He has authored other books on diverse topics, including city planning, historic preservation, Greek Revival architecture, the history of transportation, and the Peace Corps. He is proud two of his books have been translated into Chinese and Korean.

Norm has been recognized nationally as a professor and practitioner of urban planning, serving for many years as director of the Urban and Regional Planning Program at Eastern Michigan University. He has given many presentations on community planning and historic preservation at national, state, and local conferences. In 2012 he received national recognition, being inducted into the planning profession's College of Fellows.

He has been on the board of numerous community and professional organizations and has long been a community activist who ardently cares about making a difference. He served as president of the Job Tyler Family Association from 1989 to 2002, organizing a number of national and regional reunions of Association members and others.

Currently he lives with his spouse, Ilene, in a historic house in Ann Arbor, Michigan. They love traveling the world together. When home, he enjoys carpentry projects, playing piano and, of course, writing. When asked which of his books is his favorite, he replies, "My next one!"

More on Norm is available at his web site: tylertopics.com.

Introduction

Three genealogical high points

The family lineage of immigrant Job Tyler, who arrived in America in 1638, has been researched by hundreds of genealogists and family members over the past 150 years. The narrative arc of this Tyler family history is built around three high points. The first is the seventeenth-century arrival of Job Tyler, bringing an interesting family line in England to America as one of the first settlers in the Massachusetts Bay Colony. The early generations of this family line include many independent individuals who helped in the creation a new nation.

The second high-point in this family history is the culmination of the work of researcher Willard I. Tyler Brigham, who extensively documented the Job Tyler family lineage with births, marriages, and deaths. His genealogy of the descendants of Job Tyler covered the seventeenth to nineteenth centuries. His two volumes, published in 1912 and titled, *The Tyler Genealogy: The Descendants of Job Tyler, of Andover, Massachusetts,* includes data on seven thousand names, including brief biographies of many of these family members. We are deeply indebted to Brigham for this work that has become the basic genealogical resource for the Job Tyler family line. Because Brigham's Volumes I and II are readily available online and well known by many members of the larger family, the biographical information from these volumes is not repeated in the following chapters.

The third high point is the 1980s and 90s, when many researchers wrote updates on the Brigham book based on their own families. Virtually all of these more recent family genealogies were distributed primarily to their own family members, either through copy or self-published versions. Distributed more broadly was a Volume III of the Job Tyler genealogy titled *The Descendants of Job Tyler Since 1619,* written by my parents, Charles and Norma Tyler, and myself and published in 1985, with new information collected from sources across the country.

The material included in the following chapters comes from a variety of sources not so well known. They include genealogical web sites (listed in the final chapter); correspondence with members of the extended family; online research (thank you, Google); the genealogy written by Charles Tyler, etal.; other books; and anywhere else relevant material could be found. I have tried to establish reliable sources, and discrepancies between sources are described. Since some of the information is conflicting, it is presented as found and interpreted as transparently as possible. It is left to the reader to accept or challenge these sources.

The reader will find each person described in one of the following biographies has two numbers following their name. The first number is taken from the three volumes of Job Tyler genealogies (Brigham and Tyler). The second is their WikiTree ID number, the software I have selected for presenting the extended Tyler family tree online (wikitree.com). Each person has both numbers included. For example, the author's two numbers, the genealogy number and WikiTree number, would be presented as: (#9114; Tyler-5642). I trust you will find these references useful if you look up information on relatives.

Sit back with a cup of coffee and enjoy the many wonderful stories derived from the lives of Tylers in America. Welcome to the wonderful history of the Job Tyler family.

Chapter 1: Tylers in Early English History

Walter ("Wat") Tyler and the English Peasants Rebellion

We begin with a story of violence and revolt in early England. There has long been speculation regarding whether immigrant Job Tyler comes from the lineage eleven generations before of Walter "Wat" Tyler. A definite connection has not been established, but it is likely some relationship over the generations will eventually be confirmed. Because of Wat Tyler's significance in English history, his role is described in this brief background on early English history.

Some people are known as heroes of a century or heroes of a generation. Few, however, are remembered as the hero of nine days.[1] Wat Tyler was a notorious rogue who for nine dramatic days was leader of a historic revolt in England, an uprising of peasants opposing the rule of King Richard II.

Tyler was an English citizen who in 1381 helped launch a brief and unsuccessful popular uprising known as the English Peasants Rebellion (otherwise known as the Wat Tyler Rebellion). The revolt had various causes—the socio-economic and political tensions generated by the Black Death in the 1340s, high taxes resulting from the Hundred Years War with France, the establishing of a new poll tax on every adult, and the peasants' demand for individual freedom through the elimination of serfdom. The final trigger for the revolt was an attempt to collect unpaid poll taxes, which ended in a violent confrontation that spread rapidly across southeast England.

More than 60,000 people are reported to have been involved, not all of them peasants; some were soldiers and tradesmen, as well as a few disillusioned churchmen. Wat Tyler emerged as the rebellion's leader during a climactic march to London to challenge the king. During the march the peasants caused destruction in towns along the way. They burned down buildings housing government records, destroyed tax records and registers, and removed the heads from tax officials who objected to their behavior.

When they reached London the rebels found that supporters had left the city's gates open for them and they easily entered. Unfortunately, Wat Tyler soon lost control of many in the group who became tempted by the "pleasures" of the city. Their activities included destruction, looting, and some murders, including the deaths of the Lord Chancellor and Lord High Treasurer.

In an attempt to prevent further devastation, King Richard II, at the time only fourteen years old, agreed to meet with Wat. To stop the rebellion, the king gave into all of the peasant demands and asked they go home in peace. Satisfied with the outcome—a promised end to serfdom and feudalism—many did start the journey home. However, at a follow-up conference blows were exchanged. An angry mayor of London, William Walworth, first wounded Wat, and one of the king's squires fell upon Wat and stabbed him in the stomach. He died soon after.

Wat's death meant the brief revolt ultimately failed, and the King went back on his promises. However, the nine days are historically significant as the first peasant rebellion of note in English history, and it was led by one of England's first Tylers.

Stabbing of Wat Tyler at Peasants Revolt

Job Tyler's Family in England

Laurence (Lawrence) Tyler, father of immigrant Job

The following well-researched account of Laurence Tyler (Tyler #7925; Tyler-425) was found in files of the Job Tyler Family Association archives. It was written by an unknown author and included no reference resource but appears to have a high level of accuracy and so is included as part of this narrative.

Many sources cite Job as coming from Shropshire County in England. This article presents a convincing alternative, giving background describing Job's father, Laurence, living in Kent County in southeast England, rather than Shropshire in the western midlands. In addition, Laurence's burial records, shown in the following section, indicate he was buried in Staplehurst Parish, which is located in Kent, giving further credence to the following description. Future researchers will need to clarify this disparity.

Staplehurst Church, Kent County, England

"Cranbrook, Kent, in 1635 was a parish town, a market town, and the center of Kent's clothing industry. Even though it was a market town and parish town, there was only one main street and only a small part of it was paved. The rest of the town streets were very foul in the winter and very inconvenient on market days. Generally speaking, life expectancy in Kent was 35 years, with half the population dying before reaching 16. The chief causes of death were malnutrition, smallpox, typhus, and plague. Sanitation was poor and housing was overcrowded.

"In Kent, the largest landowner was the church. Followed by a dozen or so nobles and gentry. After them were several hundred lesser gentry and a large number of wealthy yeomen. There were several thousand freeholders who usually had a small farm in a single parish. Freeholders paid a nominal quit-rent, but were otherwise like modern property owners. Below these groups were tenants and various kinds of homeless people. A majority of the people were in the last two groups. Somewhere between twenty and thirty percent of the population was too poor to pay any taxes.

"There was a good deal of political and religious unrest in Kent during this period. Some nonconformists (Puritans) were refusing to tithe and were fined or jailed as a result. The Church of England was attempting to make all English citizens conform and was taking increasingly strong steps to make sure that people and money came its way. East Anglia and Kent were a part of England that had a tradition of resisting what the people there saw to be the use of arbitrary authority.

"It is in this context that we consider why Job Tyler left England and why he came to Massachusetts. The clothing industry in and around Cranbrook was in decline and would not recover. The population of the town was declining as well. Pressure from the Church of England was increasing and would culminate in the British Civil War. Emigrants from Kent had been leaving for the New World since the Great Migration had begun in 1630 and even before. Cranbrook did have a free grammar school founded in 1574 and a writing school founded in 1573. Job Tyler was literate, with literacy being defined as the ability to write his name. So he probably had attended the local school. And it appeared that Job Tyler would not inherit even part of his father's land.

"Laurence Tyler, Job's father, was a substantial yeoman. He owned land himself and rented land from Thomas Ensigne. We do not know how much land Laurence owned, but he rented 26 acres from Ensigne. This was at a time when five to ten acres would be a self-sufficient farm at a rather low standard of living. It seemed that Laurence owned and rented land in both Cranbrook and in Staplehurst, a small village about four miles from Cranbrook. In 1663, when Laurence Tyler died, he gave land to one daughter, distributed 190 pounds to various family members, and left the rest of his estate to his wife and another daughter.

"Laurence Tyler's death took place many years after son Job left for America. We can only speculate about what Laurence may have told his sons about his estate plans. Still, his will was unusual for that time and place. Primogeniture was not particularly common in Kent during that time period, so the inheritance rule was usually based on gavelkind. That is, the land was equally divided among the sons at the father's death. A less common alternative was to leave the land to one son and money to the others. Daughters usually inherited personal property. Laurence's will was almost the opposite of this practice. Two of his daughters inherited his land and his sons got cash. The third daughter got cash through her children, with the five grandchildren inheriting 100 pounds. The three sons, including Job, inherited 90 pounds in total."

An article written by Walter G. Davis in 1961 describes the will of Job's father, Laurence Tyler, written in 1663. As described in the previous section, in the will no land was given to Job; instead he was given forty pounds. This gave Job the freedom and possible incentive to emigrate to America.

"Laurence Tyler of Cranbrook, County Kent, yeoman, 'being aged and weak in body,' made his will on 10 Jan. 1663 'in our English computacon.' My son Jobe Tyler 'who is now in Old England' shall make, seal and send over a sufficient release of all his right, interest and title he or his heirs may have in a piece of land that I lately purchased of Thomas Everis of Staplehurst, wherein I joined him as purchasor with myself. For now I give the same piece of land with the house and barn newly erected thereon with a garden and other parcel of land adjoining thereto to my daughter Rebecca Page and her heirs for ever. In lieu of this I give to my said son Jobe Tyler £40. To my son John Tyler, £10. To my son Moses Tyler, £40. To my daughter Mary Potter's five children £100, namely to Mary Potter £20 on 25 Dec. 1672, to James Potter £20 on 25 Dec. 1677, to Jobe Potter £20 on 25 Dec. 1681, to John Potter £20 on 25 Dec.1682, and to Thomas Potter £20 on 25 Dec. 1684. Residue to Dorothy my wife, and Mary Potter, my daughter, whom I make executrices. They are to have the advice and consent of my two friends Mr. Hormone Sheaf of Cranbrook and Mr. John Stephens of Staplehurst, clothiers, whom I make my overseers. Witnesses: Darthy Bayly, Elizabeth Hodgkin, Richard Kingsnoth. Proved 14 March 1663. (Consistory Court of Canterbury, 32/53/201)"[2]

In this version of the Will of Laurence Tyler five children are named: John Tyler, baptized 24 June 1610 in Cranbrook, Kent, England;[3] Job (Jobe) Tyler 1619 – 1700, baptized in Cranbrook, 12 Oct 1617;[4] Rebecca Tyler born 1622; Moses Tyler 1623 – 1670. son of Laurence, bpt 30 Jan 1619 [1619/20], Cranbrook;[5] and Mary Tyler 1625 - bpt. Cranbrook 13 Nov 1603.[6]

Note the baptism dates sometime pre-date the birth date. These discrepancies are common in old records. Because the year of birth is often forgotten by families or is inaccurately recorded later, the baptism date as a church record is considered more reliable. This indicates Job Tyler was likely born in 1617, rather than the more commonly recorded 1619. Brigham established the date of 1619 in his Volume I based on a 1659 deposition stating his age as "about 40 yeares," but since this was not a firm dating but only a supposition it is possible the 1617 date would be feasible.

There is one more complication in all this dating. Although the will of Laurence Tyler shown above includes five offspring, the burial record for Laurence Tyler, found in the Staplehurst parish registers (burials, 1653-1695), states he was the father of ten children. They include: Job Tyler 1619 – 1700, Roger Tyler 1621 –

1673, Rebecca Tyler 1622 -, Moses Tyler 1623 – 1670, Mary Tyler 1625 -, Rebecca Tyler 1627 -, Abigail Tyler 1629 -, Charles Tyler 1630 – 1724, Robert Tyler 1635 – 1674, William Tyler Sr. 1644 – 1691.[7] It can be assumed the burial record accurately lists the number of offspring and the will of Laurence omitted reference to other of his children for undetermined reasons.

Minus Three Generations

Tyler family genealogist Forrest Rickly has extended the Job Tyler family lineage back three generations, well into the sixteenth century. Although his online records are extensive, he has not included the sources for this information and it is therefore subject to verification.[8]

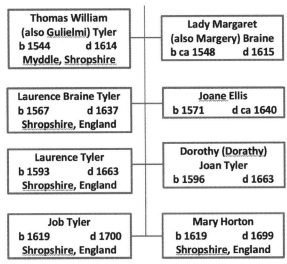

Three generations of ancestors of immigrant Job Tyler

8

Chapter 2: Immigrant Job Tyler's Arrival

Coming to America

There were many reasons emigrants from England crossed the Atlantic to get to the new land that was yet to become a nation. There were religious difficulties for many, especially under the harsh rule of the Stuarts, Kings James and Charles. America's first settlers tended to be radicals in both religion and politics, but gradually became settlers more interested in taking advantage of the opportunities in a region with unlimited land available and little oversight by an overruling power. Economic difficulties also encouraged many pioneers. The economy was poor in England and Europe, and stories were spreading of gold and silver found in the New World. Younger men desired to be part of this shift of commerce and adventure with seemingly unlimited possibilities.

As knowledge of the New World increased among the general population, opportunities seemed more varied and alluring. With limitless tracts of unappropriated land in the new land, chances of success in agriculture were great and property ownership was highly regarded as a way to wealth, as well as a basis for a respectable social and political position. There was also an inherent love of adventure at that time, with curiosity concerning unknown peoples, lands, and resources. Sometimes referred to as the Three Gs, colonial exploration by the European nations was typically based on the multiple goals of God (religious freedom and conversion of natives), Gold (finding new resources), and Glory (bringing prestige and power to the mother country).

As more settlers arrived, the goals of settlers became simpler. Generally, they were looking to build a homestead for themselves and their family in a safe environment and help establish and become members of a new community. There was inevitably hope for a better life for their children, a generation born in America that would have increased opportunities coupled with reduced hardships.

The story of the frontier is not merely one of settlements, but of institutions that were transported and transformed. Even in the early years, education was considered a priority. Governor William Bradford, a Puritan separatist who emigrated to the Plymouth Colony on the *Mayflower*, served as governor of the Plymouth Colony intermittently for thirty years. In 1624 he noted that families were educating their own children, and there was as yet no common school, even though the need for proper schooling was realized. Such facilities would soon be established in each settlement.

Why Job Tyler left Cranbrook, Kent, England

The year 1638 generally has been considered the year of the arrival of immigrant Job Tyler. However, a Tyler family historian argues there is evidence Job Tyler (16 years old) was on the Globe ship at Gravesend, England, and in Boston in late 1635, where there were several persons from Cranbrook, Kent, that Job (and his father) likely would have known. Navigation probabilities support the notion that the Globe's captain had planned to stop in Boston or got caught in an autumn storm in 1635, allowing Job to jump ship at that point before the Globe proceeded south.

New England Settlement, 1637[9]

The following section is a continuation of the article (author unknown) presented in the previous chapter on Job Tyler's father, Laurence, in Kent County, England. It describes Job Tyler (#1; Tyler-122) leaving Kent and emigrating to America.

"The bulk of Laurence's estate went to his daughters and his wife. Comparatively little went to his sons. Perhaps Job knew his father's intentions when he left England and perhaps he did not. Perhaps he was seeking adventure. But he was leaving a town where the only industry was in decline, where there was a good deal of political and religious unrest, and where his prospects could not have been promising.

"Job Tyler boarded the ship *Globe*, Jeremy Blackman, Master, at Gravesend. He had been examined by the minister of Gravesend for religious conformity and, having taken the oath of allegiance and supremacy, set sail for Virginia on August 7, 1635.[10]

"Job Tyler may have been on a ship that set sail for Virginia, but he was really headed for Massachusetts. How he ended up in Massachusetts is in question. He may have jumped ship in Boston, he may have gone to Virginia first, then on to Massachusetts. There is evidence for either of those possibilities. But from a cultural point of view, there is no doubt that he would go to New England. Massachusetts Bay and Virginia were vastly different cultures sharing the same language.

"New England was where the people from Kent were going. Charles Banks, in his *Topographical Dictionary of 2885 English Emigrants to New England, 1620-1650*, listed 198 emigrants from Kent. Seven of those emigrants were from Cranbrook, five from Staplehurst and 10 from Biddenden, a village five miles from Cranbrook and one mile from Staplehurst. Banks' sample was not all inclusive. As examples, John Biggs of Maidstone lists friends and family in New England, some of whom were from Cranbrook. Anderson mentions several children of the former minister in Cranbrook who came to America. And there is a cemetery in Scituate, Massachusetts, called the "Men of Kent" cemetery, locally called Meetinghouse Lane Cemetery. The Kent emigrants in Banks list made up 6.8% of the total. If that percentage held true for the 25,000 New England emigrants, 1,700 people in new England would have been from Kent. So Job was bound for a place where he knew some of the people and was known by them. He shared their language, religion, and cultural background.

"Our first confirmation of Job Tyler in New England was recorded by John Winthrop in late 1637. In an addendum to his history, Winthrop noted that "Job Tiler, servant to Richard Baldwin of Mount Wollaston, brought before me, and treasurer, secretary, etc. He confessed he did attempt to have carnal knowledge of the body of Jane, the daughter of the said Richard, two times, but could not. Women had searched her, and found no act committed. We committed him to prison etc. Freed from prison, Job went to Newport, Rhode Island. That destination was a result of the antinomian controversy, I suspect. [*Authors Note: the antinomian controversy pitted Puritan minister John Cotton against many of the local ministers and magistrates in a theological debate—the value of "good works" over "free grace."*]

"The following year Job was a squatter in Andover."

Other accounts of Job's arrival

It is a general rule of historical research that information should either be from a verifiable legitimate source or should be supported through at least two separate sources. There are many instances where interesting information is found from early documents but does not pass this test of accuracy. The following sections include examples of historical information on Job's arrival that, although feasible and interesting to consider, should be viewed with skepticism. They are included here to illustrate the limitations of reliable research for the seventeenth century.

Ship's Manifest

Reliable records of the arrival of immigrants are generally included in a ship's manifest. The text of the manifest of the Globe ship arriving in Virginia in August 1635 includes many misspellings but begins with basic information and includes "Jo Tyler" among its long list of passengers, listed as sixteen years old at the time. If indeed this is our Job, he actually arrived three years before the time indicated by family historian Willard Brigham. Although nothing would have been known of his activities during this three-year period, if it was Job he would eventually make his way to Massachusetts where records of his arrival begin in 1638. Then again, this could have been a different individual entirely.

Manifest of the Globe

"Globe of London to Virginia 1635

"Theis under written names are to be transported to Virginea imbarqued in the Globe of London Jeremy Blackman Master have been examined by the

Minister of Gravesend of their conformitie & have taken the oaths of Allege & Supremacie.

"... Jo Tyler, 16" [11]

Job jumps ship

It is interesting to note the many versions of Job's arrival, based on limited documents. The following record is from the Rhode Island Historical Society, sent by a Mrs. Mudgett of Montecito, California. It is included as an example of questionable information that must be sorted through by researchers:

"The ship that Job was on was headed for Virginia and contained only young ones like himself—probably delinquents being sent to relatives or as servants. He was only 16 and an orphan. (Note: It is well documented Job was the son of Laurence Tyler.) When the boat stopped in Boston he and a few others jumped ship. He sent to Rev. John Eliot, 'The Apostle of the Indians,' who acted as a guardian. Perhaps Job was being sent to William Tyler in Virginia, who was one of the few white men who escaped the Indian massacre of 1622 and may have been the William Tyler to whom Shakespeare gave a ring ('in token of our friendship') in Stratford." [12] (*Author's Note: If this account is accurate, it argues that the Job Tyler lineage is likely tied with the lineage of President John Tyler.*)

Three brothers arrive

Moses Coit Tyler was a distinguished American historian from the nineteenth century whose notable biography is included in a later chapter of this book. An account of the life of Moses Coit was discovered in a 364-page unpublished dissertation from The University of Michigan written in 1933 by Thomas Edgar Casady and edited and published by Howard Mumford Jones after the original author's death. [13] The first paragraph of this book is one of the most intriguing, for the author begins with the story of the arrival of Moses Coit's forebears, including the arrival of immigrant Job. For those familiar with the Job Tyler lineage, it sounds familiar, but also presents an interesting twist. It presents a common theory (often disputed) that Job arrived in Virginia with two brothers, each of whom traveled to a different section of the country. Although there is much argument among serious Tyler researchers regarding this account, here is how the book begins...

"Some twenty years after the arrival of the Mayflower, three brothers named Tyler landed at Plymouth after a long voyage from their native Shropshire, seated themselves on a log, partook of their refreshments, arose, embraced and kissed each other, and then went each his way, 'and it saith not that they ever again met.' One settled in Virginia, one in New Haven, and one in Andover near Boston. Unconscious of destiny, the Virginia brother, by name Henry, was the ancestor of John Tyler, tenth President of the United States. Brother Job, a restless soul, was the ancestor of Moses Coit Tyler, the historian."

This sheds new light on the theory that the Job Tyler line is somehow connected with the President Tyler line, a theory that has been under review for decades. What is the source of information the author(s) cite for this information? It is found in the first endnote of the Moses Coit biography. It indicates the authors had not yet reviewed Willard Brigham's genealogy of Job Tyler, in which Brigham began his narrative stating "he had never been able to 'find a scintilla of evidence upon which to base' the tradition that Job Tyler was a native of Shropshire, England." However, the Moses Coit biography cites two other sources worth looking into.

> "Henry Tyler of Shropshire, England was one of three brothers who settled in VA, MA, and CT. Henry settled in Charles City, VA in 1652. In Vol. III of the Virginia Land Register is the record of a Patent in Henry Tyler's name dated Jan 7, 1652, locating 254 acres in Middle Plantation, VA, due to him by and for transporting to this colony six persons. Henry is a descendant of Wat Tyler, according to G.C. Greer in his "Early Virginia Immigrants." Henry Tyler lived in the outskirts of what is now the city of Williamsburg, Virginia.

> "At June Court 1672, Ann Tyler his relic [widow], (Henry), entered a record of Deed of Gift disposing of her separate estate among her three sons, Henry, John and Daniel." (*Note: There were no heirs by his first wife paraphrased from the copy made by Moses Coit Tyler from MS of his father, Elisha Tyler, at Detroit in 1857.*)

> ". . . The three brothers are believed to have emigrated from Shropshire, perhaps as early as 1640, certainly by 1653. See the sketch of Tyler's ancestry compiled by Professor George Lincoln Burr of Cornell University in the New England Historical and Genealogical Register, vol. 55 (1901), pp. xciii-xcv; and for corroborative detail see James Savage, A Genealogical Dictionary of the First Settlers of New England (Boston, 1860), vol. IV, pp. 354-6. I have seen only certain pages of the official Tyler genealogy."

This account, although appearing to be well documented, is in direct conflict with records shown previously indicating that Job's father lived in Kent County, England, and not in the distant town of Shropshire. It is left to the reader to make of all this what they will.

Job's wanderings lead him to Essex County, Massachusetts

There is ambiguity about the date and place of Job's arrival in the eastern part of the Massachusetts Bay Colony. The Colony had been given a charter in 1630, just a few years before Job's arrival. Andover, located twenty-one miles north of Boston, was originally settled in 1636. In 1640, an appeal was made to establish a town with twenty families at the site. At that time the land had not been cleared for farming, and the local natives crudely tilled the fields and hunted and fished along its streams. The first permanent settlement was established in 1642, and four years later it became incorporated as the Town of Andover in 1646. The old burying ground, now part of North Andover and the site of a number of Tyler graves, marks the center of the early town of Andover.

There are numerous local historians in the vicinity of Andover, Massachusetts, who have written articles that include information on the early Tyler settlers, including this 2013 review: "There was a 'tradition' that Job Tyler was already in Andover when the first documented settlers arrived. That's according to Sarah Loring Bailey, whose detailed accounts of Andover's earliest happenings are incomparably described in her 1880 book, *Historical Sketches of Andover, Massachusetts*. She speculates as to whether being here first may have given him a sense of entitlement [not her exact words]. We will never know; however, it would have taken a great deal of courage to live alone in the wilderness."[14]

Historic view of Andover, Massachusetts[15]

There is very little information regarding what Job did upon his arrival in Andover in 1640. He was not included on the list of twenty-three founders of the town, so likely had little status as a young, single immigrant.

This paragraph, taken from *"Early Records of the Tyler Family of Andover,"* written by Charlotte Helen Abbott (no date) is the earliest indication of his arrival and gives an inkling of when he came to Massachusetts. "Job's early wanderings are unrecorded, but the first comers to Andover found him here, in 1640, a squatter in the Boxford section with a home in what is now the driveway of the old Wood's estate."[16] The Wood's estate referred to is the historic Tyler Homestead in West Boxford, Massachusetts, indicating Job had moved a few miles to the settlement known as Boxford, a twenty-four square mile area that was part of Rowley Village. By the 1680s only about forty families lived there, most of them farmers and craftsmen.

Describing Job

A lengthy description of immigrant Job Tyler is found the first chapter of Brigham's Volume I of *The Tyler Genealogy*. This is an excellent starting point for biographical information on him, but because it is readily available to readers the following section draws from other sources to complement Brigham's description.

Job has been described as a rolling stone, living at one time or another in Mount Wollaston, Andover, Roxbury, Mendon and Boxford, Massachusetts. He seems to have often been in trouble.[17] He is described in a letter by Ann M. Tyler written sometime before 1924,

> "He was a rude, self-asserting, striking personality. Not to be left out of account are the forces that were to possess the land. There are but few highlights in the picture; the shadows are all there. He did not, as Prof.

Tyler [Moses Coit Tyler] says, learn prudence very fast, but was himself. He had a good deal of individuality, and he gave utterance to it at times with more vigor than grace. He did not shape his words to suit sensitive ears. He resented dictation and found it hard to restrain himself from what he wanted to do through any prudential policy. Yet when you shall read hereafter what manner of men his sons and grandsons were, and what they stood for in all the places where they lived; as you come down generation by generation, and see what thousands of descendants have stood for in their homes and before the public, in peace and in war, as pioneers and as dwellers in the cities, you will realize that there must have been good stock in the ole man; and he trained a family to be useful and honored in the communities in which they dwelt. Superstitious, willful, hot tempered, independent, and self-reliant, Job Tyler lives and breathes in this record nearly three centuries after his time. He did not have saints to live with; were all truly known, it would be seen that he was on a par with the majority of his neighbors. The Puritan iron-rule, that makes no allowance for any man, met a sturdy opposition in this possible descendant of Wat Tyler of England, and it is now too late to determine whether or not he was always justified. From this old canvas there gazes steadily out, not an ideal, but a very real personage—an out and out Yankee type."[18]

Family historians can be prompted to research their ancestors in many ways. One web site, "52 Ancestors in 52 Weeks," encourages individuals to write something about one of their relatives at least once a week for at least a year and post these descriptions on this site. One relatively lengthy posting to this web site dated 2015 was particularly critical of Job Tyler, being described as "evil incarnate." The author is unknown, but he or she writes a dreadful account of Job and his family during these early colonial years. This account should be read with a great deal of incredulity.

"Job Tyler is my eleventh great-grandfather. He was born in 1617 in Cranbrook, Kent, England and baptised on October 12, 1617 according to the 'Tyler Index to Parish Registers, 1538-1874.'

"...in 1638, an 18-year-old who may have been a descendant by the name of Job Tyler became the first settler of Andover, Massachusetts. He and his brother (John Tyler) had left England when their father was beheaded by King Charles I, due to bitter debates rising from a law-making body of which he was a member. (From *The Legacy of the Tylers* by Clark L. Smithson)... He arrived in Newport, Rhode Island in 1638 and on March 20 of that year he married Mary Horton (possibly the Widow Horton).

"... What a rabble-rouser Job was. He was a fighter for what he perceived as his rights, whether he was in the right or wrong and as it seems, he was mostly in the wrong and not shy about stirring up trouble when it suited his purpose. He was evil personified with no conscience, remorse or guilt. His evilness was like a cancer that spread, and it infected the entire family most of whom were the victims, except for his son Moses Tyler, who was a little more spiteful or revengeful than his father and also without a conscience. He turned against his own family in a personal vendetta accusing many of the wives of his brothers of being witches and convincing the husbands that they were. (Jeanette Maloney)

"There are records of legal issues and complaints that go from Andover to Rowley to Mendon and around the region. It looks like Job didn't suffer fools easily and defended his family with fierce protectiveness – until he and Moses turned on his family for, it appears, not being independent enough and following the herd of social pressure.

". . . In 1671, with little more than the clothes on their backs, Job and his family moved west to the new town of Mendon, a land of apple trees and wild cranberries. They settled beyond the last garrison houses, the only places of safety during Indian raids. There, up the Blackstone River, Job helped establish the new settlement. His blacksmith son, Hopestill, was attracted by the iron ore found in the swamps. His daughter, Mary, now married to widower John Post, went with the family.'

"In 1676 an Indian raid on Mendon destroyed the town, yet again leaving the family with nothing except the pewter plates and brass kettles that they managed to bury in time in the swamps. John Post was killed by the Indians. His wife Mary (Tyler) Post and their young daughters, Mary Post and Hannah Post, survived as well as his daughter, Susannah Post, by his previous marriage. In 1678, Hopestill Tyler married Mary Lovett, daughter of Mendon neighbor Richard Lovett. In the next year Hopestill and his new wife loaded their precious feather bed and settled in the south part of Andover, where he took up his trade as blacksmith. Hopestill's sister Mary (Tyler) Post, now remarried to blacksmith John Bridges, settled in the north part of Andover.

". . . By 1680 Job and his sons, Moses Tyler and John Tyler, managed to make their way back to their original safe haven in Rowley Village, and settled there permanently. As before, they tried to avoid the taxes of both Rowley Village and Andover by settling in the area between the two centers. However, Job Tyler and his son Moses were duly inspected to see if they attended church services, with the result that they were assigned to pay rates to the Andover church.

"By 1688, Job had returned to Mendon. The last official record of him was his deed of his land in Mendon to his son Moses in November 1700.

"Job died in 1700 and was buried in Andover in the old burying ground. Job's son Moses Tyler learned and retained one important lesson from his father's experiences; witchcraft accusations represented a powerful weapon to use against enemies.[19]

Job's dispute with John Godfrey

"The first solid documentation of Job Tyler or his family occurs in 1648, when his wife was mentioned as being a victim of an accused witch, John Godfrey of Andover. [The Godfrey events occurred decades before the Salem witch trial hysteria.] Godfrey was said to cause the Devil to appear in many shapes, and one of those shapes was a bird that 'had come to suck the wife of Job Tyler, of Andover, and she and others had fallen into strange fits and sickness.' (Bailey). Godfrey was acquitted and sued his accusers for defamation, presumably including Tyler. Perhaps Tyler was ordered to pay damages to Godfrey or perhaps not, but, in 1650, Tyler mortgaged his house, land, and three cows to a Newbury man, an unusual transaction by a pioneer."[20]

The account of Job's confrontation with John Godfrey represents one of Job's earliest and most colorful longstanding disputes. It is described as part of Job's biography found in Volume I of Brigham's *The Tyler Genealogy*. The following lengthy description available online and written as part of the family history of the Duff family of Indiana complements well the earlier story.

"On November 1, 1646 permission is granted by the town elders of Dedham for Lambert Genry to sell his land 'beyond the mill creek' to Tyler of Roxbury. Roxbury church records record that on January 28, 1646 a twin infant of Job Tyler's died. The infant was probably the twin brother or sister of Hopestill Tyler who was born about 1646. Soon after the death of the infant Job returned to Andover and on March 5, 1650, he mortgaged property there to John Godfrey. This was the beginning of trouble for Job. He was indebted to John Godfrey for sixteen pounds to be paid on March 1, 1652. The payment was to be made in wheat valued at four shillings per bushel and rye at three shillings, six pence per bushel. Collateral on the loan was Job's house, land and three cows.

"On April 18, 1662, Job deeded his house and twenty-five acres of land to Godfrey. The deed was to be voided if Job paid bonds (promissory notes) from Anthony Sumerby when they became due. Currency was scarce in colonial times and Job was probably paying a debt to Godfrey with promissory notes given him by Sumerby. If Sumerby failed to pay Job on the due date of the bonds, and Job failed to pay Godfrey, Job would lose his home to Godfrey.

"Godfrey was not well liked in the colony and he was described as a hard-bitten moneylender. The Tylers apparently had some bitterness towards him since they accused him of witchcraft in 1658. The accuser and principal sufferer from Godfrey's 'wiles' was Job's wife Mary. The Tylers brought the accusation against Godfrey as part of a lawsuit they filed against him in that year. The deposition was sworn to in 1659 and brought forward again in 1665 in connection with another lawsuit. This was twenty-seven years before the famous Salem witch trials. The accusation of witchcraft illustrates the attitudes in Puritan Massachusetts.
To paraphrase, the document states, 'The deposition of Job Tyler aged about 40 years, Mary his wife, Moses Tyler his son aged between 17 and 18 years and Mary Tyler about 15 years old. These deponents witness that they saw a thing like a bird come in the door of their house with John Godfrey in the night, about the size of a blackbird, or rather bigger, to wit, as big as a pigeon, and it flew about, John Godfrey trying to catch it. The bird vanished through a chink of a jointed board. This was as they remember about 5 or 6 years later.' Apparently, the court did not give much weight to this accusation and Job lost the lawsuit in 1665.

Godfrey was not the only person with whom Job had legal difficulties. Job apprenticed his son Hopestill to Thomas Chandler of Andover in about 1655. For some reason Job changed his mind about the bargain. He went to the home of Nathan Parker, where the apprenticeship document was kept, and took it when Parker was not at home. This matter was in the courts for ten years. Finally, in 1665 Job lost the suit. The court decided that since Job was poor he should not be fined above six pounds, but the court ordered him to write a confession "in a plain legible hand" and nail it to the posts of the Puritan meetinghouses in Andover and Roxbury. Known now as "Job's Confession," it shows a personality that was always ready to challenge others. Paraphrased here, this account is taken from Sidney Perley's *History of Boxford* (1880):

"whereas it appears by sufficient testimony that I, Job Tyler, have shamefully reproached Thomas Chandler of Andover by saying he is a base, lying cozening [tricky], cheating knave; that he got his estate by cozening [trickery] in a base reviling manner and that he was recorded for a liar. That he was a cheating, lying whoreing knave fit for all manner of bawdry, wishing that the devil had him. Therefore, I Job Tyler do acknowledge that I have in these expressions most wickedly slandered the said Thomas Chandler. That without any just ground, unable to prove these slanderous accusations against him I can do no less than express myself to be sorry for them, and for my cursing of him. I desire God and the said Thomas to forgive me, and that no person should think the worse of Thomas Chandler because of any of these, my sinful expressions, and I engage myself for the future to be more careful of my expressions both concerning him, and I desire the Lord to help me to do so.

"Although the suits concerning Chandler and Godfrey were not settled until 1665, Job and his family left Andover and settled near Roxbury in 1662. In August, 1662, Job and Mary deeded part of their land in Andover to Thomas Abbot for a horse valued at ten pounds, ten shillings. Between June and August, 1662, Job and his wife Mary deeded several acres of land, their house and barn to Godfrey. Since no money is mentioned in the transaction it is probable that Job was forced to deed over his home to Godfrey for defaulting on debts he owed to Godfrey. Job and his family left Andover and went to back to Roxbury.

"The year 1665 was not a good one for Job. In addition to losing his lawsuits against Chandler and Godfrey in Andover, he found himself in trouble in his new home in Roxbury. In September, 1665, Owannamang, an Indian chief living near Marlborough complained that Job Tyler of Roxbury cut and carried off hay from his meadows. The authorities fined Job two shillings, six pence and made him pay the chief ten shillings for the hay. By 1669, Job had moved to Mendon and was soon in trouble there with the Puritan town and church authorities. On July 14, 1669, the selectmen (town officials) met and ordered the constable to summon Job Tyler to come before them the next Friday at Gregory Cook's house. Job was to answer for his contempt of their orders, and why he refused to work on the cellar at the minister's house. Job told the constable that we could not and would not come, but if the selectmen had more to say to him they could come to him.

"The town officials then resolved to take their complaint of his contempt of several of their orders to the magistrates. They also complained of Job's miscarriages of the Lord's Day [he failed to go to church]. We do not know what happened next, but the following year Job is on the list helping to confirm the Rev. Joseph Emerson, the first settled minister of Mendon. Also recorded is the fact that Job had given satisfaction for the offenses of which he was accused.

"In 1675, King Philip's War broke out in the Massachusetts Bay Colony. Philip was chief of the Wampanoag tribe. His Native American name was Metacomet, but the English settlers called him King Philip. In 1662 Philip succeeded his brother as chief and formally renewed the treaties his father had made with the Pilgrim and Puritan settlers. He honored these for some years. The colonists, however, made continual encroachments on native lands. In retaliation, Philip formed a confederation of tribes and in 1675 led an uprising now known as King Philip's War.

"When the war erupted, the residents of Mendon buried their pewter plates and brass kettles in the swamps, loaded everything else they could carry and fled to the larger eastern towns. Job and his family apparently fled to Rowley Village or Roxbury before the Indians attacked Mendon and burned it to the ground. Samuel Tyler, one of Job's sons, was drafted into the militia and was seriously wounded during the 'war.'

"The Indians burned several towns and killed many of the inhabitants. In return the colonists captured Indian women and children, destroyed crops, and promised impunity to Indian deserters. In December, 1675, the colonists won a major victory. During the spring of 1676, the Indians held out, but their numbers steadily diminished and in August, Philip was killed. The war then ended, and resistance to further colonial settlements in southern New England ceased.

"By 1688, Job had returned to Mendon. The last official record of him was his deed of his land in Mendon to his son Moses in November 1700. It is likely that he died soon after. These old documents show that Job was a stubborn, outspoken, rebellious man, who had problems with Puritan authority and trouble handling his debts. Yet, there must have been much good in him for he raised a large family, who were deeply religious, prosperous and outstanding citizens of their communities. His strong personality perhaps was passed down to his sons, grandsons and great-grandsons, several of whom became military officers in various military organizations; at least one was a high-ranking Major General. A strong personality often makes for a strong and natural leader."[21]

Chronology of Job's life

Immigrant Job Tyler had an interesting life with many intriguing and surprising turns. This chronology, based on various assumptions, dates most of the interesting events in his lifetime and describes as a whole his many controversies and challenges.

1617-19:	Birth of Job
1638:	Job arrives at Nieu-Port, Rhode Island
1640:	Job comes to Andover, Massachusetts, as a squatter
1646:	Roxbury, Mill Creek farm
1650:	Mortgage to John Godfrey
1652:	"Big black bird" incident
1658:	Witchcraft charge against John Godfrey
1661:	"Wheat Suit" against John Godfrey
1662:	Job loses farm to John Godfrey

1663:	Death of Laurence (his father) in England
1665:	Libel suit by Thomas Chandler
1665:	Suit by Chief Owannameg (stealing hay)
1669:	Job versus Mendon Selectmen
1670:	Resolves dispute with Mendon Selectmen
1680:	Job living at Rowley (now Georgetown)
1688:	Returns to Mendon
1692:	Family members involved in Salem witchcraft trials
1700:	Death of Job

Job's Memorial Stone

Because the actual grave site of Job has never been found, it is presumed he was either buried somewhere on the old farm known as the Tyler Homestead or in the North Andover Cemetery. At the first Tyler Reunion in 1896, members decided a memorial to Job should be erected. A stone was taken from the old homestead's fence and a plaque, inscribed as shown, was placed next to the grave of his eldest son, Moses. It still stands in the old North Andover Cemetery in Massachusetts.

*Charles Tyler at Job Tyler Memorial Stone,
North Andover, Massachusetts, placed in 1901.*

Chapter 3: Establishing the Tyler Homestead

The Job Tyler extended family is very fortunate the original homestead built by second-generation ancestors still remains on its original site and in largely preserved condition. Recent and current owners have been conscious of its landmark status and have recognized it is a significant physical representation of the family's history. The site has been referred to variously as Boxford House, Tyler-Wood House, and Witch Hollow Farm. We refer to it as the Tyler Homestead throughout this narrative.

The story of the Tyler Homestead begins with the community of West Boxford, which had members of the Tyler clan living there for many generations, although there are none still living in what has become a small, but upscale, New England town.

History of West Boxford

In 1880, local historian Sidney Perley wrote the definitive book, *The History of Boxford*, including detailed information on the first two centuries of this community the Tyler family called home.[22] Much of the following section is based on material from this book.

~

Rowley, Massachusetts, located to the east on the coast, was settled by a group of Puritans from Yorkshire in England in 1638. It was originally established as a plantation by Reverend Ezekiel Rogers, who had arrived with approximately twenty families. They bought a huge tract of land encompassing the present towns of Rowley, Boxford, Georgetown, Groveland, Bradford, and part of Middleton.

West of Rowley Village was the town of Boxford , which began to be settled in the 1640s. At this time Boxford was forested and had almost no residents. The farms were dispersed, and it was only later that the two villages grew up around churches. The western end of Boxford was settled by families with the names of Tyler, Eames, Blake, Pearl, Chadwick, Kimball and Porter. These families were intermarried and many relatives were interconnected.

In 1652, the General Court ordered a "highway" be laid out from Andover to Ipswich, passing over village lands. This was the first road through Boxford, and it passed the future location of the Tyler Homestead. By the late seventeenth century, the Town of Topsfield had most of the population, with a smaller number of inhabitants in Boxford. Boxford residents were required to attend church in Topsfield and were assessed a given rate to support the church. In 1689, the town of Topsfield voted "that those men in Boxford that hear the Word dispensed at Topsfield shall pay this year fifteen pounds, five of it in silver, to the ministry, and the rest of the town that go to Andover and Bradford to hear shall pay proportionably where they do hear."

Historian Perley's narrative continues: "A coldness was now creeping over the Topsfield church, which was not entirely thrown off till years after the separation—in ecclesiastical concerns—took place between the two towns. Fault was first found with the insufficient number of pews, and the seating of the Boxford people. In those times the people were seated, in respect to the position of the pew, according to their respectability, wealth, or age. Fault was often found because some had more honorable seats than others. On the 14th of January 1690 Topsfield chose a committee to 'understand' the grievances of the Boxford people, so that in some way 'peace and love' might be continued between the two towns; but the records do not inform us that any thing was immediately further done. A spirit of alleviated animosity seemed to prevail."[23]

The two towns continued to grow separately, and Boxford residents wanted to establish a firm dividing line, but Topsfield leaders were stubborn in putting off a decision. Part of the reason was that both towns wanted to have two large farms included in their side of the border. In 1699, the General Court ordered one farm to stay in Topsfield, the other to be in Boxford, and the Solomonic decision resolved the issue.

The Selectmen of Boxford wrote a petition asking for what they considered to be their proper rights. They made a plea "... to grant our town the same power and privilege to settle our bounds with all the towns that do adjoin upon us, on every side, as you yourselves had, when we were both of us one town. We have had many meetings with Topsfield and Salem men, and they refuse to settle bounds with us, unless we can show a grant, either from the General Court, or from the town of Rowley, that we have power to transact in such settlements, as other towns have. So we remain your loving friends, to serve in what we may, hoping you will be pleased to grant us our desire herein."[24]

In all, it took forty-six years before an agreement could be reached on a final boundary. Interestingly, the description of the boundary would be considered quite fluid when judged in terms of today's survey standards. In 1731, the boundary was described in the following terms: "from the apple-tree in Captain Perley's field to a stake and heap of stones at the southeasterly corner of Mr. Baker's farm, now in Boxford, and from thence to a dam, called Andrews' dam, near Mr. Thomas Gould's house, and from thence, it being the place where the water now runs under said dam, southerly to a stake and heap of stones by the Fishing Brook, on the easterly side of the rivulet running into said brook, and then as the said brook runs into the river called Ipswich River, then up said river to Middleton line."[25]

Three years later, in 1734, Samuel Tyler (#9?) and unnamed others wrote a petition to separate Boxford into two parts, arguing that many of the families had to travel too great of a distance to attend Sunday services at the township's Meeting House. By creating a separate precinct, they could build their own Meeting House. In the following winter they prepared a petition which they sent to the General Court, which is as follows:

"A petition of Samuel Tyler and other inhabitants of the Northerly part of the Town of Boxford, showing that they live at a great distance from the place of worship in said town, so that many of the families are detained at home on the Lord's Day by reason of that difficulty, and that they have erected a meeting-house in that part of the town. And at their own charge supported the Preaching of the Gospel among them; and therefore praying that they and their families and estates may be freed from the charge, (which they till now have bourne) of supporting the minister in the other part of the town and be erected into a separate precinct . . .

"The petition was read in the House of Representatives on April 10, 1735 . . . Three families were opposed and they sent to the General Court a petition embodying their views on the matter, to counteract the previous petition of Samuel Tyler and others. . .

"The committee of the Legislature came to Boxford, and after examining all parties interested and the situation of the premises, reported that the prayer of the petition of Samuel Tyler and others ought to be granted. . ."[26]

With payment of thirteen pounds, three pence to the committee, the petition was forwarded to the House of Representatives, who approved it. Officers were chosen for the new precinct, including Captain John Tyler (#11; Tyler-117) as treasurer. One of the first tasks was to build the Meeting House. Construction overseers included Daniel Wood, John Woster, and, of course, one of the Tyler family, Job Tyler (#14; Tyler-165). The new church was incorporated, with a number of Tylers as founding members transferring from the Boxford church; they included Elizabeth Tyler (#58?), Elizabeth Tyler (#83?), and Ruth Tyler. Membership soon included Richard Tyler and Samuel Tyler.

In Puritan times, attending church was compulsory, although most people were not full members. The churches were supported through taxes. At this time there was a distinction between the church (the body gathered) and the meeting-house (the building). The town had the responsibility for the meeting-house and the financial needs of the church were discussed in town meetings and are part of the town records.

Gradually the population in West Boxford continued to grow until there were more people than in East Boxford. The 1702 meeting-house in Boxford began to be in disrepair and the town meeting refused to repair it. West Boxford had a large enough population to control the town meeting, and these residents did not want to spend money for a meeting-house they didn't use. The stalemate lasted for several years.

Finally, in 1734, the people in West Boxford solved the problem by building their own meeting-house and hiring a preacher. Having proven they were obviously populous and wealthy enough to support a second church in town, forty people, led by Stephen Tyler, petitioned the General Court to be incorporated as a separate parish. Upon legislative approval in July 1735, the first meeting of the parish was held. Once the parishes were incorporated, the western end of town received the designation of Second Parish. The original Town of Boxford no longer had any say in religious affairs in the town. Instead, each parish chose parish officers. Captain John Tyler was voted parish treasurer at this first meeting. Job Tyler was on the committee chosen to obtain books for the clerk and assessors (now at the Documents Center). When the church was formally gathered in 1736, among the first members were two women, both named Elizabeth Tyler, and also Ruth Tyler. Shortly after, Richard and Samuel Tyler joined the church membership.

The Puritans recognized the hierarchical arrangement of society—the most important people obviously enjoyed God's favor, and thus were deserving of honor. They were given the best seats in the church. This recognition was based on their wealth, accumulation of land, military rank, or other title, age and length of residence. Every few years a seating committee would be appointed to "seat" the congregation, working out a formula to determine the relative dignity of each seat, as well as the status of each family, based on the head of the household.

The Tyler family served their community well. A town record from 1791 showed a number of Tylers as head-of-households in the Fifth District of the parish. They included Ensign Gideon Tyler, John Tyler, Abraham Tyler, and Broadstreet Tyler. A number of Tyler men served as selectmen for the town, including Moses Tyler (five terms), John, Job, Jonathan, Gideon, Bradstreet and John Jr. Bradstreet Tyler was a deacon of the church from 1806-1814 and held the title until his death. In 1840, the following Tylers were members of the local militia—Phineas P. Tyler, Jeremiah Tyler, and William Tyler, Jr.

In 1774, the people of the Second Parish, dismayed by the state of their meeting house, voted to build a new one, similar to that located in New Rowley, but with no steeple and a porch with stairs on each end. This meeting-house was located in the front lawn of the present church (the exact center of the parish).

Early nineteenth century West Boxford was a thriving community. Many new houses were built, often on the same site as, or even incorporating, older dwellings. The population peaked in 1855 at 1,034 and it was time to build yet another church. At a cost of $4,917.62 the present building was constructed in 1843. Pews were auctioned off to offset the cost of construction and owned individually. Since then, the sanctuary has been Victorianized, and then modernized, but it is substantially the same.

West Boxford Church

In 1872, Captain John Tyler of West Boxford died. In his will he bequeathed the remainder of his estate to the West Boxford Church. As stated in his will: "And all of the rest, residue, and remainder of my estate, after the payment of the legacies afore-named, and my funeral charges, and the charges and expenses of the settlement of my estate, I give and bequeath to the religious society in West Boxford, where I usually worship, to be held as a perpetual fund, the income of which to be appropriated annually for the support of the gospel in said society forever.

"After settlement of his estate, the fund was found to amount to about thirty thousand dollars. On receiving this bequest, the parish, April 8, 1873, passed the following resolutions:–

"*Resolved,* That the parish of West Boxford accept with sentiments of unaffected thankfulness the legacy bequeathed to them by the late Captain John Tyler,

"*Resolved,* That the parish recognize in this act of Captain John Tyler a sign of the same liberality and the same cordial interest in the religious welfare of the parish which was ever manifested by him during his unusually protracted life; and they rejoice that he felt himself prompted to crown a long life of honest industry and well-doing by such an act of liberality, which they trust will continue to be fraught with great good to the parish, and will be gratefully remembered by all coming generations."[27]

Tylers who have served as Selectmen in Boxford

In the early years Tylers had prominent roles in their community. The list below indicates Tyler men who served as Selectmen in Boxford Township over 131 years.

1691, 1694-95, Moses
1712, Moses
1714, John
1716, Job
1725, Jonathan
1728, Moses
1754, Job
1760-61, Gideon
1780, Bradstreet
1795-96, John
1817, John
1822, John, Jr.
(Note: These are from records through 1879.)

History of the Tyler Homestead

The Tyler Homestead is a very integral part of the Job Tyler family history. As described by historian Willard Brigham at the family's reunion in 1896, "The first Tyler home was built on a tract of land at the corner of Ipswich Road and Main Street. The hearth of that very early structure is still in the rear of the large white house, sometimes known as the Boxford House. The oldest part of the house is the dining room and was built (1694?) by Moses Tyler [#2; Tyler-118], son of Job. Moses had come to clear land and establish a farm, and likely Job lived and worked with him at least for a few years. Moses was probably involved with the construction of the barn and the stone wall still remaining on the property, and in some ways the barn should be considered as predating the house. Moses had an earlier dwelling on the property, but it has long since been demolished."[28]

Tyler Homestead (1988 photograph)

At the next year's reunion in 1897, Brigham included more detail on the history of the house.

"This is the most ancient family seat of the Tylers thus far identified in Essex County (Mass.), the old home of immigrant Job 1640. Job's house must have been among the first built in North Andover (he mortgaged his 'house and barn' in '1650,' and land 'fenced and unfenced,') but has not been located, and may never be.

"The eldest son of Job, 'Quartermaster' Moses settled upon the 'Captain John' place (where later Job *probably* passed some later years of *his* life) and was thus one of the first settlers of West Boxford (contiguous to northerly North Andover). The house at present standing [i.e., 1897] (that is, the *rear part*) was built by Moses' son, Capt. John Tyler, probably about the time of Moses' death, 1727. Though some 'bricks' have recently been found buried in the present driveway, which would appear to locate the old fireplace of Moses at a few rods to the east of the present dwelling; and it is not at all unlikely that when the first house was abandoned for purposes of living, it continued to be used as a storehouse, until it finally passed off the scene in decay. It must have been a very simple structure, judging from reports of the typical first settler's cabin.

"The present imposing country house is due to the kindly efforts of Gideon Tyler, son of Capt. John, who succeeded to the premises upon his father's death. The presence of *three* chimneys (very unusual in so old a dwelling) is accounted for by this interesting bit of history: Gideon had two daughters, Mehitable and Anna (commonly called 'Hitty' and 'Nanny'), who died aged spinsters, both in September, 1833, at 84 and 80, respectively. Gideon (with a paternal kindness worthy of later day imitation) built for these the west ell, with a single room upstairs and down, where for long years, in well-ordered privacy, they lived comfortably and happily. Upon their deaths, the rooms were closed, and have ever since remained unoccupied.

"Capt. John's 'rear rooms' are very well preserved and quaint, being quite low-posted, with heavy beams exposed to view, and the poem of a cozy fireplace, identical line to line with 'The days of auld lang syne.' In the front room, too, is a time-honored hearthstone, wherefrom rises the flames of domestic joys upon inclement days.

"Of the many Tylers who have lived in this dear old home, none has left a memory more quaintly attractive than 'Aunt Pru,' who was born in the house and where she passed away at the remarkable age of one hundred years. She was to have been wed in younger days, and the visitor is shown a Bible, the gift of her betrothed; though she did not marry him, nor did she pine away, one may easily see how dear he was in memory—very unusual memory of a love affair that could survive through more than the divinely allotted 'three score and ten.'"

Captain John's will provided a room for Aunt Pru on the lower floor of his house. She had kept house for him after his wife died in 1745 until he himself left eleven years later. Gideon, who succeeded Captain John, also died four years before Aunt Pru. She is buried nearby in the old West Boxford cemetery.

"When in 1800 Gideon died, his eldest son, John, fell heir to the old place; upon whose demise, in 1823, his daughters, Mehetable and Mercy, succeeded to possession. Mercy lived to so recently as 1880, 'singly' (and it would also appear *singularly*) 'blessed,' to her eighty-seventh year. Mehetable survived until 1891, aged ninety-three. Her husband was Capt. Enoch Wood (descendant of an ancient Essex County family), who left (among others) a daughter, Rebecca Tyler Wood, and a son, John Tyler Wood, born in 1830 and 1831 respectively, who carry on the premises in the old God-fearing way. Rebecca Wood, who never married, moved into the Boxford House and lived in it until she died in 1918, giving it the name of Tyler-Wood House.

"Arthur Pinkham, a Tyler descendant, learned this was his ancestral home at a meeting of the Whiting Club, a social fraternity, and then read about it in Volumes I and II. Both Mr. Pinkham and his wife had ancestors in the family ten generations back. He went to see it and bought the property with 120 acres in 1929 for $11,000. The structure was not in good condition, and the Pinkhams began making many necessary interior alterations and gradually did much of its restoration. Many antique artifacts came with the house.

"For instance, they found an oaken hand-loom older than one on display at Williamsburg. A wooden keg was found in the Tap Room which had the initials of Gideon Tyler. The biggest problem for the Pinkhams was there was not water in the well for modern plumbing. When he explained to a neighbor the only problem with the property was there was no water, his neighbor replied, 'Why, that's the only thing the matter with Hell!' They put in an artesian well, which created the lovely pond now found on the property.

"The house and barn are historically significant not only because of their important Tyler history, but also because of their age and integrity architecturally. The logs used for the walls were so hard they couldn't be drilled through to install electrical wiring. The windows still have shutters that are built into the wall, so they could be closed from the inside in case of Indian attack. The interior horizontal paneling is the oldest form found in New England and is referred to as 'thumb and feather' design.

"The barn also is a very important structure historically, and at one time was the largest barn in the country. The structure is as it was when originally built in the 1600s. The floor is made of solid wood planks 14 to 16 inches wide. When recent owners needed to replace some of them, they had great difficulty finding boards wide enough to match the original."[29]

Barn and Stone Wall at Tyler Homestead

After the Pinkhams, the Tyler Homestead property was sold to Edward French in 1958, the first owner who was not in the Job Tyler lineage. In 1970, it was purchased by David and Audrey Ladd. The Ladds continued much of the restoration work, including cleaning of the walls and chimneys and exposing the original surfaces.

"Audrey Ladd also did much toward recording the history of the place and was the first to refer to it as Witch Hollow Farm, a name given because of its association with the Salem witch trials. Boxford's witch, Rebecca Eames, was the sister of Prudence Blake, who married Quartermaster Moses Tyler. Rebecca claimed in court that she had been bewitched by the Devil in the hollow through which Ipswich Road runs. Some of the hangings are said to have taken place at the back of the property. Also, the spirit of Mary Tyler [#3; Tyler-179], sister of Quartermaster Moses [#2; Tyler-118], is still said to inhabit the house 300 years later.

"The property was then purchased by the Rich's in the 1980s. In 1997, it was designated as a historic site and the house and the remaining farmland were split. The farm was designated as a conservancy preserve and the house was bought by Lawrence and Tina Morris."[30]

Historic architectural description of the Homestead

In a local article from 2017, the Tyler Homestead was described in terms of its architectural significance by Susan S. Nelson of Goodship Research in Ipswich, Massachusetts:

"Based on the physical evidence we were able to view on our October site visit, we believe that the Tyler-Wood house, while it may rest on or near the site of an earlier building, is in its earliest iteration a fine example of Second-Period architecture with several later additions. Originally a gabled two-story structure with a central chimney and hall/parlor plan, its eighteenth-century origins are most clearly demonstrated by the undisturbed Georgian paneling and bolection [decorative] molding of its two floor bedrooms, both of which retain their original intact fireboxes. The masterly articulation of this paneling and its sophistication are suggestive of the Tyler family's high status and wealth at the time of its construction. The style of finish work in this earliest part of the house certainly suggests a construction date no earlier than about 1725, and possibly considerably later. While the Tyler-Wood House is not of First-Period construction as has been surmised, it is still a fine example of the Georgian and Federal Styles in American domestic architecture and makes a very valuable contribution to the built environment of Boxford. The use of 'American,' or trenched purlin roof framing, the continued existence of the earliest gabled roof in the attic, and the highly articulated finish work throughout the building give the house stature and make it worthy of both recognition and preservation."[31]

Rear view of Tyler Homestead

Legal Description of the Tyler Homestead Property, 1799

In the seventeenth and early eighteenth century, when a person moved into town, land was sold to him by the town. The buyer became a proprietor, or "commoner." Grants were made by all the freeholders in a town. "Portions of land necessary for settlers were set off from time to time to individuals in proportion to expenses, or taxes, paid by each, and their division recorded in the town book. The first house lots were small, seldom larger than ten acres. Wood, plough and swamp lands (the last for hay) were distant and granted in small lots. As a result, few large modern farms are compact."[32]

The following is a full description of "The Homestead of the Tylers" as given in the "Valuation Book of 1799." It delineates various sections of the overall property and their boundaries based on what properties or roads are adjacent.

"In literal verification of which, it is permitted us to study 'The Homestead of

"John Tyler Chaise House, 8x15 (Dwelling House 45x18 and 35.x19, 2 stories high (500 or 550) Windows) 394 panes of glass 7x9, 3 chimneys

"One acre and ½ valued therewith bounded Northerly by the County Road.

"One Barn 69x30; Cider House 20x28; One Shop 14x18; One Barn 41x30

(One Farm bounded Northerly by the County Road, Easterly by John Kimball, Nathan Kimball and others, Southerly by Stiles Pond, so called, Westerly by Tyler Porter Ephraim, Foster Jonathan Foster, and Others— 130 acres—last mentioned Barn standing on the above—16 dollars per acre.

"One lot of Woodland bounded Westerly and Southerly by Ephraim Foster, Easterly by Amos Spofford and Abraham Tyler, 30 acres, 20 dollars per acre.

"One tract of Mowing and Woodland bounded Southerly by the County Road, Westerly by Nathan Barker and Stephen Tyler, Northerly by Samuel Spofford and others, Easterly by Nathan Kimball and others, 70 acres, 19 dollars per acre. First barn standing on the same.

"One tract of Meadow land known by the Name of the Great Meadows, 20—4 dollars per acre.

"One tract of Meadow and Wood lying in Andover known by the name of shoe meadow, 10 acres—

"One lot of Thatch bank in Rowley, known by primes Island,—5 acres—

"Thus we see 'the lay' of a conspicuously large old Essex farm divided among three townships (West Boxford, Andover and Rowley), scattering over *several miles* of surface; *seven* parcels in all, aggregating 266-1/2 acres, showing the ancient division into 'House lot, wood plough and swamp land.' And otherwise characteristic of the specifications set out by brother Abbot."[33]

Memories of the Homestead by Arthur Pinkham

The following is a short excerpt from a recollection of life in the Tyler Homestead written by Arthur Pinkham, who lived there for many years beginning in 1929. He wrote a paper, "Memory Hold the Door," for a presentation he gave in 1944 to the Whiting Club. Excerpts from this humorous account give a wonderful feeling for stories relating to this the Tyler Homestead.

"When my wife and I first discovered this house and peeked in the windows, we were not in the least impressed. These old oak beams and rafters were covered with beaver board, the hand-hewn horizontal paneling was shrouded with faded wallpaper, and the fireplaces were closed with sheets of metal into which projected smoke pipes from air-tight wood stoves.

"The last regular occupant of this house was Rebecca Tyler Wood who died here in 1918, aged 88. . . After Rebecca died, the property went to her brother's widow, Mrs. Louise Wood of Hyde Park.

"It was quite an event in the lives of all of us that 19th day of April 1929, when we met to close our deal on purchasing the property. We had agreed on the purchase price of the land and buildings, but couldn't come to terms on the personal property, so I made an offer that was accepted.

"I must confess that the value of the residue which we bought, but which we did not know was there, was far greater than what we saw and included in our original estimate. For instance, there were such things as the corner barrel-backed cupboard and two of the old tavern tables which we uncovered under a pile of boards in the woodshed; the oaken hand loom which now stands on the scaffolding in the barn, which is older than the one on exhibition in Williamsburg and which was stored away and forgotten in the attic of the old workshop; also spinning wheels, coils of flax, and bags of wool which were mute evidence of the thrift and independence of these sturdy colonial ancestors: balances, Bibles, casks and rum bottles, empty these many years but which were reminiscent of those pre-Volsteadian days when a bounteous supply of hard cider and of New England rum was not inconsistent with the customs of the community and the manners of a gentleman. . . .

"The dining room is the oldest part of this house. It was built as a separate unit about the year 1700. The oak beams, pinned together with dowels more than two hundred and forty years ago, have become so hard that you can't drive a nail into them without bending it. Mr. Guilford, a builder from Topsfield, says that the horizontal paneling with the thumb and feather design in this room is the oldest form in New England. Some of the panes of glass in the windows have been worn so thin by the storms they are like tissue paper. Dr. Gus Esselin says that glass of that vintage was slightly water soluble. While the present windows are about two hundred years old, it appears from the frames that the originals were casements. There is a front door with original locks and hinges, stairs going to the cellar and others going to the two bedrooms, one on the second floor, the other in the attic. . .

"Many times during these last fifteen years, I have sat alone within these sound-proof walls and shuttered windows. Around me, as I gazed into the fire, have been those memorials of days and of men long vanished. On such occasions my mind has slipped back into the past and I have witnessed the panorama of life during these last nine generations.

"From amidst the flames of those burning embers emerged the figures of Moses Tyler and Robert Eames whose ages were 24 and 30 respectively, and who looked as if they might be woodsmen or rough and tumble Indian fighters—certainly ingenious youths who gave promise of great power. They had married Prudence and Rebecca Blake, sisters from Gloucester, Massachusetts, and they, as well, were our ancestors nine generations back.

"The Tylers built a cabin in 1666 where now is the woodshed and a few years ago several bricks from its foundation were unearthed when the present yard was being repaired. . .

"During the next twenty years, Moses Tyler was surveyor, constable, and selectman in addition to being a successful farmer, and acquired large holdings of real estate. In January 1689 he was ordered by the town selectmen to lay in a stock of ammunition in anticipation of Indian hostilities. It was not long after that that he had become custodian of "10 pounds of powder, 60 pounds of bullets, and 50 flints." For such services he acquired the title of Quartermaster. . .

"After John Tyler had served his time in the French and Indian War, he went to sea. There he acquired the title of Captain because he was the Master Mariner of a Merchant Ship. In 1708 he also acquired by deed from Moses, his father, 107 acres of land and the oldest part of the present dwelling which, as I have already said, is the dining room.

"The next owner of this ancient domicile was Captain John's son, Gideon, who was born here in 1712. In 1748, in anticipation of his wedding, his father joined the two small houses together into the present arrangement.

"Gideon Tyler was a member of the Continental Army with an ensign's commission and was at Cambridge when Washington took command of the troops. While many of the items which we listed fifteen years ago in the inventory of personal property were once owned by Gideon, the most prominent one and the one about which there can be no doubt, is the wooden keg in the tap room. That bit of antiquity bears his initials. He used to fill it with rum and water and carry it into the fields to cure snake bites. . .

"Gideon's son John, one of the twins, succeeded his father in the ownership of this property. Then John's daughter, Mehitabel, born here in 1797, became the owner. When she married Capt. Enoch Wood in 1826, the farm's name became hyphenated into the Tyler-Wood Homestead.

"Mehitabel Tyler Wood left as her heirs to the property a son, John T. Wood and a daughter, Rebecca. Since Rebecca outlived her brother John, she left the farm to her brother Enoch's widow, Louise, and Louise's three daughters and a son. All of which goes to show that, in the history of this property, the last three owners, not to mention this one, have been women.

". . . The stories were always about our ancestors, and one which I insisted upon here repeating was the legend that at the base of the main chimney they kept hidden a pot of gold. . . old English sovereigns of which Captain John Tyler always had a bountiful supply.

"Which was the main chimney…there were three…was always the stumbling block and she was the sort of little old lady who wouldn't think of allowing a small boy to explore.

"Well, I grew up and in 1918 Aunt Rebecca died, leaving the property to my mother, sisters and myself. They occupied it summers, but the old house was left many months in the year to itself.

Tyler Homestead Fireplace (1988)

"One spring I was visiting in Chicago and my friend took me to see a famous clairvoyant who was all the rage at the time in that city. When she began on me, the affair became a revelation instead of just an amusing way to spend an evening, for she said at once, 'Young man, you come from the East. You've come into some family property lately. I see a large white house, set well back from the road. There are huge chimneys with many fireplaces, blocked up. Near the base of the main chimney there is a hiding place. Back through the generations, it has been used for money and once for jewels. You had a sea-faring ancestor who used to make voyages to New Orleans and, well, there were many beautiful creole girls there and I think the jewels, which were topazes, were for one of them. That's all I can tell you! Am I right?'

"It didn't take long for my friend and me to decide that we were starting for Boxford, and that very night we set out, arriving at the old farm a few nights later. I had no key, but I knew of a second floor window latch which never worked and with the aid of a ladder we were soon in the house. The ladder we hauled up and then standing there in that upper bedroom, we tried to figure out which was the main chimney. This we decided was the center one, and since matting in the clothes closet next to it was far easier

33

to rip up than carpets, we started in on that. We had to work by candlelight, and when a trap door was disclosed, my hands and knees began to tremble and we both almost had the jitters. We lowered the ladder into the darkness and followed with our candles. It didn't seem to surprise us very much to find a neat hiding place on the chimney's side, but to our great disappointment we found no golden sovereigns, nor the beautiful topaz necklace...we found nothing but a very old pewter candle-stick.

"It didn't take us long, after Franklin Wood and his mother and sisters departed on the 19th of April fifteen years ago, to make up our minds that we were going to take up the search where Franklin and his friend had left off many years before. Since we, also, were undecided which of the three was the main chimney, we started on the dining room one first. Back of the chimney in the attic we found two loose wide boards which we lifted up. We couldn't drop down lower than the second floor level, but there we found a small room large enough for two or three people to sit down in comfort. On the floor were bits of homespun, some buttons and other evidence that the space was once a hiding place, but there were no signs of treasure. Then we tackled the chimney at the west end of the house. There we were a little more successful in that we could crawl down to the first floor level. Behind the paneling we found a powder horn, bullet mould and various other things which Captain John must have brought back from his voyages about the time that part of the house was built.

"Finally, we tackled the middle chimney and went down through the trap door on the second floor to the cellar level. There was the ladder and resting on the chimney ledge was the pewter candle-stick just as the boys had left them...but still no pot of gold.

"There is no cellar under the parlor floor and we hated to rip up the hearth, so we have started to tunnel from the further cellar. Some day, I have no doubt, we shall find the pot of golden sovereigns and when we do, you shall hear about it in a paper before the Whiting Club."

There has been conjecture over time that the small hidden room found by Pinkham was part of the underground railroad, a network of secret routes and safe houses established in the United States during the early to mid-1800s and used by African-American slaves to escape into free states and Canada. No support for this hypothesis has been found, however.

Who lived at the Homestead? A timeline of owners

Moses Tyler had come to clear land and establish a farm.

- There was an earlier dwelling on the property at the beginning.

- Moses was probably involved in the construction of the barn and stone wall that is still on the property.

- Job lived on property for some time.

First section of Homestead probably built by Captain John Tyler (3rd generation)

- He was "Master Mariner" of a merchant ship; son of Moses.

- Assume house was built with some assistance from Moses, although Moses may have been in his 70s or 80s.
- It is said that Mary, sister of Moses, has been a spirit in the house for 300 years.
- Rebecca, daughter of Moses, was acquitted as a witch during Salem Witch Trials.
- Some have claimed some of the hangings were on the property behind the house.

Gideon Tyler (son of Captain John) built an addition when married in 1748.

- It joined the two sections of the house together.
- Gideon was a member of the Continental Army.

Ell addition was added for Gideon's daughters, Mehitable and Anna.

- They were spinsters; each had a chimney built for them.
- Both died in 1833, in their 80s.
- Their rooms were closed off and unused for many years.

Prudence (Aunt Pru) was born and died in the house.

- She lived there for 100 years.
- Captain John's will provided a room for her.
- Gideon passed house on to his son, John.
- John's daughter, Mehitable, married Captain Enoch Wood. Enoch Wood came from another old Essex County family.

Last regular Tyler family occupant was Rebecca Tyler Wood

- John T. Wood lived there, died in 1906.

- Rebecca was daughter of Enoch Wood.
- She kept records for Second Congregational Church.
- She died in 1918.

Enoch Wood's widow receives property in 1921

Rebecca Wood left all her property to Louise M. Wood, widow of Enoch Wood, and her children, Annette M. Bryant, Louise W. Delano, Florence M. Bryant, and Franklin T. Wood.

Arthur Pinkham learned this was his ancestral home.

- Louise W. Delano sells property to Ruth Griffith Pinkham, wife of Arthur Pinkham; passed down to their son, Charles Pinkham II and his wife, Marie.
- Pinkham discovered the house's history at a meeting of the Whiting Club (a social fraternity).
- He then uncovered information from Volumes I and II of *The Tyler Genealogy* that he had ancestors 10 generations back.
- He went to see property in 1929 and bought the house with 120 acres for

$11,000.

- He used it as a summer house for entertaining. At that time, house was not in good condition.

- It had had many interior alterations.

- Many antique artifacts came with the house.

- ...oaken hand loom older that one on display in Williamsburg.

- ...antique spinning wheel.

- Biggest problem was no water in well for modern plumbing.

- Pinkham put in an artesian well and a pond to provide water.
- He moved out in 1958, the last of the Tyler line to live there.

House bought by Edward L. French in 1958

Sold to David and Audrey Ladd in 1970

- Audrey Ladd said she had an experience with a male spirit on her first night at the house, but realized it was a friendly spirit.

- Audrey gives name, Witch Hollow Farm, to property

Bought by Steve and Jean Rich in 1980s.

- Jean Rich sensed spirit of Mary Tyler in house many times, she has said.

Larry and Tina Morris bought Homestead in 1997.

- Farm had been designated an official conservation area and house was designated as a historic property.

Saving the Homestead

The Tyler Homestead is recognized as one of the most historically significant structures in the region. Its history is well documented, but as with many historic homes they sometimes stand in the way of progress based on developers who view older structures as not constituting the "highest and best use" of a property. Such was the case with the Tyler Homestead property in the 1990s, when the West Boxford community had become the location of many large, upscale new homes. Surrounded by new residential development, there were numerous offers for sale of this favored site. Although the owners at the time, Steve and Jean Rich, recognized its historic significance, they recognized there needed to be some resolution to the problem of how to preserve the property while retaining its economic value.

This issue was picked up by members of the Job Tyler Family Association, a national organization of approximately two hundred families. The Association published in its newsletter a description of the situation at that time.

Job Tyler Family Association Newsletter: September, 1994

"We are bringing you this special edition of the Job Tyler Family Association newsletter for an important purpose.

"One of the reasons we have the Family Association is to inform Tylers of things that are happening that are of general interest. This special edition of the newsletter is being sent because we have recently been made aware of an event of considerable significance to the family history. As explained to us by Melanie Shepard, who lives in Georgetown, Massachusetts, the Tyler Homestead is up for sale. This important landmark has been sold in the past and was sold out of the Tyler family about 35 or so years ago after being in the family almost 300 years. New owners have always taken very good care of it. The current owners, the Rich's. recognize the historic significance of the house and barn, as well as the property, and have done a wonderful job of maintaining the house, barn, and 23 acres remaining of the original much larger farm.

"However, they are now putting it up for sale, and there is a real threat of the 23 acres being split into developable parcels, essentially destroying the character of the site and thus the structures as well. The Rich's are not proposing such a subdivision. In fact, they have been cooperative in finding an alternative solution. But the threat this to landmark property, now listed on the National Register of Historic Places, is something that we should all be concerned about, since it is our family's most important landmark as well. Those who were at Reunion '88 in Massachusetts, when we opened the house and grounds for tours and we saw the significance of the place and began to relive the history of its early residents, can recognize what would be lost if the homestead and barn were surrounded by large, contemporary homes.

"The problem is especially large because of simple economics. This area of northern Massachusetts has become a very desirable residential area, and real estate values have skyrocketed in recent years. This puts tremendous economic pressure on parcels of any size that are put on the market. As a result, the Rich's are asking a price that reflects its development potential as much as it reflects its value as it now exists.

"Because of its significance to the Tyler family and also because of its great importance to the local history of this area of Massachusetts, a number of local residents recently formed an group calling themselves "The Friends of Witch Hollow Farm, Inc." The group's purpose is to find an alternative use for the Homestead which would preserve its historic integrity. At their request, the Rich's have agreed to hold off sale of the property for twelve months to give the group a chance to develop a proposal for its purchase. It's a huge undertaking for them. They have become incorporated and have initiated ideas on converting the property to a historical and cultural center. Their proposal is outlined on the following pages.

"When the group heard of the existence of our Association, we were immediately contacted and sent material describing their activities. As a response to their request for assistance, this special edition of the newsletter presents you, as a member of the Association, with the available information, and is asking for your help.

"The newsletter first lays out the history of the house and property and explains its significance to all of us. It next describes the group, The Friends of Witch Hollow Farm, and fills you in on their activities and thinking. Finally, it asks you to seriously think about how we as an Association, or you as an individual, can help in this effort. We are not asking for money (that is for others to do), but we are asking for advice and ideas. Read the following, and then write to us and tell us your thoughts.

"Thanks.

"Norma and Norman Tyler"[34]

The Tyler Homestead was originally a much larger farm, and by 1995 the property with the house and large barn, with its small pond and broad fields, had been reduced to twenty-three acres in size. The surrounding township had become an attractive area for expensive modern country homes, and the Boxford property was to be sold for almost one million dollars to a developer to be split into subdivision lots. Under state law, in Massachusetts a community has a 120-day option period with the right of first refusal for agricultural land at the time of its sale. The Boxford Open Land Trust, a non-profit conservation group, looked for other resources. The state would not protect it under its agricultural protection program, since it was considered a "hobby farm." A Friends of Witch Hollow Farm tried to raise money to purchase it but came far short of the funds needed. Ultimately, the small township didn't have the financial resources to outbid the developer.

However, the local efforts, supplemented with extensive lobbying activities, stirred interest among other state and local agencies and organizations. In the eleventh hour, a guardian organization with extensive experience with just this kind of problem stepped forward, and the situation changed literally overnight. The Trust for Public Land (TPL) is a national organization created in 1973 with the specific mission to buy threatened historic properties, sell such properties to public or private entities and put the proceeds from sales into a revolving loan fund, with which the Trust purchases more land for public use. Because the TPL can act independently of a membership or board, it is able to act quickly when needed, such as was the case with the Tyler Homestead.

After discussions between the TPL and local leaders, the Trust agreed to purchase the property in its entirety, including the house, the barn and all 23 acres. After the purchase, the house, barn and three acres had a historic covenant put on them to protect them and were then sold to a private family. The remaining acreage was purchased by the township, with half of the funds coming from the state, and with a conservation restriction placed on it to keep it as farmland, rather than being developed.

This arrangement took a significant threat to the historic homestead and turned it to advantage, since the homestead will continue to be lived in by a compatible family and the farm property will be public land used by the township as a conservation area.

Rear of Tyler Homestead farm

Today the property, known as the Witch Hollow Conservation Area, remains a seventeen-acre wildlife meadow near woods and just off Main Street and Ipswich Road. It is privately managed as a native New England prairie and provides habitat for native species. Connected to an adjacent parcel, it now is part of a contiguous wildlife corridor.

Other historic Tyler houses in and near Boxford

The Dwellings of Boxford, a book written in 1893 by Sidney Perley, gives an early history of the Tyler Homestead during the period of its occupancy by the Wood family, when it was referred to as the John T. Wood Residence. The well-dated book is useful because it also describes other Tyler houses in the vicinity, briefly included here. Many no longer exist.

Old Tyler Cellar: Across the highway from the Adams House is an old cellar. A Tyler family lived there, and the late Mrs. Enoch Wood thought it was that of the grandfather of the late Captain John Tyler. The house that stood over the cellar has probably been gone a century.

Old Cushing (Job Tyler, son of Moses Tyler) Cellar: At the southwest corner of the junction of the roads near the residence of the late Capt. Enoch Wood (Tyler Homestead), stood the residence of Job Tyler, son of Moses and Prudence (Blake) Tyler, born at the Tyler Homestead in 1675. By his first wife, Margaret, he was the father of several children, one of whom, Job, settled at what is now referred to as the Job Tyler Cellar.

Job Tyler Cellar: On the same farm and a short distance in the rear of the Peter Pearl house is what is known as the "Job Tyler cellar." This is the site of the house in which Job Tyler resided early in the eighteenth century. How long the house was standing has not been determined.

Job Tyler (son of Job Tyler) House: This farm was originally in the possession of Job Tyler, a son of Job Tyler, who lived at the Old Cushing Cellar. He was born in 1705, and married Elizabeth Parker of Bradford in 1730. He had a negro woman servant, who was called "Notur." Mr. Tyler was the father of Abraham Tyler. His son Phineas, born in 1736, was the first baptized in the first West-parish church, the service occurring in 1736. After living in Boxford many years, Phineas removed to Leominster. Bradstreet Tyler was another son. There were twelve children in all— eight sons and four daughters. Mr. Tyler probably moved to another house in Boxford. Bradstreet Tyler lived here after his father. In 1802, Stephen Tyler, whose wife's name was Patty, who had owned the place some years, sold to James Fletcher of Ashby. The farm consisted of a hundred and twenty acres.

Abraham Tyler House: This place on "Old Shaven-crown hill" was probably originally settled by Abraham Tyler, son of Job and Elizabeth (Parker) Tyler, born in Boxford in 1735. He married, first, in 1756, Abigail Stickney, by whom he had fifteen children; and second, in 1780, Jerusha Mersay, by whom he had one child. Of his children, William succeeded him at the homestead and farm. William married Abigail Barker of Haverhill in 1799, and had a son William, and a daughter Salenda, both of whom resided on the place. The children obtained the title to the property and forced their parents in their old age to seek a home at the almshouse, where they soon after died.

The son William married Mary S. Dorman and had two daughters both of whom died young. He lived only a few years after his marriage, and during that time resided here, replacing the old buildings by those now standing about 1850.

The daughter Salenda married Nelson Bodwell in 1826, and after living in Summersworth, N. H., Methuen, Mass., and in New York state, settled on this place after William's death. They continued to live here until 1868, when they sold the place to Mr. Jeremiah Dacey, from Ireland, the present owner and occupant.

Joseph Stickney Tyler House: Joseph Stickney Tyler, born in 1776 in the Abraham Tyler House, being son of Abraham and Abigail (Stickney) Tyler, probably built this house. He married, in 1798, Hannah Nelson of Rowley, who lived with her parents a few rods beyond the old turnpike gate in Linebrook parish. They had eight chidren, three of whom died in infancy, and five lived to be old. Mr. Tyler resided in this house awhile, and then removed to the Dollof House. It ultimately came into the possession of Bradstreet Tyler, who in 1832 sold it to Benjamin McLaughlin of Rowley.

Asa Tyler House and farm: Before 1770, Asa Tyler owned this farm, and probably lived there. He sold the place to Jonathan Wood. In 1822, Eliphalet Wood of Loudon, N. H., probably a brother and an heir of Mr. Wood, sold the farm to Wingate Ilsley of Rowley. Mr. Ilsley, still of Rowley, conveyed it to Richard Spofford of Boxford in 1824, and on the sixth of the following month Mr. Spofford was married in the house to Hannah Tyler. A part of the land was purchased in 1889, but the remainder of the farm still belongs to Mr. Spofford's heirs. The house has been unoccupied for many years.

Jonathan Foster House: This house was in the possession of Zebediah Foster, son of Jonathan and Abigail (Kimball) Foster, who was born in 1702. He married Margaret Tyler in 1723-24, and settled here, where he died in 1772, at the age of sixty-nine.

Bradstreet Tyler House: This house was owned by Bradstreet Tyler before 1795, as in that year he conveys the place, with the buildings thereon, to Daniel Kimball of Boxford for 350 pounds. Mr. Kimball removed to Newbury, and in 1803 sold the place to Moody Perley, who removed here from the old Killam house. Several of his children were born here.

In 1820, Mr. Perley sold out to Bradstreet Tyler of Boxford, and removed from the place. In 1824, on Christmas Day, Mr. Tyler sold the farm to Flint Tyler of Boxford, a shoemaker by trade, and originally from Bradford, where he had married Jerusha Hardy of that place in 1815. Flint Tyler sold out to James Nason of North Andover in 1858.

Recognizing the Bradstreet Tyler family in West Boxford

In 1971, a special dedication was held in West Boxford to celebrate the history of the Tyler family in the community. This section from a two-page personal paper written by Mrs. Charles Austin describes the historic significance of the homestead of the Bradstreet Tyler family.

> "A new sign of colonial appearance and old lettering was set up this week at the corner of Main Street and Lake Shore Road in West Boxford by Mrs. Charles Austin and her grandson Malcomb Fowler. Selectman Harry Cole gave his blessing on behalf of the town and donated the cedar post on which the sign is mounted. The sign reads, "Tylers Corners 1791" and was set up to serve as a memorial to the Tyler family, of which there are some dozen descendants now living in the immediate vicinity of the corners. Mrs. Austin at 90 is one of the community's oldest residents. Though not herself a Tyler family descendant, her husband's family came from the Tyler clan and her children are of the seventh, eighth, and ninth generations.

> "In 1791, the date on the sign, a descendant of the original settler Bradstreet Tyler bought a tract of land with a house and barn on what was known then as Haverhill, or Academy, Road. Around 1860 the town and county wished to straighten the road and cut directly through the Tyler farm, leaving the homestead on one side of the road and the barn on the other. The barn that goes with the Tyler house is still across Main Street from the homestead. It is however "new," having been built in 1868.

> "Bradstreet Tyler's daughter Mary married Joshua Day and they settled near the brook just north of the present Everett Chadwick farm, where they erected a grist mill, stones of which have been recently unearthed. They in turn purchased some forty acres across the street so that Tyler descendants owned all four corners.

> "Today (1971) about a dozen families, all being descendants of Bradstreet Tyler, are still settled around the Tylers Corners."[35]

Sale of Lot to Hopestill Tyler

Hopestill Tyler purchased a subdivided lot in Mendon, Massachusetts, probably in the year 1692. The following section is included largely to let the reader appreciate the use of the English language at that time for formal documents. Spelling is shown from that time, including the use of the letter "u" to represent "v."

> "Hopestil Tylers ten Acre hous Lott with A quarter of his father Job Tylers Lott being A fiue Acre Lot With all the Rights and Priuiledges thereto belonging or Apertaining to A fifteen Acre Lott In all the diuissions both of upland Medow and swamp Land Now Samuel Torrys as Apears by A deed of Sale baring date.

The Ten Acre house Lott and Dubling Lott being laid out together and the fiue Acre Lott and the Dubling Lott which was Part of Job Tylers second Deuission begin ten Acres the whole being Thirty Acres with the swamp Lott Laid out Together with the swamp Lott belonging to the Ten Acre Lott being one Acre and three Quarters Laid out Joining together upon the West sid of the Ten Rod Highway Leading to the North Medow bounded Easterly upon sd Ten Rod Way Southerly upon the Land of John SPrage westerly upon the way Leding from the Simon Pecks to the North Medow Northerly upon Common the NorWeast Corner begin A marked Tree on the west sid of the old siller the north East Corner being A stake by the Ten Rod byway Aforsd."[36]

Chapter 4: Documenting the Tyler Lineage:

Willard I. Tyler Brigham

Many of us are familiar with Willard Irving Tyler Brigham (#7154; Brigham-811) simply as the author of Volumes I and II of *The Tyler Genealogy: The Descendants of Job Tyler, of Andover, Massachusetts, 1619–1700*.[37] But who was this researcher who drove himself to an early grave in his search for information on our family and who didn't live long enough to see it completed? The following account is taken from an article written early in the twentieth century by Emma E. Brigham, who co-authored the book, *The History of the Brigham Family*.

"Willard Brigham was born in 1859 in Montpelier, Vermont, to Dr. Gershom Nelson and Laura Elvira (Tyler) Brigham. He was descended from eighty different immigrants, including Richard Warren, who arrived in 1620 on the Mayflower, as well as Governor Simon Bradstreet, and Governor Thomas Dudley. His lineage, then, included many prominent early settlers, as well as our own not-so-prominent Job Tyler.

"He attended school at the University of Michigan and was elected class historian. He then studied law in Grand Rapids and Petosky, Michigan, where he rendered services to the Pottawatomie Indians, and was adopted by the tribe under the name of "Kenoshaus" ("bigmouth"—hence, orator).

"Because of his oratorical skills, he was asked to tour the United States for five years as an actor with a well-respected Shakespearean troupe. Physical ailments sent him back to law, and he practiced in Minneapolis, where he helped write a history of the city.

"During this time, he interested his Tyler relations in forming a family association. Brigham served as both secretary and historian of the American Tyler Family Association during its most active period, from 1896 to 1901. (He also served a similar role for the Brigham family.) Although he was a talented lawyer, he spent relatively little time with his practice, and worked instead on completing the two volumes of the Tyler family genealogy. He gathered Tyler material as quickly as he could, with the intent of publishing it.."[38]

Brigham's Trip to England

Brigham described his trip to England to continue his in-depth research in a lengthy speech given the American Tyler Family Reunion in 1900.

"I suppose all will wish to hear something of my researches in Great Britain. You will please not think I have been through all the public records of that country, with a very old history; it would have taken much greater than the few months at command. Besides, many records are illegible, or were put away so securely that nobody knows where to look for them at this time. They are greatly improving the 'getatableness' of their records, however; for which I believe, we Americans, because of our great curiosity to know of our forebears, are largely responsible. Everywhere I received courteous treatment, and ofttimes they seemed really eager for me to find what I sought. Professional researchers told me 'tipping' the attendants was not to be encouraged, but I found better service after doing so. And it was not to be wondered at, for it now and then seemed rather laborious for clerical labor, when, for instance, you requested a clerk to lug out and back a volume of parchment wills, which might be over a foot thick, and weighing approximately '5 stone.' i.e., 70 pounds.

"The Library of the British Museum, you know, is the largest in the world, and the circular work room for students is perfectly equipped. A great amount of research is constantly being done here, and the freedom with which they allow one access to priceless books and manuscripts is very admirable. They have an excellent 'Authors' Index' in many volumes; but they lack a complete 'Subject Index,' such as we are accustomed to in our 'card catalogues.' A few fragmentary attempts at publishing something in this line only add to the prick of the thorn. Thus, while I learned much in a general way of the Tylers, I am convinced that a great deal (possibly of the highest import to my work) lie locked up, simply because there is no index to point out the volumes.

"Having learned by this time that the leading Tylers of British history had mostly come from East Wales, and knowing of the American tradition that several of the American Tyler emigrants were from West England, I went thoroughly to work in that direction, and personally visited and examined probate records at Exeter, Taunton, Wells, Bristol, Gloucester, Llandatt, Shrewsbury, St. Asaph and Litchfield. Exeter contains Devon County wills, which, at an earlier period, were probated in no less than eight local courts of limited jurisdiction, While the name- Tilly, Tully, Taylor, and others of near sounds were found, not a single Tiler or Tyler estate was described during the period in question. This, while disappointing, was not wholly unexpected; for it had been gleaned from Westcote's work ('A View of Devonshire in 1630, with Pedigrees of Most of Its Gentry') that the Tylers did not scorn to figure at all in the affairs of that county. The effect of those records is rather perplexing; in the light of the record of the Heralds' College, London; to the purport, that Thomas Tyler, founder of the Boston line, sailed from 'Budleigh, Devon.'

. . .

"In all my wanderings and searches, I never ran across a Job Tyler; until at last, I became certain, that should I ever find one by that name, it must be he who was in New England in 1638. I am still looking patiently for Job!

"The adage runs, 'labor omnia vincit'—labor accomplishes everything! We are still hopefully working, and must abide by what the future has in store."[39]

Brigham likely never found records for Job Tyler's family in west England because, as has now been shown, his family came from Kent in eastern England. He returned to the United States, but his further research was disrupted in 1901 when his doctor insisted, for health reasons, that he move to the southwest, where he died in 1904 before his volumes had been published.

Recognition from publishing partner

Emma Elizabeth Brigham was responsible for compiling and editing the Brigham volumes. In 1908 she wrote a brief tribute to the man and his work.

"Picture him now, with two histories on his hands, on each of which money had been pledged and paid, dependent on the small and very irregularly paid income from the Brigham work, such sums as interested Tylers might advance him, and—his wife's chicken yard. If you know anything of the constant small demands on the pocket book in genealogical work, you will recognize that it was something like the old tale of bricks without straw.

"Had health been given him and life spared, think not but that every obligation he had made would have been met. Willard Irving Tyler Brigham was a high-minded, honorable man, but misfortune came to him from out of a clear sky, in a form which it was impossible for him to foresee or to provide against, and it found him at a point in his work where he needed health and a prolongation of life to fulfill the obligations resting upon him. He did the best he could. No one conversant with all the circumstances can doubt this. How bravely he battled for life that he might finish his noble tasks can never be sufficiently known to his kinsmen. His editors marvel at his erudition and industry. He toured New England and New York State on his bicycle more than once, going to large and small places for records. One summer he traveled in this way more than 2,000 miles. The summer of 1900 he spent in Great Britain and France in researches. In fact, he contracted the disease from which he died in the damp stone buildings in London, searching for Tyler origins."[40]

In 1906 The Houston Post published an announcement regarding the publishing of Brigham's *The Tyler Genealogy*. It referred to the death of Brigham before his extensive work had been published and how the final work would be covered by The Grafton Press.

"The Grafton press, publishers, New York, whose specialty is genealogical and historical work, announce that they have undertaken the editing and compiling of a great mass of manuscript of 'The Tyler Family in America,' originally gathered by the late W. J.[sic] Tyler Brigham who, after many long years of labor, died leaving the matter incomplete. The editorial work is in charge of the genealogical expert of the Grafton press, Mr. Frank Allaben, who will be glad to hear from any member of the family. After the manuscript has been complete, it will be published in two handsome, illustrated octavo volumes."[41]

Rollin U. Tyler and C. B. Tyler continued the effort to realize the publication of Brigham's two volumes. At considerable financial cost, the books were published in 1912 and since that time have remained the major resource for the history and genealogy of the Job Tyler family lineage. The efforts of Rollin U. and C. B. Tyler are included here:

"*The Tyler Genealogy* now (June, 1912) ready for distribution has passed through many vicissitudes. W. I. T. Brigham, the author, spent an enormous amount of personal work on a labor of love, besides spending some thousands of dollars advanced to him by various members of the clan. On his death in 1904 he left an incomplete manuscript.

"The Grafton Press took this and contracted to complete editing and publishing it. In order to help the publication generous members of the clan again contributed money. Some pre-paid their subscriptions. A guarantee fund of over $1,700 was raised to be paid back in the future. Most of this was spent in necessary editing and other work. Early in 1911, the Grafton Press assigned for benefit of creditors. By its insolvency, it carried with it the printer, the Binghamton Book Co., which had in page proof 784 pages of the Genealogy for which it had not been paid. In order to prevent destruction, the undersigned purchased this from a bank that had taken it on foreclosure, and at a new expense of about $1,000 we had the book indexed and publication completed.

"To our friends who have lost by the failure of the Grafton Press, we suggest the following:

"The book as finally published besides more than a score of years service without pay, has cost probably over $5,000 cash. The sale of the book would never under any circumstances pay back any large part of even this latter amount. Somebody had to lose. The undersigned being among the largest contributors have lost most. In completing the publication, we have no desire to make anything. If we do not collect enough to pay our last $1,000 disbursement, we will stand the loss. If we collect more, we have intended to distribute it where we thought it most equitably belonged, namely, to the contributors to the guarantee fund raised for the Grafton Press, and those who had already prepaid the Grafton Press for copies of the book, and now pay again. Meanwhile we have such satisfaction as is obtainable from the knowledge that the genealogy is in much more accurate and handsome form than would have been possible had only such money been spent as the sale of the book would have yielded. Also, we have lowered the price to $12, hoping to reach a larger public and grant wider distribution.

"Rollin U. & C. B. Tyler"[42]

Chapter 5: Notable Kin and Their Stories

There are many members of the extended Job Tyler family line who individually have had either significant impacts in American society in one way or another or have had personal lives of consequence. Many stories of notable Tylers were included in Brigham's Volumes I and II of *The Tyler Genealogy*.[43] Because these volumes are well known and readily available in print and online, it is not necessary to include biographies from those volumes in this narrative. However, there are many other notable stories not as accessible or well known. It has been a gratifying experience to discover the wealth of biographies, stories, and anecdotes describing the centuries of contributions made by the Job Tyler family in America since 1638. Many of these biographies are included in the following pages.

On the following two pages the lineage is shown of each biography included in this chapter. The first chart indicates the lineage on the Moses (#2; Tyler-118) side of the family; the second chart shows biographies from the lineage of Job's other children. A darker box indicates an individual whose biography is included on the following pages. The biographies are ordered chronologically according to distinct eras of American history. However, the reader should feel comfortable in reading them in any order they wish.

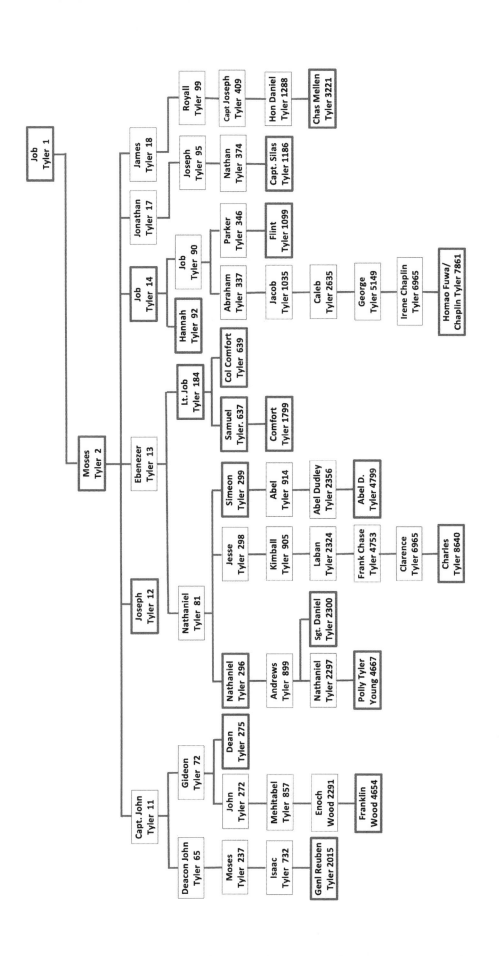

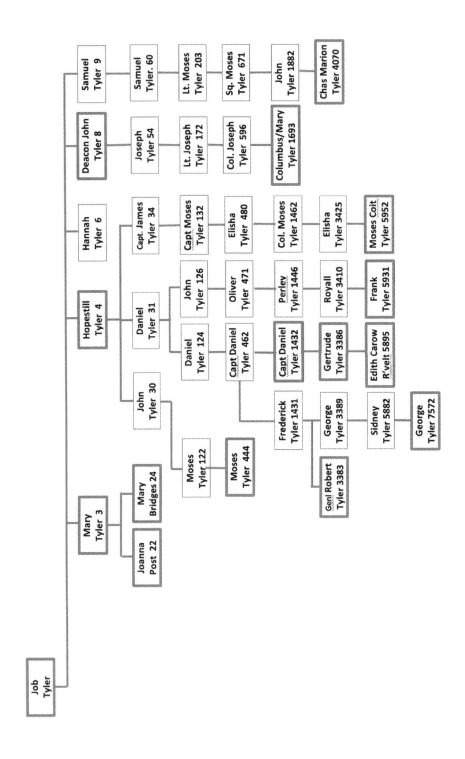

Colonial Era (1600s–1770s)

In the late sixteenth century, England, France, Spain, and the Netherlands launched major colonization programs in America. England made its first successful colonial efforts in the early 1600s as a commercial enterprise, because of over-crowding in England, and a continuing desire for freedom of religion. English settlers came from a variety of social and religious groups. Most immigrants to Colonial America arrived as indentured servants, young unmarried men and women seeking a new life in a much richer environment. In New England, the economy was organized around small family farms and urban communities engaged in fishing, handicrafts, and Atlantic commerce, with most of the population living in small compact towns.

During the late seventeenth and early and mid-eighteenth centuries, the colonists became embroiled in a series of contests for power between Britain, France and Spain. By the 1760s, after Britain had decisively defeated the French, the colonists were in a position to challenge their subordinate position within the British Empire, and the colonists began efforts for more freedom and independence from their mother country.

Many of the prominent Tylers from this period significantly helped establish early communities. Most of the Job Tyler family settled in Massachusetts, especially in Essex County in the northeast corner of the what was then the Massachusetts Bay Colony.

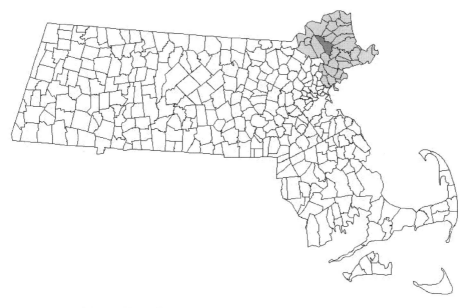

Map of Massachusetts, Essex County, and Boxford Township[44]

"Quartermaster" Moses Tyler (ca. 1641–1727)

Brigham's Volume I includes an extensive biography of Moses Tyler (#2; Tyler-118), Job's oldest son. Moses may be considered the most noteworthy and prominent of Job's offspring because of his contributions as an early settler in his community as well as having many offspring. This brief section includes additional information not included in Volume I.

Moses was born in Andover, Massachusetts, but moved with his parents and family to "Rowley Village." In Rowley Village he cleared land for a farm, reared a family, and became a locally conspicuous citizen. His father Job spent some time there. The main settlement of Rowley Village is now the village of Old Boxford, Massachusetts.

Moses kept his church affiliation at Andover for a while. He served the town as selectman, committee-man, surveyor, constable, etc. He became the custodian of "Ten pounds of powder, sixty pounds of bullets and fifty flints." For such services he acquired the title of "Quartermaster." In 1691, he was one of five men who were selected to find a central site for a local church edifice. It was completed in 1695 and was presented to the town, being in the "East Parish." Most of his sons and their wives are listed as members. He was the Minister from 1692 to 1726.

Based on deeds in Salem, Massachusetts, we know he was the proprietor of large lands, acquiring and seldom parting with properties. His will was written in 1725 and was probated at Salem in 1727 (Case #28452). His sons by his first wife, Prudence, had been provided for before the will was written. He had given them their full portion out of the estate. He left all of his homestead in Andover to his youngest son, Jacob, who was his son by his second wife, Sarah, and her three daughters, Martha, Catherine, and Mary, who he had raised as his own.

Moses Tyler gravestone with Job Tyler Memorial plaque,
Old North Parish Burying Ground, North Andover, Massachusetts[45]

Moses Tyler's gravesite is found in the Old North Parish Burying Ground at North Andover, Massachusetts, next to a memorial plaque for his father, Job, whose gravesite is unknown. "This spot is peculiarly interesting, being the place of interment of the immigrant Job's eldest son. (It is altogether safe to assume that Job's last resting place cannot now be identified.) It is located near the north wall of the old North Andover burying-ground, about opposite the center of the cemetery, under the drooping west boughs of a giant spruce, which here in numbers have been allowed to attain unusual size and add a weird attractiveness to their surroundings. The patient seeker will be rewarded by the sight of a venerable slab, whose thickness suggests importation from England, after the custom of early times. Though eroded and cracked by the elements for nearly two centuries, it is still distinctly legible, and retains with wonderful exactness all its essential details, even of quaint ornamentation. More ornate than most of its fellow, with tracery, foil and courses, it must have been an envy in its day. In its center chief is an effigy, which fancy translates to represent a winged cherub (common on ancient slabs), but so primitive in execution as vividly to suggest the craft of contemporary Indians. The inscription (and let him who seeks to read the stone beware of poison ivy) runs as follows:

"HERE LYES BURIED
the BODY OF Mr.
MOSES TYLER WHO
DIED OCTOBER Ye 2nd
1727 & IN the
86 YEaR OF HIS AGE."[46]

Joseph Tyler (1671–1699)

Joseph Tyler (#12; Tyler-188) was the grandson of Job and son of Moses. As a young man, he decided to travel to the Caribbean Island of Barbados, looking for adventure and opportunity. His six years on the island, working and eventually managing a sugar plantation, is described by Colonel O. Z. Tyler in his 1987 book, *Sweet Land of Liberty: One Family's Saga in Colonial America.*[47] The book is a narrative based on the history of the Job Tyler family, with the author changing the last name to Williams to make it a fictionalized history. Colonel Tyler explains in the Introduction: "It is substantially the true story of a real pioneer family in early America." Following are two excerpts from the book that are based on research on the Job Tyler family by Colonel Tyler and others. It describes a young man in the seventeenth century in search of adventure who eventually finds rewards and dangers inherent in traveling far from his home in Massachusetts.

~

"As you know, Joseph was the third son of Moses Williams, Job's eldest son. He was born September 18, 1671, in Andover. He had been involved in the Witchcraft Trials in 1692 as a very young man. With two cousins, Martha and Joanna Williams, he was one of the confessed witches. They were said to have been led into the witchcraft hallucination by Abigail Faulkner, the leader of the bewitched girls who were the principal witnesses.

"But I must not get ahead of my story.

"I—Barbados, 1693

"The decision of Joseph to go to Barbados came as a surprise to everyone. Of course, all of the family were aware of Joseph's ordeal of trial and acquittal in the infamous witchcraft trials. And they were sympathetic with his desire to get away to some place where he could make a new start.

Joseph was known and liked as a smart lad who showed great promise. His involvement in the witch trials came as a shock and surprise to everyone. Of course, everyone knew about his association with Abigail Faulkner and his half-sisters, Joanna Post and Mary Bridges, who were star witnesses in the courts. It was the testimony of these girls, coupled with their convincing fits and seizures, which proved to be so damning in the witchcraft trials. But no one really considered Joseph as being seriously implicated.

"Joseph's selection of Barbados as a destination may have had some connection with the trials. Tituba, the black servant in the kitchen of Reverend Samuel Parris where the witchcraft girls played, was from the islands. It was felt that Tituba may have had something to do with the witchcraft hallucinations. [Note: Tituba will be described later in the section on the Salem Witch Trials.] It would be pure speculation however to think that Joseph was influenced to head for Barbados by Tituba. Nevertheless, the fascinating Tituba was replete with stories and information about the islands as well as a catalogue of voodoo lore together with spells and incantations. No doubt all this may have entered into Joseph's decision.

"Suffice it to say that Joseph decided to leave Andover and go to Barbados. He went first, of course, to Boston, where the ever-helpful John Ford, his grandfather Job's faithful friend, assisted him in booking passage on the *Lion*, sailing soon out of Salem for Barbados. Joseph had never in his twenty-one-year life been farther afield than Boston. But here he was in the spring of the year, embarking for a tropical island that he had barely heard of, but which promised new experiences, opportunities, and high adventure!

"Not the least intriguing possibility was the thought of earning his fortune, possibly by running a sugar plantation. He had heard of the Barbados plantations in the stories of Tituba. He was an experienced farmer. He felt that he could grow anything. He had heard stories of the English colonization there, which began, he remembered from his books, in Barbados around 1627, soon after the colonization of new England. And he also knew of the plentiful slave labor, which worked the fields and operated the sugar mills. In the pattern of the young, not once did he give thought to tales of literally thousands of pirates that swarmed the warm Caribbean waters between him and his destination. If he did think of such things, he was comforted by the eight guns of the *Lion*, four on each side, that seemed adequate to meet any contingency although he had never himself heard a cannon fired.

"At the family gathering that was held prior to Joseph's departure, white-haired Job and Mary presided a little more soberly than usual. There was laughter and gaiety enough, and more than a plenty of wonderful things to eat and drink. But the two elders seemed to enjoy, sitting a little apart and letting Moses and Hopestill, the elder sons, do the major share of the talking. Job's daughter, Mary, old before her time because of the scars of the witchcraft trials, just sat and watched the jollity.

"Job did take time during the festivity to talk to Joseph about his decision to leave Andover.

"'No doubt you have given this matter much thought,' he said. 'I do not blame you a bit for leaving what you must feel is a small, backbiting town.

But there are lots of people here who love you and would like to see you stay around.'

"'I know, grandfather, but there is a big world out there, and I aim to find out something about it,' his grandson replied seriously.

"Before the evening was over, Job also contrived to slip his departing grandson an appreciated 50-pound note."

The author continues the narrative with Joseph's time on Barbados, from 1693 to 1699. Within a year Joseph had become part of the English society of Barbados. He had been selected for a job as plantation bookkeeper and, eventually, manager. He prospered on the island, and eventually took a native islander as his mistress and partner. Unfortunately, his demise came during a trip to another island to purchase a new sailing vessel when their ship was attacked by pirates. The author's final story on Joseph concludes with this attack.

"Joseph and Samuel were both good sailors, so they enjoyed the spanking breeze and the roughed-up water. The captain of their own ship, the *Barbara*, provided them with the best cabin on the little vessel. He also instructed the cook to make the meals extra special and to break out the very best wines aboard.

"The *Barbara* was sailing smoothly on her northerly course when all at once a cry from the lookout rang out: 'Sail-ho! Brigantine bearing down on the starboard bow,' the sailor on watch chanted.

"Joseph and Samuel were out of the cabin and peering out northward and to the right. They wondered who this stranger might be. They did not have to speculate very long. They could see a puff of smoke from the bow of the approaching vessel, and almost at once the muffled boom of a cannon was heard. The warning shot whistled over the bow of the *Barbara* and splashed into the water nearby.

"'Not a very friendly greeting,' Joseph thought out loud.

"'Do you see anything familiar about that ship?' Neither Samuel nor the captain answered the query.

"The captain of the *Barbara* hove his ship to as the warning shot had directed.

"'It looks like they are loading a small boat to come aboard,' said the captain, somewhat alarmed.

"'Secure arms and stand by to repel boarder,' he commanded his crew.

"By this time the two vessels were both hove to, within fifty yards of each other. Three additional small boats were loading and shoving off from the dinghy-looking vessel.

"'Pirates!' screamed several crewmen. One man had spotted the gruesome black flag at the masthead.

"'That looks like Stede Bonnet's flag,' one of the crew yelled. 'See that single bone beneath the skull? That's his sign!'

". . . As small-boats began to arrive, shots rang out! The *Barbara*'s crew dutifully tried to deal with the swarming buccaneers. Joseph and Samuel stood near the cabin, muskets in hand. There was no stopping the cut-throat intruders. Joseph and Samuel both fired at point-blank range. Each shot took its toll, the invaders going down to redden the deck with spurting blood. They reloaded their muskets and courageously fired again. But the attackers kept coming. Cutlasses and knives came into play. Joseph was mortally struck with a knife from behind, by a ruffian he did not even see. Samuel survived to make a bargain with Stede Bonnet. The entire melee took only a few minutes.

"'What a way to have it end,' Joseph breathed to the small cluster who gathered in shocked silence to see this prominent man expire. Even the ruffian pirates were for the moment quiet and impressed.

". . . Samuel did get back to Bridgetown. He was able to pay the large ransom Bonnet, the pirate, demanded. And he did write back to Job in Andover, telling of his admiration and affection for Joseph and of his sad and useless demise.

"It was a tragedy for his family, especially his grandmother, who set such a great store by Joseph. But who can say that this New England lad who carved a niche for himself in far-off Barbados did not live spectacularly!"

Job Tyler, son of Moses (1675–1754)

The early Tyler family was connected with the prominent Bradstreet family in the third generation as a result of Job Tyler (#14; Tyler-165) marrying Margaret, a granddaughter of Governor Simon Bradstreet. Job Tyler was born on 16 December 1675 in Rowley, Massachusetts, the son of Moses Tyler (#2; Tyler-118) and Prudence Blake. Job was a model citizen. In 1706 he served as constable of the recently erected municipality of Boxford, as selectman in 1716 and 1744, and served on town and church committees. In 1735, he was on the committee of three to oversee and manage the building of the Second (i.e. original West Boxford) church.

But perhaps his most notable tie to local history was his marriage to Margaret Bradstreet, the granddaughter of Governor Bradstreet. In the Tyler Family Reunion of 1896, one of the events scheduled as part of the program was a visit to the Bradstreet House. It represented the close ties between the Bradstreet and Tyler families. The visit was described in the Reunion brochure as follows:

"BRADSTREET HOUSE. One of the most conspicuous dwellings of Massachusetts Bay Colony. To this home from Ipswich, about 1643, moved Simon Bradstreet, ten years Governor of Massachusetts Bay under its first and second charters, being 89 years of age when he vacated the gubernatorial chair. He married Anne, daughter of Thomas Dudley, four times Governor of the Colony. Anne, who died here, was the very first American poetess. From her are descended such literary lights as Dr. O[liver] W[endell] Holmes, Wendell Phillips, Richard H. Dana and Dr. Channing."[48]

Colonel Dudley Bradstreet has an important tie to the Tyler family. Born in 1648 in Andover, Massachusetts, he was the son of Simon and Ann Dudley Bradstreet. Simon Bradstreet was Governor of the Massachusetts Bay Colony from 1670 to 1686. Bradstreet also is an ancestor of United States President Herbert Hoover. Like his father, he was a prominent early citizen—an attorney, a colonel in the militia, schoolteacher, and serving as a selectman and town clerk in Andover. He would also serve as a Deputy to the General Court of Massachusetts, and later was a member of the Governor's Council.

Though he opposed the entire witchcraft delusion, he found himself in the unenviable position of Justice of the Peace in Andover during the witch hysteria. For eight weeks in 1692, Bradstreet gave arrest warrants and committed to prison some thirty Andover residents for supposed witchcraft. Under substantial pressure, and after overseeing a ludicrous "touch test" (in which accused individuals were pricked to see if they felt pain; if they did, they were considered innocent), he dutifully wrote out an additional eighteen warrants. However, after he had issued those warrants, he refused to grant any more. Not long afterwards, both he and his wife Ann were themselves accused of witchcraft, with the claim they had killed at least nine people. In response, Bradstreet and his wife fled the area. However, he later returned to Andover and his name appears first on the petition presented to the Superior Court of Judicature at Salem at its opening session in 1693.

During this time, Colonel Bradstreet married Mary Wainwright and they had three children. One of them, daughter Margaret, was a neighbor and friend of the Moses Tyler family. Margaret took a special interest in Job Tyler, and they were married. Margaret's marriage to Job gave the Tyler lineage connection to Dudley Bradstreet, and thus the tie between the Bradstreet/Dudley line and the Tyler lineage has increased significance.

The Book of Maggie Bradstreet

In 2012, contemporary author Gretchen Gibbs wrote *The Book of Maggie Bradstreet*.[49] It is a fictionalized history depicting the underlying fear in the Andover, Massachusetts, community during the period of the witch trials in 1692. She uses as her literary device the diary writings of a thirteen-year-old girl, Margaret ("Maggie") Bradstreet, who historically was the daughter and granddaughter of two generations of the distinguished Bradstreet family in the Massachusetts Bay Colony. Over the course of a year Maggie writes in her personal diary descriptions of what is happening to her, her family, and others in her community. During that year she becomes a special friend with Job Tyler, and although details are fictionalized, in actuality Job and Margaret became married in later years and had six children. As the author states, "All of the book's characters from Andover were real people, taken from the records of the time brought together by the historical Societies of Andover and North Andover. I used nicknames for Margaret Bradstreet (Maggie) and Mary Bridges (Polly), as I thought it was too confusing to have a Margaret, Mary, and Martha as main characters." The following is a revealing and intriguing section from the book focusing on the relationship of Job and Margaret during this difficult period.

~

"I enjoy going to Tyler's because I might see Job Tyler, whom I like, though he is a friend of Dudley's. I like his eyes, which are blue and still. He looks at things closely, like he is seeing them true. I would that he had dark hair to go with them, but his hair is not too different from my own, only a few shades lighter brown. I would not like Dudley to read this passage."

". . . Something jumped inside me when I saw Job throwing a ball in the yard with the young boys. When Job looks at me with his blue eyes, I know he sees only Dudley's small sister, however. He talks to me as though I were a child."

In the following excerpt from the book, Maggie's father is the local magistrate during the represented year of 1692. Part of his responsibility is to complete paperwork designating who is to be tried as a witch. In this lengthy diary entry, the locals are attending Sunday service, but the service serves as an opportunity to expose alleged witches.

"We passed down the aisle, past the Tylers. Martha [*Note: Historically, Martha is Job's stepsister*] and the Hussy seemed not to note me, but Job looked up and was startled. I could see that he was sorry I was there, and his fear for me first made me happy, and then it added to my own fear. I had been thinking so much about Hannah and the children, I had given little thought to myself. I know I am not a Witch, and I had felt Father's name would protect our family. [*Note: Margaret's father was Dudley Bradstreet, son of Governor Simon Bradstreet and grandson of Thomas Dudley, who also served as Governor of Massachusetts Bay Colony.*] . . . Mother handed Father his papers across the aisle before we took our places.

"The Reverend Barnard spoke out loudly and firmly. He called upon God to be present and to help us in our work and to be with us in each step of the proceedings. He said that we should now, with God's help and the help of the poor afflicted girls from Salem, root out the evil that had lain among us for too long. (pp. 135-6)

". . . Reverend Barnard commanded us to stand, and he brought forth a large a quantity of handkerchiefs. He began to go up the aisle handing handkerchiefs to some. I knew not what the handkerchiefs were for, but I knew they did not bode well.

"When he passed up the aisle without handing one to me, or Mother, or Dudley on the other side, I began to breathe again. I had not realized I had stopped breathing. I turned and watched the Reverend go up the aisle, whether or not it was rude to stare. Everyone was staring. He gave handkerchiefs to many, perhaps more than half of the women. Hannah's mother received one, Eunice Fry received one. A number of children were given handkerchiefs.

"He gave none to Job. Job's eyes met mine again after the Reverend had passed, and we spoke without words our relief for the other." (p. 137)

". . . Reverend Barnard commanded all who had received a handkerchief to come forward and to stand facing the congregation. He told them to tie the handkerchief about their eyes so they could see nothing. . . . There were many there facing us, perhaps thirty.

". . . Father was busy writing and writing, as more and more women were brought forward. His face looked blank and angry.

"I knew that the girls were play-acting, that they were as bad as Martha, and yet in spite of that they struck me with fear. Ann screamed that she had lost her sight. She stared around as blindly as the women behind her in their blindfolds. She began to scream more hoarsely than before that her throat closed up upon her and she could not breathe. I was frightened to my bones. I could not help it. I had to pass water, I was so frightened and it was hard to sit still, it was also fearsome to see the looks upon the faces of the accused as they were forced to touch and as they were pulled away.

". . . Job's aunt, Goody Tyler [*Note: Goody is actually Mary Tyler, wife of Hopestill Tyler*], was called, and the girls stopped writing at her touch. I looked back at Job as she was hauled away to the back benches, and his face was tight with wrath. Now three of his aunts had been taken.

"Then there were his cousins, the children of Goody Tyler. The twins are but 11. They clung to each other piteously though they did not understand well what was happening. Joanna [*daughter of Hopestill*] peed upon the floor, she was so frightened. The smell was strong. I could hardly control my own need, but I knew I could not leave.

". . . Father still wrote. I thought he looked more angry than I had ever seen, and very cold.

"The noise of the crying and wailing of those taken was now louder than the noise of the Salem girls, and Reverend Barnard commanded that all those arrested be brought outside. We could still hear them, but the wails of the Salem girls were the louder noise in our ears, and the smell was less.

"There were others. Captain Osgood's manservant was taken. Father was writing slower than before. I kept looking at the Eye of God upon the pulpit. And wondering how God could abide this.

"There were still many more in front with handkerchiefs over their eyes. Till now, the girls had found all who had been brought forward to be witches. All who had been asked to touch the girls had been arrested.

"Joseph, Reverend Dane's servant, was called. I heard a sound in back, and I turned about to see Ruth covering her mouth with her hand, and her eyes wide with fear. Joseph moaned, as he was guided forward to touch Ann. She sighed like she had just recovered from the worst illness one could ever have.

"Reverend Barnard nodded to the Constable to take Joseph [*servant of Reverend Dane*] away. Reverend Barnard nodded to Father, who began to write. He seemed to hit a snag in the paper, as he stopped, and dipped the quill again into the inkwell. He picked it up again. Then, as Reverend Barnard was looking at the group of blindfolded folk remaining, deciding whom to pick next, Father flung his pen down upon the table. A large gob of ink flew from the quill in an arc like that an arrow makes from the bow, and landed upon the Reverend Barnard's hand.

"'Fie upon this travesty of justice!' Father shouted louder than I have ever heard him. 'You have called upon God, but He is not in this chamber! I shall write no more.'

"There was silence. Even the Salem girls were quiet, though they had begun their moans again after Joseph was taken. Then from the back Francis Dane called,

"'You have spoken true, Dudley Bradstreet. God bless you.'" (pp. 139-140)

Maggie and her family quickly escape to rural New Hampshire to escape prosecution. Their knowledge of what is happening in Andover and Salem is limited, but Maggie thinks often of home, as represented in this brief excerpt from her diary.

"Father says that the court has just begun its fall session, and that some may be undergoing trials right now. I wonder if there were more arrests, and if there is a warrant out for our arrest.

"I think also about Job. I wonder how he can abide living in the same house with Martha and to know his relations have been shut in prison by her doing. How do they speak to each other? I wonder if Job thinks about me." (p. 151)

The Bradstreets remained in New Hampshire until December. However, in October they received a letter (fictionalized) from Job Tyler describing the current situation in Andover. The letter was addressed to Maggie's brother, Dudley, but she feels it is really intended for her, especially since it includes the story of what happened to her dog, Tobey.

"Fifteenth of October,
"Year of our Lord 1692
"My dear Dudley,

"I think often about you and your family and hope for your health and safety. I have been told by Reverend Dane that should I write to you Grandfather, he would forward it, and I hope you shall receive this missive and my good wishes.

"I know not what news you have received, and I think you must know this, but I shall tell it again in case. I was not there, but have heard fully from several who were. When the crowd came, armed and angry, to arrest your uncle, they were angrier yet to find him not at home. They came upon Tobey, who was protecting the house. Martha Sprague waved a stick at him, then hit him hard on the back. He bit her under her skirts on the ankle. Martha began to shriek, 'Witch! Witch! He has been bewitched!'

"Henry Chandler, who is sweet on Martha, spoke to the others and they picked up Tobey, muzzled him and took him away in their own carriage, to be charged. What role Constable Ballard played I do not know.

"On the way back, Tobey managed to free himself from his restraints, and he bit Martha again. Martha began to scream and rant. All in the carriage were incensed, and they stopped upon the way at Woodchuck Hill and hung Tobey from a tree.

"The next day, the town could talk of nothing else. 'Did you hear, they hung the Bradstreets' dog for a Witch?' It went around and around. Folk said, 'What think you, how remarkable that Tobey, who seemed a good dog, could be a Familiar of Satan?'

"I could not abide that Tobey should hang there on Woodchuck Hill for passersby to see, and I told my father that I wished to take the wagon to cut him down. Father tried to prevent me, and Martha and her mother were wrathful. I went regardless.

"I do not think that Tobey suffered, for his neck was broken clean. I was angered to see him, as well as sorrowful. Instead of coming straight, I drove around the town at a slow pace before coming back into the village. Then I buried Tobey in your yard, under the elm tree in the front, for all eyes to see. Reverend Barnard came out of his house and told me I should not, but I did not regard him and he went away. It took a time, as I dug a hole three feet deep, so no animals shall disturb his rest. I thought what

Maggie would like and I cut a branch from the Rose of Sharon to place upon him. Several folk gathered to watch and mutter. Reverend Dane came by and said, loudly, that is was right that Tobey should have a decent burial.

"By the time I went to Peters' store the next day, the talk had changed. When I came up, Andrew Peters was saying, 'How could folk be so witless as to suppose that good dog was a familiar of Satan?' All were agreeing, and blaming Martha and the others who hung him. It was like the way the wind shifts in a nor'easter. Who can honor the doings of folk who would hang a dog?

"Other things have occurred to help. People have been saying in private that they do not think that your father and mother could be Witches, that many in the prison could not be Witches, and they have asked why all Reverend Dane's family has been taken. Also, the fall rains came, some crops were saved, and it looks no longer that we shall starve. One other thing of import has occurred, one of the women testified that it was Reverend Barnard himself who told her daughter the words to use when casting spells. I trust that has shaken the Reverend's faith in spectral evidence. I have heard that Reverend Cotton Mather has also revised his view of spectral evidence. [*Note: Spectral evidence is evidence based on dreams and visions.*]

"At all events, a letter was written to the Salem court requesting leniency for some of those taken. Many signed, including the Reverend Barnard.

"The good news is that today many have been released on bail, mainly children. These include the children of Martha Carrier, and several other children, and best news of all, for me and for Maggie, Polly Bridges!

"Our family shall take Polly in and care for her. I shall send news of her after I see her. Please give my regard to all your family, and be sure to give this news to Maggie. I know you all, and Maggie especially, grieve for Tobey. I believe Tobey has helped to play a role in the sea change in our town, and perhaps it could be a comfort to think that he died in a worthy cause. Like a small soldier, perhaps.

"With humble respects,

Job Tyler" (pp. 155-158)

Witchcraft Comes to Andover: The Salem Witch Trials, 1692 to 1695

It is difficult for society in this century to understand the rationale used in the seventeenth century to justify the witch trials and executions. There are a number of theories, none of which is conclusive. Such theories include:

- Puritans had a strong belief in the witches making an alliance with the devil and they saw any personal disorders as evidence of this.
- The winters preceding the witch trials were especially cold with hardships resulting from crop failures, with the blame placed on certain individuals.
- Rye grains contaminated with a fungus could cause convulsions and hallucinations.
- Devastating losses suffered by the colonists in the wars with Indians on the northern frontier traumatized many of the accusers and the general populace alike, making them (and the judges) search for explanations in the "invisible

world" of witchcraft, since witches and a native peoples were both thought to be devil worshippers, and thus logical allies of each other.

- Stress from the challenges of colonial living led to mental anguish, eventually realized with a psychogenic disorder with physical symptoms.
- Reverend Samuel Parris of Salem and his supporters used witch accusations to settle accounts with individuals they saw as a threat to Puritan values.
- The arrest and confession of Tituba, a Caribbean worker who practiced occult rituals, led to her stating she worked for the devil and there were other witches like her in Salem.

No general consensus has ever been made as to the cause, but to put ourselves in the mental state of society at that time can perhaps better explain the reasons for this misuse of rational justice. Belief in the supernatural–and specifically in the devil's practice of giving certain humans (witches) the power to harm others in return for their loyalty–had emerged in Europe as early as the fourteenth century and was widespread in colonial New England. We now have the benefit of more analytical and thoughtful rationales, but at that time there was a universally prevalent belief in witchcraft.

Salem Witchcraft Trial[50]

Mary Tyler and the Witch Trials

Mary Tyler, wife of Hopestill (#4; Lovett-160), got caught up in the web of suspicion that swept out of Salem Village and into surrounding towns and villages, until more than 150 persons found themselves accused of witchcraft. The following account is taken from the "Ron and Sue Wall's Family History Site."[51]

"In the fall of 1692 the wife of Joseph Ballard of Andover fell sick. Ballard, as did many others, believed that a sick person could tell who or what was the cause of their illness. Ballard or his wife apparently accused several persons in Andover of causing her sickness by witchcraft. Ballard, either on his own or at the urging of others, brought two of the "afflicted" girls from Salem to Andover. The people accused of witchcraft were ordered to come together at the meeting house in Andover where the Salem girls were being kept. A strange test was conducted. It was believed that if the hand of a witch touched the body of the person whom they had bewitched, that person would immediately become well and could identify the witch.

"Mr. Barnard (the local minister?) prayed and then blindfolded the accused. The afflicted girls fell into their fits when the accused person came into their presence. Then the hand of the accused was placed on each of the afflicted girls. The girls would immediately come out of their fit and identify the person touching them of being the one who afflicted them. This evidence was enough to cause the arrest of the accused as witches. The authorities immediately seized the men and women and sent them to Salem for trial. Among them were Mary Tyler (sometimes identified as Martha in the documents) and her daughter Johanna (Hannah).

"Those arrested were dumbfounded, knowing, of course, that they were completely innocent of anything as hideous as witchcraft. They were respected members of the community and pious members of the church. How could they be even suspected of such a thing.

"Events in Salem were not encouraging. People who refused to confess were being executed. Many of the relatives of the accused pleaded with their family members to confess in the hopes that their lives would be spared.

"At first Mary Tyler was unafraid, convinced that nothing could cause her to confess against herself. When she was brought to Salem, her brother Bridges rode with her. All along the way from Andover to Salem, he kept telling her that she must be a witch, since the afflicted had accused her, and at her touch they were raised out of their fits. He urged her to confess to being a witch.

"Mary constantly told Bridges that she was no witch, that she knew nothing of witchcraft, and begged him not to urge her to confess. When they reached Salem, Mary was taken to a room, where her brother on one side, and Mr. John Emerson on the other side, told her that she was certainly a witch, and that she saw the Devil before her eyes at that time. Emerson would attempt to beat the devil way from her eyes with his hands. I assume that this means Emerson beat Mary about the face. Eventually, Mary was in such a state that she wished herself in any dungeon, rather than be so treated. Emerson told her, again and again, 'Well, I see you will not confess! Well, I will now leave you; and then you are undone, body and soul, forever.'

"Mary's brother urged her to confess, and told her that, in so doing, she could not lie. Mary answered, 'Good brother, do not say so; for I shall lie if I confess, and then who shall answer unto God for my lie?'
Bridges still asserted that she was a witch and said that God would not suffer so many good men to be in such an error about it, and that she would be hanged if she did not confess. He continued long and violently to urge Mary to confess.

"Finally, Mary began to believe that her life would go from her, and she became so terrified in her mind that she confessed, at length, to almost anything that they propounded to her. At the same time, she felt she had wronged her conscience in doing so; that she was guilty of a great sin in belying herself, and desired to mourn for it for as long as she lived. In the meantime, ten-year-old Dorothy Faulkner and eight-year-old Abigail Faulkner, children of Abigail Faulkner of Andover confessed to being witches and stated that their mother along with Mary Tyler, Johanna Tyler, Sarah Wilson and Joseph Draper had lead them into witchcraft. Knowing what poor Mary Tyler went through in her inquisition, one can imagine what these children were put through."

The Story of Mary's Confession

"Goodwife Tyler did say, that when she was first apprehended, she had no fears upon her, & did think, that nothing could have made her confess against herself. But, since, she has found to her great grief, that she had wronged the truth & falsely accused herself. When she was being taken from her home in Andover to prison in Salem, her brother-in-law Bridges rode beside her; and, during the memorable ride, told her that she must be a 'witch,' because the afflicted were raised out of their fits 'by her touch.' She stoutly denied the accusation and begged him not to urge her to confess. But, arrived at Salem (shall we not rather say, temporary 'Pandemonium'?), she had to combat, not only a stubbornly misguided brother on one side, but also on her other side, 'John Emerson'; which latter stoutly took up the cudgel of accusation, on calling her a witch, declaring he could see the Devil before her eyes, whereupon, with his hands, he proceeded to beat him off. In short, her persecutors so harassed her for confession that she would have 'preferred a dungeon' to their presence. Finally, they threatened to leave her; declaring that, in such event, she would be undone body and soul forever. To their reiterations, that she 'could not lie by confessing,' she retorted, 'I shall lie, if I confess; and then, who shall answer unto God for my lie?' Their final resort always was, 'You will be hanged, if you do not confess!' In short, they so protracted their unmerciful treatment, that the poor woman began to doubt her very life and reason: whereupon they proceed to have her 'agree to say' what they should 'suggest.' But, in her real 'confession' to Rev. Mather, she insisted, 'she wronged her conscience in so doing, was guilty of a great sin in belying herself & desired to mourn for it so long as she lived.' And the said Mather adds, 'Her affliction, sorrow, relenting, grief and mourning, exceeds any pen to describe and express the same.'"[52]

As a way to appease the judges, Mary and Johanna (Hannah) Tyler confessed to being witches. Mary confessed to making a covenant with the Devil and signed the Devil's book, promising to serve the Devil as long as she lived. She confessed to being baptized by the Devil and renouncing her former baptism and thus became a witch. On about September 7, 1692 and other times she practiced the "detestable Arts called witchcrafts, and sorceries" wickedly, maliciously, and feloniously used them in Andover. Mary confessed to using witchcraft against Hannah Foster, wife of Ephraim Foster of Andover, and Ralph Farnam, Sr. of Andover, who were "tortured, afflicted, pined wasted, consumed and tormented."

After their confessions, the women were held in the jails in Salem awaiting their trials. In October 1692 nine men of Andover, including Hopestill Tyler, sent a petition to the General Court in Boston begging that their wives and children, having confessed, be released from Salem jails back to their homes so their families could care for them until their trials. Condition in the overcrowded jails was appalling and the inmates were suffering from lack of proper food and clothing, and winter was fast approaching.

In December 1692 another petition was sent by the men of Andover, including Hopestill, to the Governor and Colonial Council sitting in Boston begging that their relatives be released to their families. The petition states that the families were sensitive to the extreme danger the prisoners were in of perishing if they were not speedily released. They begged the Governor and Council to consider the distress and suffering of their friends and family members in prison and grant them liberty to come home, under whatever terms as judged should be met by the petitioners. "If we might be allowed to plead their innocency, we think we have sufficient grounds to make such a plea for them, and hope their innocency will in time appear to the satisfaction of others, however they are at present under uncomfortable circumstances. So craving pardon for the trouble we have now given your Honors, and humbly requesting that something may be speedily done for the relief of our friends."

Finally, on January 13, 1693, Mary and Johanna were released to their family until their trial date. Hopestill and John Bridges posted the sum on one hundred pounds to guarantee their appearance at court. By then, Mary and Johanna had spent more than four months in prison in Salem. Their trials apparently took place in February. Both women pleaded not guilty, recanting their confessions. The juries found both Mary and Johanna not guilty of all charges and their long, terrible ordeal was over.[53]

Mary Tyler's Verdict Statement

"MARY TYLER wife of Hopestill Tyler of Andover, Blacksmith, being Indicted by the Jurors for or Soveraigne Lord and Lady the King and Queen upon these Oaths. try these Severall Indictments. That is to say; 1st—For that shee the said Mary Tyler wife of Hopestill Tyler of Andover in the County of Essex, Blacksmith, about seaven Years since in the Town of Andover aforesaid wickedly Malitiously and ffeloniously a covenant with the Devill did make and signed the Devills Book, and promised to serve the Devill as long as she lived &c. &c. The Jury went out to agree on their verdict, who returning did then and there in open Court deliver their Verdict. That the said Mary Tyler was Not Guilty of the ffellony by witchcraft for which shee stood Indicted in & by the said Indictments, and each of them. The Court ordered Mary Tyler aforesaid to be discharged paying her ffees."[54]

Mary Tyler's Unhappy Life and Death

In a 1981 article from a local newspaper written by Joe Hurka, the ghost of Mary Tyler is described by individuals whose claim to have experienced her presence has been consistent over many years. The text of the article begins: "She is usually seen dressed in 17th-century elegance, standing in ghostly transparency at the edge of the nearby meadow or wafting through the master's bedroom.

"If family legend is to be believed, Mary Tyler never rested after her death three centuries ago. According to some accounts, she has practiced her transparent trickery on the grounds and interior of the Witch Hollow Farm in Boxford since a little after her witchcraft trial in 1692.

"'I do at times feel a presence,' Jeanne Rich, who owns Witch Hollow with her husband Steve, says reflectively.

"She says the spirit is 'a positive one,' although she has never sighted her. And she recalls the visit to Witch Hollow of a psychic who spent a weekend at the farm.

"'The first night he didn't sleep, because he felt someone was watching him,' she says. 'But the second night he felt that he was accepted and could sleep.'

"Details one history of the Tyler clan: This is the Mary Tyler who supposedly returns to haunt the homestead only in the wee hours of the morning, when the mists rise from the meadow and the master of the house is alone in the house. There is some story of her carrying a curry comb (used for grooming horses) as she goes her way. She supposedly rattles papers in the attic and then descends the old stairs to the bedroom and proceeds through it and down the front stairs.

"Witch Hollow, according Rich, was so named because that area of Boxford (bordering North Andover) was allegedly populated with alleged witches in the late 1600s.

"The farmhouse is both romantic and peculiar in its architecture. It was built between 1666 and 1720 as three separate houses and finally connected with the third addition. The large, white structure has three chimneys, six stairways, two secret passageways (used in case of Indian raids), and nine doors leading to the outside. To the left of the house stands a giant red barn.

"The first Tyler on Boxford soil (or what was then Rowley and later Andover) was an interesting sort. He was an immigrant and a rowdy, crass individual, according to some reports.

"Recent excavations have found bricks on the Witch Hollow driveway, where the family patriarch and his wife probably had their first dwelling before he built the farmhouse. There they settled, prospered, and had children.

"Then came Mary Tyler, who was born in 1644. There is no record of her childhood, but the family tree shows she married Richard Post in 1662 and moved to what was then Mendon, in the Shelburne area.

"She returned to the homestead after her husband was killed in an Indian raid in 1675 and married again, this time to John Bridges. The next date which surfaces in her history is January, 1692 when she was accused of witchcraft and tried in Salem."[55]

The legend of Mary Tyler continues through an article written by Paula Tracy for *The Salem News* in which she has interviewed people living currently that claim to have experienced Mary's spirit. She described how Mary has been reportedly seen by the former owners roaming the house and grounds carrying a curry comb. Noise such as a loud banging and the rustling of paper have also been heard in the attic. A black pitch-like substance of an unknown source has also been seen dripping from the living room ceiling. The Riches and their five children have lived at Witch Hollow Farm for the past seven years, and although none have actually seen Mary, they say they've had some close encounters.

The late Ed French, who lived in the house in the 1950s, said he had seen Mary several times walking outside the house on moonlit nights.

The late Arthur Pinkham, who purchased the farm following World War II, wrote that he had seen Mary walk through the pine panels in his bedroom and when he reached out for her, disappear. In his study of the history of the house, he deduced the ghost was Mary, who lived at the farm in her youth.

The witch trials are today largely misunderstood as to the motivations of those judging their own citizens on these horrible accusations. To give more historical perspective, in 1884 a Judge Story described in a Centennial Address in Salem, Massachusetts, his explanation of the thinking of the times: "We may lament, then, the errors of the times which led to these prosecutions. But surely our ancestors had no special reasons for shame in a belief which had the universal sanction of their own and all former ages; which counted on its train philosophers as well as enthusiasts; which was graced by the learning of prelates as well as the countenance of kings; which the law supported by its mandates, and the purest judges felt no compunctions in enforcing. Let Witch Hill remain forever memorable by this sad catastrophe not to perpetuate our dishonor, but as an affecting enduring proof of human infirmity—a proof that perfect justice belongs to one judgment-seat only—that which is linked to the throne of God."[56]

~

In all, eleven members of the Tyler family were accused.

July 28 Mary Tyler Post Bridges, 48; Job's daughter, Moses' sister
August 2 Mary Post, 28; Mary's daughter
August 25 Susannah Post, 31; Mary's stepdaughter
August 25 Hannah Post, 26;Mary's daughter
August 25 Sarah Bridges, 17; Mary's stepdaughter
August 25 Mary Bridges, Jr., 13; Mary's daughter
August 31 Mary Parker, 55; John Tyler's (Job's son) mother-in-law
September 7 Mary Lovett Tyler, 40; Hopestill Tyler's wife
September 7 Hannah Tyler, 14; Mary and Hopestill's daughter
September 7 Joanna Tyler, 11; Mary and Hopestill's daughter
September 7 Martha Tyler, 11; Mary and Hopestill's daughter[57]

Nathaniel Tyler (1747–1829)

The following brief biography, included in the genealogy blog, "Aunt Roma's Family History," interestingly includes Nathaniel Tyler's spiritual beliefs; he is said to have died in the presence of an angel. To understand Nathaniel, it is requisite to better understand the foundational role of the bible in the colonial period. Angels are referred to many times in the bible as messengers between God and humankind. The belief in angels goes back to ancient times, and angels are found within three major religions: Judaism, Christianity, and Islam. Guardian angels provide comfort to those experiencing trials and tribulations; for example, the archangel Raphael was associated with the protection of travelers; archangel Michael gave protection during times of war. To early settlers in a strange land, angels provided better access to understanding the unknowable supernatural world that was very much part of the Puritan belief system.

Nathaniel Tyler (#296; Tyler-3988), the son of Nathaniel and Sarah Wood Tyler, was born in 1747 in Boxford, Massachusetts, and died in Springfield, Pennsylvania, in 1829. He was married in 1770 to Abigail Andrews of Boxford, Massachusetts, and they were the parents of seven children. Nathaniel had eight month's service in 1775 at Lieutenant in the Continental Army in the Revolutionary War. He lived in Metheun, Massachusetts, and moved to Cayuga County, New York, and also Herkimer County, New York. He later moved to Springfield, Pennsylvania.

"About 1823 there seemed to be a conflict in the minds of the people of Springfield regarding religion. Nathaniel, who lived with his son Andrew, became unusually interested in reading the scriptures and talking about them to their neighbors. One day Andrew happened to open to Mark 16, Chapters 16 & 17 verses, Quote: 'He that believeth and is baptized shall be saved, but he that believeth not shall be damned. And these signs shall follow them that believe. In my name shall they cast out devils; they shall speak with new tongues;'

"After reading them several times carefully he said: 'There is not a true believer in the world.' He showed the passage to several Ministers, mostly Methodists and argued with them. The more he argued the more convinced he was that the Gospel was not on the earth, and he was able to confound the most learned divines, although he was quite illiterate. Nathanial, [sic] aged 76, also had the same view and he prophesied that he would die, but his son would live to see the true church organized with all the Apostolic gifts and blessings.

"For this cause, much unfavorable comment in the neighborhood was indulged in, and Nathaniel was often asked, usually in a derisive way, why he did not have his dislocated shoulder, which had been out of place for some thirty years, replaced by the power of faith. He argued that it would be done if he had sufficient faith.

"One morning he came from his bed-room and told his son's family, that the Lord had revealed to him that 'whereas physicians had said your shoulder could not be set. He would let them know it could be done, for He would do it Himself.'

"It happened not long afterwards, that while he was lying in his bed at the dawn of day, thinking quietly of the blessings of God to him, his shoulder slipped into place with a snap that he thought might have been heard for a distance of one or two rods. Previous to this he carried his arm in a sling most of the time and could not raise his hand to his head, but from that time it was as limber as the other and had its full strength. This was a testimony that could not be impeached. Outside of the family, however, it was looked upon as a mere accident; but the previous revelation to him convinced the family that it was done by the power of God. This was in 1827 and in 1829 he died.

"During his last illness an angel clothed in white appeared to him and told him he would not recover for his sickness was unto death. Ten days later he died. To save ridicule this vision was kept a secret."[58]

Revolutionary Period (1760s–1790s)

During the eighteenth century, the British had spent a great deal of money defending the Colonies against attack by the French and others. As a result, the British had very high taxes in their country. They decided to shift some of their financial burden to the colonists. The Stamp Act of 1765, which taxed all legal documents, newspapers and other documents, was met with a great uproar in the American colonies. In 1766, this tax was repealed, but it was just the beginning of serious problems between the colonists and the British. The Boston Tea Party in 1773 was an act of revolt against the British and their tax on tea in the colonies.

Tensions such as these eventually led to the writing of the Declaration of Independence in 1776. A year earlier, the War of Independence, also known as the American Revolution, began. When the British finally surrendered on October 19, 1781, Americans were officially independent of Britain and set about establishing their own government.

Many Tylers with interesting stories lived during this period, some involved with the revolution, some with establishing a homestead and becoming contributing members of their community.

Moses Tyler (1734–1811)

Moses Tyler (#444; Tyler-6274) is noted primarily for his active role in opposing the British as they tried to impose unfair taxes. He was born in Boston in 1734, "descended from an honorable English ancestry." His great grandfather was Thomas Tyler, who came from England soon after the Pilgrims and settled in Boston. His great grandmother was Miriam Simpkins, daughter of Pilgrim Simpkins of the Mayflower party. He was the son of Moses Tyler (#122; Tyler-6270) and Hannah (Luther) Tyler of Boston.

As a young man he moved with his wife, Elizabeth Adams, to Barrington, Rhode Island, where he became a prominent citizen. Inheriting the thrifty habits of his Tyler ancestry, he became in early manhood a freeholder and at middle life was one of the largest owners of real property in the town.

"The sturdy virtues and independence of character of his Pilgrim ancestors were prominent in Moses Tyler's life, and while yet a young man he took an active interest in the affairs of the town, and was always to be found in favor of all measures that had for their object the general welfare of the people."[59] He noted with concern and anxiety the disposition of the British Parliament to enact measures of oppression towards the American colonies and was among the first to raise his voice and exert his influence in resisting them. He never hesitated to affirm that "the instincts of freedom are inherited from the Creator, and the oppressive edicts of a tyrant King and his Parliament must be resisted even to the sacrifice of life and fortune." In 1774, a town meeting was called by the people of Barrington to consider the action of the British Parliament in placing a duty upon all tea exported to the American Colonies. Moses took an active part and was appointed a member of a committee to arrange for concerted action in opposition to receiving or using from any source or under any circumstances any of the "dutied tea." He was elected a deputy to represent the town of Barrington in the General Assembly in 1776-77 and was also elected by the General Assembly a justice of the peace.

In 1778, Moses actively tried to prevent an invasion by British and Hessian soldiers into Barrington. As described later by Moses, the story of this confrontation is as follows:

"The British had already blown up the powder magazine, burned the Baptist meeting-house, and the adjoining parsonage, and several other buildings in Warren. During this work of destruction and pillage, a few of the Hessian soldiers made their way to the north part of the town, but soon returned to Join the main body. Two Hessian soldiers, more adventurous than the rest, secured a small boat and prepared to cross the river to the Barrington side to continue their work of destruction. Mr. Tyler, with musket ready, and with ammunition prepared by the hands of his wife and daughter, hastened to the bank of the river just below his house, ready to dispute the passage of the two red-coats across. As they pushed off into the stream he hailed them, and warned them of their peril, and of the fate that awaited them. They replied to his warning with derisive oaths, and, nothing daunted, continued their course. Waiting until they got within range, Mr. Tyler took aim and fired, instantly killing one of the soldiers. The other, realizing that the same fate awaited him, hastily turned the boat about, and pulled for the Warren shore. Mr. Tyler, jumping into his own boat, pursued but could not overtake the fleeing Hessian, who, in his haste to escape, was only too glad to abandon his dead comrade to his pursuer. When he reached the abandoned boat, Mr. Tyler took possession of the dead Hessian's musket and accoutrements, and with the assistance of a neighbor, gave him a decent burial and returned to his home."[60]

The tract of land on which he resided in Barrington extended between Palmer's River on the east and to Barrington River on the west and has ever since been known as "Tyler's Point." The Tyler Homestead at this location was passed on to his son and grandson, and originally included all the land between the two rivers. It was here he built ships. On the upland of this land is one of the old burying grounds of the town known as the "Tyler Burial Ground," where three generations of Tylers are laid to rest side by side. At the gravesite of Moses was placed a marker of the Society of the Sons of the American Revolution.

Simeon Tyler (1754–1840)

Simeon Tyler (#299; Tyler-6302), a son of Nathaniel Sr. (#81; Tyler-1875) and brother to Nathaniel, Jr., (#296) described above, was involved in many ways during the Revolutionary War period. He was born in Boxford, Massachusetts. Despite his British ancestry, he was a true rebel and despised the British rule. At that time, Boston was occupied by British troops and many of the Americans there were Tories.

Simeon joined a company of "Minutemen," who were not considered soldiers, but civilians pledged ready to respond should our country be threatened. They were known for being ready at a minute's notice, and provided a highly mobile, rapidly deployed force that allowed the colonies to respond immediately to war threats.

Some towns in Massachusetts had a long history of designating a portion of their militia as "minute companies" constituting special units within the militia system whose members underwent additional training and held themselves ready to turn out rapidly for emergencies. They became a body distinct from the rest of the militia and, by being more devoted to military exercises, they acquired skill in the use of arms. Minutemen, who were generally younger and more mobile, were the first armed militia to arrive at or await a battle.

"In 1775, when the British troops marched to Concord to confiscate powder and munitions stored there, fraction began in Lexington between them and the militia. When Simeon Tyler and his company of Minutemen heard the news, they grabbed their muskets and headed for battle. Later, when requesting a grant of land to which everyone in the Revolutionary War who enlisted and served for three years should be entitled to 200 acres, this is what he said:

"'I, on the 14th day of February, 1775, volunteered as a Minute Man and on the 19th of the following April, chased the enemies of our beloved country from Lexington to Concord and from there back to Boston. Then went into camp and was stationed in Cambridge and served until the 19th of December, same year under Colonel James Frye, when I was honorably discharged. Without loss of time I enlisted again for six months and was stationed on Prospect Hill in the winter of 1776. In the spring, went on to Castle William, now called Fort Independence fortifying that place till the last of June under the direction and superintendence of the late Governor Hancock. July 1st, same year, I enlisted again under Eliphlet Bodwell, Captain, for five months and marched into Saratoga, as in Colonel Titcomb's regiment of Newburyport, served until 1st of December 1777. I enlisted again on the first of December under Captain Nathaniel Marsh of Haverill for the term of four months and marched to Danbury in Connecticut from there to White Playnes near New York, from there to Bound Brook in the state of New Jersey and then was stationed there 'til the first day of April; and then hon. discharged and home sometime in April. August 1st, I enlisted again under Captain Page, Colonel Johnson's regiment, marched to Saratoga, and was in the battle at the capture of John Burgorne, Guarded the prisoners down to Bunker Hill, went on to Boston and was stationed there 'til first of April, 1778, when I was discharged, June about the tenth, enlisted for three months under Captain James McLoon, Colonel Peleg Wadsworth regiment, marched to Rhode Island, was at General Sullivan's retreat, returned home. Then XX of September same year, 25th of September under Captain John Davis of Metheun, Colonel Cogswell's regiment, marched to Boston, was stationed there 'til first of January, 1779. I enlisted again, the 1st of September 1779 for three months under Captain McLoon and marched to serve on Fort Independence, served about 19 days was taken sick and sent home."

"'I served those three years and upward without fines, or bounty or clashing and I may say without wages as old paper money was good for nothing. . .'"[61]

Colonel Comfort Tyler (1764–1827)

Comfort Tyler (#639; Tyler-6346) was a major figure in the early history of America. The lengthy account included here gives the story of an individual with great initiative who was unafraid of exploring new pathways. He served in the Revolutionary War and the War of 1812, was one of the first settlers of Onondaga County, New York, was the primary promoter of an early turnpike, served in many capacities of local government, and also played a critical role with Aaron Burr in a dramatic "conspiracy" against the federal government. He was a colorful and controversial figure. Much of the information on his life is taken from the book, *Pioneer Times*, written by Carroll Smith.[62]

~

Comfort Tyler, brother of Samuel (#637; Tyler-6344), was born in 1764 in Connecticut and came to Onondaga County, New York, in 1788. He claimed to be a descendant of Wat Tyler, the British revolutionary in the time of Richard II, so he may have felt he had revolutionary blood in him.

Tyler served in the American Revolutionary War in 1778 at the age of 14 and was stationed at West Point, New York. In 1783, he Joined General James Clinton, father of future governor DeWitt Clinton, as a member of the expedition that established a boundary line between New York and Pennsylvania. At the age of 24 he traveled across the wilderness of New York State as a member of a "Lessee Company."

As the result of his travels, he decided to be one of the first permanent settlers of Onondaga County in upstate New York. The year of his arrival in Onondaga County, he was shown a salt spring by Indians, who had for their own uses been taught by the Jesuits a primitive mode of procuring salt. Before that time the spring had been held in superstitious awe, as accursed by a demon, who makes waters bitter. Comfort Tyler took an iron kettle of fifteen gallons capacity and in nine hours had made thirteen bushels of salt. This was the natal day of the American salt trade, and the enterprise quickly grew to become the major salt provider in the country. A one-mile-long lateral canal was constructed to service this successful industry. This salt, found in Salina, a settlement just east of Montezuma, was considered superior in quality to imported salt, and with easy transport on the canal to the east coast. Comfort's salt manufacturing at Salina provided a half million bushels each year, representing one quarter of domestic salt production. At the time salt was selling for 50 cents per bushel, with virtually all of it imported and subject to a twenty cent per bushel tariff. As DeWitt Clinton said at the time, "I consider the salt manufacture of Salina the most important establishment in the United States. . . Without the canals its usefulness would be very circumscribed—but now the facilities of inland navigation enable the conveyance of this indispensable mineral to the remotest regions of the west, and to the shores of the Atlantic Ocean."[63]

Colonel Comfort Tyler

Comfort became a very prominent and well-respected citizen. He was surveyor of the Cayuga reservation, and leading promoter of the original Seneca Turnpike Road and Cayuga Lake Bridge. He personally felled the first tree to build the Seneca Turnpike and became its biggest promoter, procuring a charter for the Seneca Turnpike Company and receiving $100,000 for its construction. In the 1790s he kept a tavern on the turnpike that was the scene of great activity for travelers on this thoroughfare extending across New York State, from Albany to Buffalo.

He had a busy and successful career serving multiple roles—local supervisor, justice of the peace, sheriff, coroner, county clerk, the county's first postmaster, being elected to the New York State Legislature, and serving as a Colonel in the War of 1812. Local Native Americans were fond of Tyler and named him "To-whau-ta-qua"—one who can do two things at once, capable of work and, at the same time, being a gentleman.

Comfort Tyler and the "Burr Conspiracy"

Comfort Tyler's acquaintance with Aaron Burr was the beginning of a shadowy chapter in his remarkable biography. In 1800, Burr ran for the United States presidency against Thomas Jefferson. Because they each received the same number of electoral votes, members of the House of Representatives were left to determine the winner. When the House met to discuss the election, Burr's rival, Alexander Hamilton, vocalized his support for Jefferson and his disapproval of Burr. In the end, Jefferson secured the presidency and Burr, because he had the second highest total of votes, by right became vice president. However, Burr was incensed at events, believing Hamilton had manipulated the vote in Jefferson's favor.

After Burr left the Vice-Presidency at the end of his term in 1805, he journeyed to the Western frontier, areas west of the Allegheny Mountains and down the Ohio River Valley, eventually reaching lands acquired in Jefferson's Louisiana Purchase. Burr had leased 40,000 acres of land from the Spanish government along the Ouachita River in Louisiana. Starting in Pittsburgh and then proceeding to Beaver, Pennsylvania, and Wheeling, Virginia, and onward he drummed up support for his plans.

Burr tried to secure money and conceal his true intention, which was to help Mexico overthrow Spanish power in the Southwest. He intended to establish a dynasty in what would have become Mexican territory. Based on the Neutrality Act of 1794, which Congress passed to block filibuster expeditions against United States neighbors, Burr's action was a misdemeanor. Jefferson, however, sought the highest charges against him.

Burr had met with the British Minister to the United States and suggested the British could gain control in the Texas Territories. Burr intended to raise a western army and form a separate government. In 1806, Burr contacted the Spanish minister and told him that his plan was not just western secession, but the capture of Washington, D. C. Spain and Mexico were concerned about the growing domination of the new American government, but the Spanish government gave no support to Burr.

Burr then devised a scheme whereby he intended to attack Mexico and acquire land in Texas. The plan was to form an expedition against Mexico with five hundred men and descend upon the Orleans Territory in light boats, hopefully creating a revolution. "The money in New Orleans banks would be seized in order to fit out the expedition, which would sail for Vera Cruz about 1 February. . . They expected naval protection from the British, and the officers of the American Navy were so disgusted with the Government they were ready to join."[64]

During this period Comfort Tyler had relocated to New York City, where he had represented Onondaga County in the New York State Legislature. In 1802, he was the Federalist candidate for Congress, but was defeated. He then served as county clerk back home, but "falling upon evil days," had gone back to New York City and was arrested for vagrancy.[65]

In October, Comfort Tyler joined with Burr in recruiting young men to his cause. Comfort served as Burr's local agent. He received funding and clothing from Burr, who sent him to New York and Ohio for this purpose. Comfort Tyler was one of Burr's primary assistants, recruiting locals to join the group. Burr made a contract with Tyler to deliver $40,000 worth of provisions to an island headquarters in the Ohio River. Comfort had sub-agents who provided goods in Pittsburgh that were shipped in canvas-covered keelboats, appearing to be an activity of normal business.

Comfort was reportedly having a very successful recruiting effort. "It was said that amazing numbers of 'Yankees' were arriving at Pittsburgh by every stage and were inquiring for the rendezvous of Comfort Tyler. . . [A Spanish agent] reported he saw 100 men in the city under command of a colonel who declared openly that an attack on Mexico was their aim. . . One Western informant reported that 300 young gentlemen descended the Ohio at this time, . . . A 'high authority' in Washington reported that between August and December 1806 more than 1,000 young men had passed through New York and Pennsylvania on their way to join Burr on the Ohio."[66]

Burr's ally in this plan was to be American General James Wilkinson. Unbeknownst to Burr, Wilkinson was being paid by Spain to protect its territorial interests. In pursuance of the best interests of Spain, Wilkinson informed President Jefferson that Burr was planning to use his army against the Western territories held by the United States. Jefferson declared Aaron Burr a traitor and used the United States Army, under the command of General Wilkinson, to arrest various people whom he believed to be aiding and abetting Burr to commit treason.

When Jefferson received notice of the recruiting activities of Comfort Tyler, he called a cabinet meeting where specific measures were adopted for meeting the threat. Letters were written to governors advising them to watch Burr and have him arrested and tried if he committed any overt act. It should be noted, however, that a few years earlier Jefferson had considered a two-state situation as acceptable. This was noted in an 1804 letter to Joseph Priestly Washington, where he wrote: "Whether we remain in one confederacy, or form into Atlantic and Mississippi confederacies, I believe not very important to the happiness of either part. Those of the western confederacy will be as much our children & descendants as those of the eastern, and I feel myself as much identified with that country, in future time, as with this; and did I now foresee a separation at some future day, yet I should feel the duty & the desire to promote the western interests as zealously as the eastern, doing all the good for both portions of our future family which should fall within my power."[67]

When Jefferson received notice of the recruiting activities of Comfort Tyler, he called a cabinet meeting where specific measures were adopted for meeting the threat. Letters were written to governors advising them to watch Burr and have him arrested and tried if he committed any overt act.

During that time Burr added to his team Harman Blennerhassett, a wealthy Irishman who had emigrated to the United States and purchased an island in the middle of the Ohio River. He built an enormous mansion on the island and entertained many distinguished visitors, including former vice-president Burr. The island became headquarters of Burr's plot to separate the American west from the Union, take Mexico from the Spanish, and create a new country, supposedly with Burr as its leader. During this time of preparation Tyler was providing recruits and Blennerhassett was providing funding and the headquarters.

Blennerhassett Mansion[68]

John Graham, from Pittsburgh, described in a letter written to James Madison in 1806 the activity underway: "An expedition inimical to the interests of the United States was about to set on foot; that a flotilla was being prepared; that young men were being inveigled into joining by promises of pay and rations from the time of their engagement, and by the assurance of future fortunes. They were to capture New Orleans and its dependencies; possess themselves of the money in the banks and treasury (which amounted to $2,000,000); erect a government independent of the United States under a foreign power and force the West to secede. He had been informed that two boats loaded with artillery, muskets and bayonets had passed down the Ohio and that there were men on board who spoke French; but for want of legal authority they could not be arrested."[69]

By December, Tyler had reached Blennerhassett Island with four boats and twenty men he had labeled as "settlers," some of whom were armed. (Going armed would not seem in itself unusual in a pioneer region.) Tyler wrote to Mr. Blennerhassett, "My calculations have at all times been to leave Beaver on the first of next month. The only difficulty that I have encountered is the procuring provisions necessary for my settlers, some of whom are behind, and I fear they will not arrive in time, but I shall be off with the few that may happen to be with me, and trust to those behind to follow on."[70] As the result of the president's call for the arrest of Burr, Tyler and Blennerhassett got word that the Virginia militia they would be approaching the island. The decision was made to head downriver in the middle of the night with the boats, men, and provisions that were available.

Colonel Phelps of the Virginia militia arrived the next day to find nothing on the island, so the mansion and island were occupied and plundered. The militia then took an overland route to intercept the flotilla. But the sentinels, "pouring spirits down to keep spirits up," fell asleep and the boats passed unnoticed. In Cincinnati, officials prepared to attack one of the boats, but when a local fired a bomb at the suspect vessel, it turned out to belong to a local merchant and was loaded with dry goods. The Burr expedition boats had already passed. Orders were sent to stop all boats on the Ohio River, and the militia was sent to enforce this decree of the State.

Surprisingly, Tyler and Blennerhassett met no further obstructions with their four boats and were joined by additional boats further downriver. Burr's fleet now had nine boats and less than sixty men as a force to take over control of New Orleans. Although militia had been instructed to check all boats, the orders were not carefully observed. One dispatch noted, "On or about the thirty-first ultimo Colonel Burr, late Vice-President, passed this way with about ten boats of different descriptions, navigated with about six men each, having nothing on board that would even suffer a conjecture more than that he was a man bound to market. He has descended the river towards Orleans."[71]

Andrew Jackson, who was overseeing the militia effort, decided there was nothing alarming and deemed it appropriate to dismiss the troops, allowing the boats to proceed into the bayou area. Jackson was not concerned that Burr was doing anything inimical to the country. Jackson, always one to impetuously exercise the dramatic, wrote," If he is a traitor, he is the basest that ever did commit treason, and being tore to pieces and scattered to the four winds of heaven would be too good for him."[72]

Comfort Tyler gave a brief account of the voyage at this point in time in Mississippi, and the reception received: "At the mouth of the Cumberland I met Colonel Burr, expecting to proceed on with him to our intended settlement, but to my chagrin, the approach of Colonel Burr [produced] the most terrible confusion and alarm—hundreds under arms have turned out to meet him, and about fifty unarmed, defenseless, and peaceable fellow citizens, of whom I have the misfortune to be one. Conscious of the purity of my intentions, [I] hope the suspicions will not rest on me or my friends."[73]

His expeditionary force was finally overtaken by a force of 375 men. Burr was presented a letter from the governor, attributing hostile intentions to the flotilla. Burr responded by saying he would have contacted the governor but had heard reports of assassination. He covered the plot by insisting the boats were being used for emigrants who would be settling land he owned in Louisiana. He pointed to his boats, asking if there was anything warlike in their appearance. He then submitted himself to local authorities and agreed to an interview the next day, as long as he was kept safe. He was next taken to a territorial judge, where he was put on trial. Such was the end of Burr's inglorious expedition.

Erick Bollman, who had received an appointment from President Jefferson to serve with an Indian agency in Louisiana, also served as Aaron Burr's agent in New Orleans. He admitted to Jefferson during an interrogation that Burr planned to raise an army and invade Mexico. He said that Burr believed that he should be Mexico's monarch, as a republican government was not right for the Mexican people. Bollman did not think Burr's activities conflicted with U.S. interests, and expressed these thoughts in an interview he requested with Jefferson.

Ultimately, charges were brought against Burr:

> "First. For a high misdemeanor, in setting on foot, within the United States, a military expedition against the dominions of the King of Spain, a foreign prince, with whom the United States, at the time of the offense, were, and still are, at peace.
>
> "Second. For treason in assembling an armed force, with a design to seize the city of New Orleans, to revolutionize the territory attached to it, and to separate the western from the Atlantic States."[74]

Burr adamantly denied and vehemently resented all charges against his honor, character, or patriotism. The case went to the United States Attorney General, where it was argued there was no treason because there had been no act of war. As argued: "First, it must be proved that there was an actual war. A war consists wholly in acts, and not in intentions. . . An intention to levy war, is not evidence that a war was levied. Intentions are always mutable and variable; the continuance of guilty intentions is not to be presumed."[75]

Burr's trial was presided over by Chief Justice of the United States John Marshall on August 3. Article 3, Section 3 of the United States Constitution requires that treason either be admitted in open court or proven by an overt act witnessed by two people. Since no two witnesses came forward, Burr was acquitted on September 1, in spite of the full force of the Jefferson administration's political influence thrown against him. Burr was immediately tried on a misdemeanor charge and was again acquitted. Many historians believe the extent of Burr's involvement may never be known.

Comfort Tyler was accused of participating in the conspiracy. He responded that he was conscious of the purity of his motives, and that he respected the laws of the United States and treason had never entered his mind. In fact, at one time Comfort had planned on settling on Burr's land in Louisiana but had abandoned the idea when he realized the title might be bad. One witness testified that Tyler had insisted that the men "would not resist the constituted authorities, but . . . would not be stopped by a mob."[76] His men were accused of being disorderly, committing any mischief, and guilty of misconduct, but the judge was sympathetic, writing, "I am strongly inclined to think him entirely innocent."

Others implicated in the Burr conspiracy also had prominence nationally. One person had been told by Tyler that the project was supported by "some of the first men in the United States, including several gentlemen of rank, . . who were honest, well-meaning men."[77] They included Ohio Senator Jonathan Dayton; a former United States senator from New Jersey; John Smith, a current senator from Ohio; John Adair, another former senator and a general in the Kentucky militia; Erick Bollman, the German doctor who had tried to rescue the Marquis de Lafayette from and Austrian prison; and Thomas Truxton, a former naval commander.

After the trial Comfort returned home, but this affair greatly impaired his fortunes and blighted his political prospects. Whenever he was accused of treasonable intent, he indignantly denied it, but the episode embittered and saddened the remainder of his life. He once said to his little grandchild, "Whenever persons refer to this matter, you are to tell them, whatever might have been contemplated, 'You know that no harm to our country was intended by Mr. Tyler.'"

Tyler moved to Montezuma, New York, in 1811. In the War of 1812 he served as assistant commissary general (with the rank of colonel) to the Northern Army. Tyler was also indirectly involved with the construction of the Erie Canal. In Montezuma, Dewitt Clinton, who was governor of the state and prime supporter of the canal, came across construction of a boat for the canal. As Clinton described it, "The whole expense of each of these boats, furniture included, will not exceed 900 or 1000 dollars. They are principally designed, and partly owned, by Colonel Tyler, of this village—a gentleman who unites kindness of behaviour and benevolence of disposition, with intelligence and enterprise."[78]

In his later years Comfort's home was the regular scene of cordial hospitalities, and he was described as affable, original, intelligent, and benevolent. He died in August 1827 and is buried in Oakwood Cemetery in Montezuma. Many years after his death his remains were moved to Syracuse, New York.

Memories of Onondaga Hollow are recorded in this final scene of George Kasson Knapp's series of paintings, "Pioneers of Onondaga." Colonel Comfort Tyler, after service as assistant commissary general in the northern army, stands with axe in hand, looking out over the community that has grown up around the fields he and Asa Danforth first cleared in the wilderness only a quarter century ago.

Comfort Tyler painting in landscape

"The village, with its sixty-five or more houses, stretches for a mile along the turnpike from East Hill to West, a thriving center for store-keepers, artisans and professional people. Tyler's tavern now is kept by his son-in-law, Cornelius Longstreet. There are two other inns, an "elegant meeting house" and a grist mill. Just this September young Lewis H. Redfield, defying the uncertainties of the times, arrived from Canandaigua, opened a book store and printing office and began publishing a weekly newspaper, the *Onondaga Register.* . .

"John Gridley's impressive stone house, along with Job Tyler's and Deacon Joseph Swan's houses on the north side of the turnpike, and George Olmsted's two-story home opposite them will survive all the changes and hazards of coming decades and stand to celebrate the Bicentennial of the Nation. At the right, from its terrace on the East Hill, the Onondaga Arsenal dominates the scene. We see it, "in its glory when all was trim and neat and the arsenal had it intended uses." No one was thinking in the mid-1800s of the preservation of historical sites. The deteriorating stone building served as a hay barn until the 1880s, when its roof was blown away. In 1894, proposals were made to acquire the Arsenal and restore it as the community's only military vestige of the past.

"Tyler's tavern was kept by his son-in-law, Cornelius Longstreet. It was a trying year for the pioneers at Onondaga and others on the frontier. December brought word that Buffalo and all the other settlements along the Niagara River had been overrun and burned. In June, news of the defeat and exile of Napolean brought fears that the British armies engaged in the European war would be transported to America."[79]

General Daniel Tyler IV (1799–1882)

Daniel Tyler IV (#1432; Tyler-1038) had a long and distinguished career both as a dedicated soldier and prominent industrialist. Among his other achievements he became a West Point cadet; was president of a number of railroads; became a war hero as brigadier-general during Civil War; established the town of Anniston, Texas; and met world leaders as he traveled throughout Europe.

Daniel was born in Connecticut in 1799. As a young man he prepared to attend Yale University, but secured instead an appointment to the United States Military Academy at West Point in 1816. In 1817, the Academy was transformed with upgraded academic standards and military discipline that focused on honorable conduct. It also emphasized civil engineering, and gave training in construction of roads, rail lines, and other public infrastructure. This served Daniel later in life when he became superintendent of a number of railroads.

The following section describes his career, beginning with his early years in the military:

"In 1815 I visited one of my brothers, then an officer in the army in New York, and was so taken with military life that I determined, if possible, to procure a cadet's warrant, which I accomplished in the spring of 1816 by writing a personal letter to the then Secretary of War, Mr. Dallas. I received my appointment, if I recollect right, in the month of July, 1816, and on or about the last of September of that year I reported to the Superintendent of the United States Military Academy, Capt. Alden Partridge, for duty; and without any examination, either physical or educational, was admitted as a cadet and turned over to Assistant Professor Davies for mathematical instruction.

"In 1819, he was commissioned Lieutenant of Light Artillery, and in 1824, he was offered to the Artillery School of Practice at Fortress Monroe. He tells how 'On joining the School of Practice I was attached to Saunders' Company, First Artillery, and entering heartily into the object of the school I devoted myself ardently to all the means within my reach to acquire professional knowledge,—importing books both from France and England relating to the artillery service, general science of war, court martial, etc., until I had the best military library my pecuniary means would secure. Among other books imported from France, I acquired a copy of the *Drill and Manoeuvers*, published in Paris in 1824 for the use of the Garde Royale, which was the most complete compend published to that time, and I devoted all my hours that could be spared from daily service to translating it into English and making it ready for the printer; mutilating the original copy by removing all the plates and placing them in their proper position in the translation.

"His translation was used by the American army, and in 1828 he was sent to France to make further study of the French system. Finding the French system far superior, he proceeded at great expense to obtain copies of every drawing and treatise on the French system and to translate their latest manual of exercise and instruction for field artillery. "He was sent to Europe to study the French system of artillery training, bearing with him letters of introduction from his cousin, Aaron Burr, to General Layfayette. Having in Paris placed himself in a French family for a couple of months to improve 'my West point French,' he entered the School of Practice in Metz. He threw himself with all his energy and ability into his profession. 'During the twelve months I was at Metz, besides my other work, I collected copies of every drawing, and the memoirs connected with the construction of the system of Artillery adopted for the French army, including the Field, the Siege, and the Coast Batteries, and Mountain Artillery, which I brought to the United States and disposed of as herein-after stated.'"[80]

Upon returning to the armory in Springfield, Massachusetts, as superintendent of inspectors of contract arms, he rejected as defective most of the muskets delivered by manufacturers. When the Ordnance Corps was reorganized, he was recommended for the commission of captain, but President Jackson, doubtless owing to political pressure, refused to appoint him. Tyler then resigned in 1834.

In the early 1840s, as president of the Norwich & Worcester Railroad and the Morris Canal & Banking Company, he rescued both from bankruptcy. He was then asked to complete the construction of a railroad from Macon, Georgia, to Atlanta, then for sale at $150,000, scarcely one-tenth of the capital already expended. Through Tyler's financial aid and the backing of a group of Macon men, the re-chartered Macon & Western Railroad was opened for traffic in ten months and was soon paying a dividend of eight percent. During the next decade he reorganized and improved a number of railroads in Pennsylvania, New Jersey, and Kentucky— superintendent of the Cumberland Valley Railroad, general superintendent of the

Dauphin & Susquehanna Railway and Coal Company, president of the Auburn & Allerton Railway Company, and president of the Schuylkill & Susquehanna Railway Company. He also went to England to study the application of blast furnaces in smelting iron ore. He was a pioneer in the iron industry in this country, establishing furnaces in Pennsylvania and later in Alabama.

With the outbreak of the Civil War, in 1861 Tyler was chosen to command the 1st Connecticut Regiment, and in May he was commissioned brigadier-general. Shortly before the Bull Run campaign, he was given command of a division. He was in action at Corinth in 1862 and in command of Maryland Heights and Harpers Ferry during the summer of 1863, and he also aided in recruiting, prison-camp administration, and army investigations.

An officer who knew him well during the war, General Donn Piatt, wrote the following description of him:

> "I came to know, and be known, to General Daniel Tyler of Connecticut, in the brief campaign that terminated at the disastrous battle of the first Bull Run. Our intercourse was not cordial, or indeed in the slightest degree intimate, for he was a General in command of a division, and I only a captain, and of the volunteers at that. Our brigade,—for I was serving in the staff of General Schenck, as Assistant Adjutant-General,— was under the immediate command of General Tyler, and I had been pretty severely trained, in what was known as the three months service, into a fair recognition of his soldierly conduct, that excited among us volunteers more admiration than love. To others under him he made himself offensive by insisting on a more perfect discipline and better drill, but I had been through a schooling that made me appreciate his thoughtful efforts, and so was well prepared to believe in, and admire, the soldierly bearing and brave conduct of the man. At first Bull Run, I saw him ride under fire, with all the composure of a veteran although he was no more a veteran than the men he commanded. He seemed to be not only without fear, but clearly possessed of a knowledge of his duties, and a will to carry them in execution."

General Piatt goes on to relate the following incident that took place several years after the inception of the war; at the close of the lengthy court-martial of General Don Carlos Buell, a Union general. General Tyler was a member of the court.

> "'Not long after our so-called court finally adjourned, General Tyler and I were in the ante-chamber of the War Department, when President Lincoln unexpectedly entered.

> "'Well, gentlemen,' he said, 'you did not out-last the war, and now have you any matter worth reporting after such a protracted investigation?'

> "'I think so, Mr. President,' replied General Tyler. 'We had it proven that Bragg [a senior commander in the confederate army] with less than ten thousand men, drove your eighty-three thousand under Buell, back from before Chattanooga down to the Ohio at Louisville, marched round us twice, then doubled us up in a depot at Perryville, and finally got out of Kentucky with all his plunder.'

"'Well, now Tyler,' said the President, 'what is the meaning of this; what's the lesson? Don't our men march as well and fight as well as these Rebels? If not, there is a fault somewhere. We are all of the same family—same sort.'

"'Yes, there is a lesson,' said General Tyler. 'We are of the same sort, but subject to a different handling. Bragg's little force was superior to our larger number, because he had it under control. If a man left his ranks he was punished; if he deserted he was shot. We have nothing of that sort. If we attempt to shoot a deserter you pardon him, and our Army is without discipline.'

"The President looked troubled. 'Why do you interfere?' General Tyler continued. 'Congress has taken from you all responsibility.'

"'Yes,' said the President impatiently, 'confound it, they have taken the responsibility and left the women to howl about me.'"[81]

After the war he traveled extensively year after year in Europe and the South. He was in England at the outbreak of the Franco-Prussian War and, of course, took an immense interest in its progress. In a letter home he wrote: "We went ten miles into the country to see a camp of eleven thousand French prisoners, and I was glad to note how well the Prussians were treating their captives. They were camped in regular Sibley tents, well fed and clothed; and seemed as happy as their enemies who guarded them. Verily, civilization is softening the barbarities of war, 'and it is time.' I have nothing to say as to the war; you get news almost as soon as I do here within a hundred miles of the operations. I meet American correspondents of the *Herald*, *Times*, and *Tribune* almost every day. Yesterday I encountered two just from the front with a pocket full of speculation and very few facts."

Tyler spent a year travelling through Holland, Belgium, Switzerland, Germany, and Italy, taking a keen interest in everything and everyone, as the following entries in his diary attest: "Nice, March 27th. We left Rome for Florence and thence to Leghorn; and from there to Caprera on purpose to see Garibaldi. [Note: Italian Guiseppe Garibaldi was described as one of the greatest generals of his time, who contributed to Italy's unification and creation of the Kingdom of Italy.] I dined with him of the 2d, and he talked freely of matters on this side of the water, and spoke kindly of the United States and General Grant. He gave the health of Grant as a toast, and asked me to communicate his good wishes, etc."[82]

In 1872, he met Samuel Noble in Charleston, South Carolina, who induced him to examine the iron deposits of Eastern Alabama. They explored the country on horseback. Noble gives this picture of Tyler during this period, when, at seventy-three years of age, he was on a prospecting tour in Alabama preliminary to taking on a new mining venture: "Familiar as I thought I was with the whole country, I found when with him how much there was that I had not looked into or thought of investigating. Nothing escaped his observation. In his company I made the most thorough and exhaustive exploration of the country I ever made before or since. I was surprised at this knowledge and practical ideas concerning the requisites for iron manufacture. We rode for three days in succession, returning to the hotel in Oxford after dark—I thoroughly tired out, but the General was fresh as ever. He would go down from his room, and with some choice tea (a present from an English sea captain), make a hot cup for both; at that time the hotel people did not know how tea was 'cooked.' Sipping our hyson [a Chinese green tea] we talked over what we had seen during the day, and planned for the next."[83]

The upshot of the visit was the organization of the Woodstock Iron Company by Tyler, Noble, and Tyler's son, Alfred. Furnace No. 1 was erected immediately with a cash investment of $200,000 and gave rise to the town of Anniston, Texas, named for Tyler's daughter-in-law. A cotton mill with 10,000 spindles was added to the town, as well as a water tower, a car factory, and an agricultural improvements business. During his last years he served as president of the Mobile & Montgomery Railroad in Texas, where he invested in railroad lands.

In 1874, General Tyler traveled once more to Europe. As described by his niece, who was also there, he left a good impression: "When he arrived in Paris, old Mr. Le Vasseur came up from where he lived to renew the acquaintance of fifty years ago. He was a bent decrepit tottering old man to whom Uncle Dan, erect, tall, and alert, had to give his arm as they walked together. They went to Galignani's [an English library in Paris opened in 1800 by Giovanni Antonio Galignani] and looked up the old files of newspapers, to read about a dinner at which they had been present given by the Americans in Paris to General Lafayette in 1829 or 1830, fifty-five years before. If I remember rightly, Uncle Dan had a letter of introduction to Lafayette from Aaron Burr. This meeting made a great impression on me as it seemed to take one back so vividly to almost Revolutionary times, and I was proud of Uncle Dan, so handsome and so alert in contrast with the tottering Frenchman with his brown wig."[84]

General George Washington Cullum, a Civil War general and Superintendent of the United States Military Academy, wrote an appreciation of Tyler for the annals of the West Point Alumni Association: "Tyler was a very distinguished civil and mining engineer—bold, enterprising, skillful, and eminently successful in whatever he undertook. It seemed to be his delight and pastime from dead carcasses to produce living, breathing realities. Broken-down railroads, moss-grown coal companies, collapsed iron works, crumbling canals, and such like financial ruins, his wizard touch suddenly transformed into engines of power and profit. We have already recorded the skillful surgery of this master-healer of diseased corporation, and even in old age how he made a solitary desert in Alabama voluble with spindles, glowing with furnaces, and teeming with busy life."[85] General Daniel Tyler died in New York City in 1882, but was buried in Anniston, Alabama.

Era of the Young Republic (1800s–1840s)

The young American republic saw growth of the federal government during the early decades of the nineteenth century. This growth included organizing the executive branch, creation of the Bill of Rights, the establishing of two political parties, and a growing sense of nationalism.

Conflicts between the new nation and England escalated, with the British regularly seizing American ships at sea, kidnapping sailors to serve in the British navy. Americans in the West also accused Britain of inciting Native Americans to attack white settlers. These led to the War of 1812, finally settled by the Treaty of Ghent in 1814, which increased America's prestige overseas and generated a new spirit of patriotism, referred to as the "Era of Good Feelings."

During this period the United States was the special promised land as the nineteenth century took its dynamic course. Fewer than 8,000 immigrants per year landed on American shores between 1783 and 1815, but 2,598,000 came in the next forty-five years: 1,500,000 in the 1840s and 3,000,000 in the 1850s. The immigrants helped push the United States population from 4,000,000 in 1790 to 32,000,000 in 1860. In the following decades, sectional disputes began as industry developed in the North while Southern agriculture depended on slavery. As the nation expanded west, sectional conflict continued to escalate.

The Tyler biographies from this period include individuals with possibly less impressive, but just as interesting, stories. After the War of 1812, Americans felt good about themselves, and these biographies reflect this optimism in the period before the Civil War tears the nation apart.

Flint Tyler and His Fire Alarm (1782-1870)

Sometimes it is the small, anecdotal stories that give character to the many personalities found in the extended Tyler lineage. Such is the case with this brief description of Flint Tyler and his unhurried nature when faced with an emergency.

"In 1827, Flint Tyler (#1097; Tyler-6365), an old man who then lived at the Adams house (formerly owned by Bradstreet Tyler), was one morning going home from Topsfield way, and when near the Savage house saw that this house was on fire. A storm had been brewing for several days, and a strong easterly wind carried the cinders from the chimney to the dry, parched roof, which immediately ignited. Mr. Barnes was then living at the Savage house, and Mr. Tyler leisurely got out of his wagon, went to the door, and knocked. Capt. John Peabody, who was there, came to the door, and being informed by Mr. Tyler of the cause of alarm, hastened to the wagon, got in, and hurried Mr. Tyler to follow his example and drive as fast as possible to the fire. But the beast was never known to hurry, nor be hurried, not Mr. Tyler either. About half-way across the plain, Mr. Peabody jumped from the wagon, being exasperated at the slow jogging of the animal, and ran to the scene of danger. Mr. Spofford's family was at dinner. Mr. Peabody burst into the room where they were eating, and hurriedly called for an axe, stating that the house was on fire. The Deacon was perfectly bewildered, and throwing up his arms, shrieked: 'Where! where!!'

"But one of the daughters was more composed and, getting an axe, she showed Mr. Peabody to the garret, where by a few minutes of quick chopping he cut away the burning boards, and saved the house. As he cut away the last fragment of blazing board, he looked out of the aperture he had made, and saw Mr. Tyler just tying his horse to the garden fence. By prompt and decisive action, the house and much other valuable property was saved."[86]

Mary Elizabeth (Sawyer) Tyler and Her Lamb (1806-1889)

Mary E. Sawyer (Sawyer-5658), a fifth-generation American, was born in in Sterling, Massachusetts, in 1806. Mary became famous as the Mary in the poem, "Mary Had a Little Lamb." Mary and her lamb became noted at the time through the surprising, popularity of the poem, which has remained popular to this day. The rhyme was the first audio recorded by Thomas Edison in 1877 on his newly invented phonograph. Later, Henry Ford bought the Redstone School structure referred to in the poem and moved it to nearby Sudbury, Massachusetts. In 1991, a bronze statue of a lamb monument was installed on Main Street in Sterling.

In 1835 Mary married Columbus Tyler (#1693; Tyler-6368) of Somerville, Massachusetts. They were esteemed citizens of the community. This first section of the narrative is taken from the description found in Volume I of Brigham's *The Tyler Genealogy*. Mary Sawyer Tyler (wife of Columbus Tyler) was the heroine of the verses, "Mary Had a Little Lamb."

"When she was a child in Sterling [in 1817], a little new-born lamb was one of twins; the mother refused to nurse both and abandoned one of the lambs. Mary found it nearly dead one day and nursed it back to life, sitting up all night to keep it alive. One day the lamb followed Mary and her brother, Nathaniel, to school. At her brother's suggestion they took the lamb into school, having considerable trouble to get it over a high stone wall. They had high seats, boarded up, in the schoolroom and Mary placed the lamb inside this enclosure at her feet on a shawl. When she it was Mary's turn for recitation the clatter of little hoofs was heard on the floor and the lamb appeared following Mary up front. The teacher laughed and the children giggled, but Mary was very much ashamed and led the lamb to a shed outside in the schoolyard, where it stayed until she went home. A young man named John Roulstone, visiting the school that day, was greatly pleased with the incident. The next day he brought three stanzas of a poem he had written. Two stanzas have been added since then by another hand. From the lamb's fleece, Mary's mother knit two pairs of stockings, which were kept until Mrs. Tyler was about 80 years of age. The ladies of Boston were then raising money for the preservation of the Old South Meeting-house, and Mrs. Tyler contributed these stockings, which were unraveled and small pieces of the yarn sold, thus realizing a considerable sum from the pair of hose."[87]

Redstone School (1798), believed to be the schoolhouse mentioned in the nursery rhyme[88]

A full description of the story is found in the article: "The Story of Mary and Her Little Lamb: As told by Mary and Her Neighbors and Friends."[89] It is likely the poem written by Roulstone had verses added by neighbor Sarah Hale, who had it published. The schoolhouse was bought for thirty-five dollars and fifty cents and brought to Sudbury, Massachusetts, in 1926 and located not far from Longfellow's Wayside Inn, where it was restored by Henry Ford as a schoolhouse. Two boulders on the site have bronze memorial plaques with images of McGuffey's Reader pages giving the "Mary's Lamb" lesson.

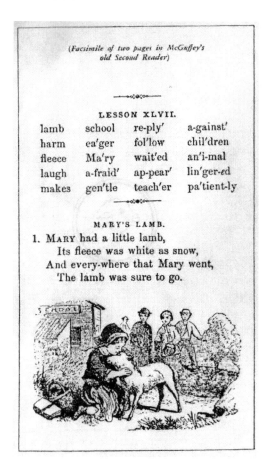

Page from McGuffey's Reader

And what happened to the weakling lamb? As it grew, Mary would dress it in pantalets and play with it in the fields. It grew to be an ewe with three lambs of its own, and Mary said the sheep's devotion to its family was as strong as could be.

Mary related the story of the day she and the sheep were in the barn together. Unfortunately, a cow in the barn lowered its head and gored her special companion, who died in her arms. Mary Sawyer Tyler described those remaining moments as follows: "I took it in my arms, placed its head in my lap, and there it bled to death. During its dying moments it would turn its little head and look up into my face in a most appealing manner, as if it would ask if there was not something that I could do for it. It was a sorrowful moment for me when the companion of many romps, my playfellow of many a long summer's day, gave up its life; and its place could not be filled in my childish heart.

The story from 1928 continues . . ."'Well, if I had known,' Mrs. Tyler smilingly said to a visitor at her home a few years ago, 'that the interest I took in my little pet was to have given me so much notoriety, I do not know that I would have carried out the plan I did; but I think I should, for then I was too young to understand much about notoriety, though not too young to take an interest in dumb animals, especially when I saw them suffering.'"

Mary Had a Little Lamb

1. Mary had a little lamb,
        Its fleece was white as snow,
    And every-where that Mary went,
        The lamb was sure to go.

2. He followed her to school one day;
        That was against the rule;
    It made the children laugh and play,
        To see a lamb at school.

3. And so the teacher turned him out;
        But still he lingered near,
    And waited patiently about,
        Till Mary did appear.

These first three verses were written by John Roulstone, Jr., a member of the freshman class at Harvard University, who died soon after at the age of seventeen. A later version of the poem added three verses, including a conjectured conversation the lamb had with Mary, as well as conversation between the students and their teacher, adding imagination to the original facts represented by Roulstone. The additional verses read as follows:

4. And then he ran to her and laid
        His head upon her arm,
    As if he said–"I'm not afraid–
        You'll keep me from all harm"

5. "What makes the lamb love Mary so?"
        The eager children cry–
    "O Mary loves the lamb, you know,"
        The teacher did reply–.

6. "And you each gentle animal
        In confidence may bind,
    And make them follow at your call,
        If you are always kind."

Years later, Henry and Clara Ford decided to research the origin of the poem and its writer and found that John Roulstone, Jr., who lived in Sterling at the same time as Mary, died in 1822 at the age of seventeen. In a magazine Ford came across

Mary's personal story of what happened to the fleece from the lamb: "From the fleece sheared from my lamb, mother knit two pairs of very nice stockings, which for years I kept in memory of my pet. But when the ladies were raising money for the preservation of Old South Church in Boston, I was asked to contribute one pair of stockings for the benefit of the fund. This I did. The stockings were raveled out, pieces of the yarn being fastened to cards bearing my autograph, and these cards were sold, the whole realizing, I am told, about one hundred dollars. After the first pair were thus sold, the ladies wanted more yarn; and they were so anxious to have the other pair . . . that I gave them also. Now all I have left in remembrance of my little pet of long years ago are two cards upon which are pasted scraps of yarn from which the stockings were knit."[90]

The Village Blacksmith (ca. 1830-1910)

It has been a longstanding family story that Henry Wadsworth Longfellow's poem, "The Village Blacksmith," was written about Thaddeus Tyler (#4722; Tyler-6385) of Lynn, Massachusetts. This poem was immensely popular and routinely memorized by American school children through the 1950s. It is a sympathetic portrayal of an unassuming but moral workman grieving for his late wife and taking joy from his work and his family.

The Village Blacksmith[91]

As once described on the Gulf Coast Blacksmith Association web site: "The ballad, 'The Village Blacksmith,' was written in the fall of 1839 and appeared in 1840 in the *Knickerbocker* magazine. The inspiration for the poem is commonly believed to have come from Thaddeus Tyler, a blacksmith who worked the forge of the Cambridge Smithy on Brattle Street which the poet passed every day as he walked to his position at Harvard College. Longfellow told his father he wrote it in memory of their seventeenth-century ancestor, Stephen Longfellow, who was a blacksmith. The tree in question was a horse-chestnut tree near Longfellow's home in Cambridge."[92]

"The Original 'Village Blacksmith' Dies

"Boston, April 11 - Longfellow's 'Village Blacksmith' is dead. He was Thaddeus W. Tyler of Lynn, aged 76. To his children, Tyler often told of his acquaintance with the poet while he worked at the forge in a Cambridge blacksmith shop. Longfellow showed him 'The Village Blacksmith,' he said, after he had written it.

"He was born in Warren, New Hampshire, and in 1844 came to Boston, where he learned blacksmithing, being apprenticed to John Tuttle, the man who fashioned the first wagon springs. Then he went to the village smithy in Cambridge. Later he engaged in shoemaking in Stoneham, ran the first engine ever used in the manufacture of shoes, and originated the molded stiffening for shoes."[93]

As we look deeper into this story, it is seen that such historical assumptions can be precarious. A counterargument on the identity of the Village Blacksmith was found on the web site, M. E. Bond. There is validity to this author's argument, since Thaddeus Tyler was born in 1833 and the poem was written in 1839 and Thaddeus could only have been a young apprentice at the time.

"In my research I came across two candidates for the blacksmith who inspired the poem. The first is Dexter Pratt, who lived and worked near Longfellow's home in Cambridge, Massachusetts. Wikipedia backs this man, citing Literary Trail of Greater Boston (Houghton Mifflin, 2000).

"However, in an obituary of April 7, 1910, The Daily Times calls Thaddeus W. Tyler the 'original smithy.' (We'll have to ignore the fact that the smithy was the building, while the man was called the smith.)

"The Gulf Coast Blacksmith Association also states that Tyler was the inspiration behind the poem and provides a link to his obituary (this one from the Boulder Daily Herald).

"So who was the real 'village blacksmith'?

"In this debate I'll have to side with Wikipedia because the Daily Herald obituary says that Tyler didn't move to Massachusetts until 1844, four years after the poem was published. Moreover, another source (a record in the archives of the Maine Historical Society) calls Tyler the apprentice of the 'Village Blacksmith.' Mystery solved." [94]

Era of Early Westward Expansion (1780s–1860s)

During the nineteenth century, much of the focus of United States diplomacy was on territorial expansion. To President Jefferson, westward expansion was the key to the nation's health. He believed that a republic depended on an independent, virtuous citizenry for its survival and that independence and virtue went hand in hand with land ownership, especially the ownership of small farms. ("Those who labor in the earth," he wrote, "are the chosen people of God.") In order to provide enough land to sustain this ideal population of virtuous yeomen, the United States would have to continue to expand. The westward expansion of the United States is one of the defining themes of nineteenth-century American history.

Major land acquisitions followed Jefferson's Louisiana Purchase; other acquisitions included Florida, Hawaii, Texas, Oregon, California, Arizona and New Mexico, and Alaska. By 1840, nearly 7 million Americans—40 percent of the nation's population—lived in the trans-Appalachian West. Most of these people had left their homes in the East in search of economic opportunity. Thousands of people crossed the Rockies to the Oregon Territory, which belonged to Great Britain, and thousands more moved into the Mexican territories of California, New Mexico, and Texas. When gold was discovered in California, acquired through the treaty that ended the war with Mexico in 1848, waves of treasure seekers poured into the area. The California Gold Rush was a major factor in expansion west of the Mississippi. That westward expansion was greatly aided by the completion of the Transcontinental Railroad in 1869, and passage of the Homestead Act in 1862. That act provided free 160-acre lots in the unsettled West to anyone who would file a claim, live on the land for five years and make improvements to it, including building a dwelling.

Many Tylers followed routes from New England to the new territories to the west during this period, especially across New York State to the Great Lakes region. The following biographies are individuals in the extended Job Tyler family who moved to new areas and established a significant presence with their activities.

Dean Tyler (1755–1802)

Once in a while we come across a star-crossed love story that affects an entire lifetime. Such is the case with the story of Dean Tyler (#275; Tyler-6640). Dean was born in 1755, probably at the old Tyler farm where his parents, Gideon (#72; Tyler-1294) and Mehitable Tyler, lived for their entire lives together in West Boxford, Massachusetts (although some sources indicate he was a native of Haverhill, Massachusetts). In his will, Gideon bequested land to daughters Mehitable and Anna and "convenient room in my dwelling house and in the cellar under the same so long as they live a single life, they not admitting any family to live with them," which is likely the reason the sisters remained unmarried throughout their lifetime.[95] Gideon's other offspring received acreage and cash amounts ranging from £40 to £400. But Dean received in Gideon's will a relatively measly £5 (worth about 22 dollars in 1800) out of an estate valued at over $12,000. One can only speculate why Dean was not favored by his father. But he successfully moved forward with his life, attending Harvard University and graduating in the distinctive year of 1776. Family historian W. I. Tyler Brigham described him as follows: "He had a brilliant mind, an agreeable person and refined manners."[96]

During this time, he formed a liaison with a young lady and the two were described as being deeply in love. Although it was an intense relationship, at one point they had a significant disagreement and Dean made the decision to take a cooling-off period. Surprisingly, he decided to leave Massachusetts and embark on a trip to Europe. As described by historian S. P. Hildreth, this period was especially difficult for the young man: "A misunderstanding occurred, which induced Tyler to embark for Europe, to flee from that which had really become necessary to his happiness. He took passage in a letter of marque [official authorization for travel as a privateer] for Bourdeaux. On the voyage out and back, he met with some fighting, some storms, and had several narrow escapes. These incidents probably helped to cure him of his jealousy, or whatever it was that caused him to go on this adventure. He returned with a full determination to confess his fault and unite himself with her whom he had so abruptly parted from. But it was too late; he had broken the heart of his loved one, and the first news he heard on landing was that she was dead—had died of a broken heart. The shock entirely overcame him; he was attacked with a violent illness, followed with delirium, and narrowly escaped that death he would willingly have suffered, could it atone for his error."[97] Dean's recovery was slow. He went into a depression and it was a long time before he could attend to any of his business.

Eventually, as part of his recovery he decided to leave Massachusetts and explore new areas. In 1786, ten men gathered at the Bunch of Grapes tavern in Boston to develop plans for establishing a new settlement in the enormous wilderness known as the Northwest Territory. A year later the Northwest Ordinance was passed by Congress, including a contract tied with the Ohio Company, a newly formed land speculation company that received one-and-a-half million acres of land for settlement. It was truly one of the most far-reaching acts of Congress in the history of the country. Many people in New England were interested in being part of a first expedition to this distant wilderness, among them Dean Tyler. He was intrigued with the prospects of this new group called the Ohio Company, whose goal was to support some of the first settlers in the Ohio Territory.

He joined the first group of pioneers, a selected group of surveyors, carpenters, boat builders, common laborers, and a blacksmith. Although Dean had none of these skills, he was still invited to join them on the trip from Massachusetts. Leaving in December, during the winter of 1788, they traveled across the frozen lands of New York and Pennsylvania. That winter was especially harsh, and their travel was described as "excessive bad." They spent time at the Youghiogheny River, southeast of Pittsburgh, and built a flotilla of boats to transport themselves and their goods to the Monongahela and eventually to the Ohio River. They arrived at a bend in the Ohio River at the mouth of the Muskingum River on April 7th and formed a settlement that would become the city of Marietta, Ohio. During this first year, times were tough in the new settlement. The few provisions the settlers had brought were spent, the hunting season was over, and very little meat had been salted as provisions. It remained difficult even during the first summer as the settlers took care of the many burdens of establishing new homesteads.

Little is known of Dean Tyler during this initial period. One Ohio historian described his traits as insufficient to cope with the needs of a frontier existence: "He had been liberally educated. He possessed abilities, but his genius was eccentric; he had been exclusively confined to handling books and found it difficult to become accustomed to the ax-handle and the hoe, and without the means to live without, there were few implements which offered the means to keep the pot boiling, and instead of growing up with the settlement and becoming a guide and benefactor, he became worse than indolent, buried his talents, and his errors should not be remembered."[98] But more out of necessity than anything, Dean gradually became a more useful citizen. In one instance, the arrival of settler Ichabod Nye, with his wife and children, was a concern because of their lack of a shelter. Dean, who had a small cabin at that point, offered to share his space in return for help with his patch of corn and cucumbers.

The next summer required construction of shelters and clearing of farm land, but as fall approached there was once again a real shortage of food for the settlers. In an attempt to gain provisions, Dean utilized Ohio Company funding to acquire a flatboat and take it to Pittsburgh for a supply of flour to get the settlers through the winter. However, the river froze before he could return, and Nye wrote about how they were all starving for bread. It is unclear when Dean was able to return with provisions, but his effort indicated he was ready to provide leadership in the new community. Fortunately, by the following summer, the land was much more productive for the new community, and crops were planted and harvested with greater success.

Marietta was located at a key bend in the Ohio River (referred to by the natives as the O-Y-O). At this point it received the waters of the Muskingum River, a smaller, clearer, and smoother-flowing river. Some miles upriver on the Muskingum, a second community was established, and in 1789 Tyler was one of thirty-nine men to form the Second Association of the Ohio Company to settle what became the town of Waterford, Ohio. Tyler quickly attached himself to this community, receiving from the Ohio Company a donation of one hundred acres of land. A twenty-six-acre section on the northern portion of his property, located along the river, eventually developed to become the center of the town of Waterford.

Possibly because of the personal tragedy in his youth, Dean Tyler never married. As a settler, he remained more interested in intellectual pursuits than in farming and building, and his habits were described as rather studious and sedentary. However, he became an active member of the community, serving as its first constable. He also taught school and served as chaplain on Sundays when the church's minister was elsewhere.

The first two years in Waterford were peaceful for the settlers, but in 1791 the town was threatened by an attack from one of the more warlike Native American tribes that was upset about the taking of their lands and the loss of hunting grounds. Tyler responded to this threat by helping construct a garrison on the south side of the river, which was to include a structure known as Tyler's Blockhouse, part of Fort Tyler, which enshrined his named as part of local history. As Major Dean Tyler, he commanded an effort to build mills under the protection of the fort, leading to a skirmish that led to the death of three men, who were buried on a bluff near one of the mills.

Unfortunately, the colorful life of this Harvard graduate who became a pioneer eventually led to a period of depression, likely caused by his being a single man living far from his birthplace. In his later years he became intemperate, presumably hoping to drown his melancholy through inebriation. Indeed, one historical resource noted the county sheriff was given orders in 1794 to take him into custody, although the reason has never been shown in historical records. He died a bachelor in 1802 in Marietta, Ohio.

Samuel Tyler (1759–1825)

Samuel Tyler (#637; Tyler-6344) was born in Ashford, Connecticut, in 1759. With his brothers, John and William, he and his wife, Deliverance, moved to Onondaga County, New York, in 1794 as one of its first settlers. They built in an area that became known as "Tyler Hollow," where Samuel built a saw mill and grist mill. He was the town's Supervisor in 1797 and became Justice of the Peace two years later, when he held sessions in his home as a common practice.

In 1806, Samuel became one of the incorporators of the Skaneateles Turnpike, a "corduroy road" constructed with logs. This was a period when there were few road systems, and many resulted from the private initiative of early settlers. The turnpike charter was repealed in 1847 to make the route a state road.

The following, taken from an article in the Marcellus, New York *Post Standard* in 1934, adds more information on his life:

"TYLER HOLLOW AS FOUNDED IN 1794

"Samuel Tyler, a native of Ashford, Connecticut, built a pioneer home for his family in the hollow destined to bear his name, now home of George E. Manahan, just south of Route 20.

"Samuel Tyler was a brother of the more famous Comfort Tyler, remembered with Ephraim Webster and Asa Danforth as one of the first white settlers of this county.

"With his wife and son, Samuel Tyler established himself in "Tyler Hollow" in 1794. Three years later he was appointed supervisor, and in 1798 he became the first Justice of the Peace in the township of Marcellus. His home was the scene of the first courts of common pleas and federal sessions held in the county.

"MANY MOVED WEST

"Throughout the first half of the 19th Century, descendants of this sturdy pioneer kept alive the name of Tyler in the little farming community south of Marcellus, but as years slipped by many of the Tylers responded to the urge to move further west. Jared Whiting Tyler, grandson of the pioneer Samuel, is said to have been the last Tyler to leave the old family homestead. The date of his departure, however, is uncertain.

"Ebenezer and David Tyler, twin sons of the pioneer, were born in 1792. Ebenezer was unfortunate in that he drowned in his 14th year in the mill sluice of his father's mill. Other sons were Job Tyler, who died at sea, Comfort Tyler, who moved to Colon, Michigan in 1834 and died there in 1873, and James Tyler. The last of the Tyler Hollow Tylers died in Jordan in 1898 and was buried in Marcellus where according to The Tyler Genealogy published in 1912 'four generations of Tylers sleep.'"[99]

Samuel died in 1825, a week after visiting his sick brother Comfort in Montezuma, New York. He is buried in the Old Marcellus Village Cemetery.

Captain Silas Tyler (1795–1875)

The Middlesex Canal was a 27-mile barge canal connecting the Merrimack River with the port of Boston. Because of extremely poor roads, the cost of bringing goods such as lumber, ashes, grain, and fur to the coast could be quite high if water transport was unavailable. The first boat operated on part of the canal in 1802, and the canal became one of the main thoroughfares in eastern New England. People viewed the canal as a wonder. United States Treasury Secretary Albert Gallatin called the Middlesex Canal "the greatest work of its kind that has been completed in the United States."

In 1899, Mabel Hill wrote an article in *The Lowell Book* describing life along the Middlesex Canal through Lowell, Massachusetts. Her essay refers to Silas Tyler (#1186; Tyler-6394), one of the best-known captains of any Middlesex Canal packet-boat.

"Silas Tyler was born in 1793 in what is today called Lowell. His father, Nathan Tyler, who was also a Captain, moved about in 1821 to Middlesex Village and soon was one of its largest landowners. He was engaged in fisheries of the fish business. Silas lived all his life in Lowell and it was here that he and his wife raised their family. . . He arrived at Middlesex Village by the canal boat, then plying between that village and Charles-town three times each way every week. . . There was a large business done in summer by boats from Concord and other points on the river and canal in transporting goods, wood and lumber, and in floating rafts. Soon after the opening of this canal, a packet-boat was built and run between Middlesex Village and Charlestown, for the accommodation of passengers, propelled by horse-power at a speed of about four miles per hour. This boat continued to run in Summer up to 1835 or 1836 and was under the management for many years of our respected townsman, Silas Tyler, as captain, who informs me the fare was fifty cents for the whole distance, or about two cents a mile, and that is was a paying business.

"Captain Silas Tyler, the man of genial nature and courteous manners, who for so many years commanded the packet-boat walked up and down the deck, bidding his guests make themselves comfortable. He was indeed regarded as a good Captain and was more—for he was known to all as a 'jovial' man. Nearby the stages emptied their passengers into the Boston packet-boat commanded by the jovial Captain Silas Tyler.

"Captain Tyler worked as a skipper—or as he is sometimes called 'Master'—for two decades on the canal and sailed the 'Governor Sullivan' passenger boat for seven. J. W. Meader in his book on the Merrimack River says this of him: 'Mr. Tyler followed the Merrimack many years as pilot and was connected to the Middlesex Canal for twenty years, being for seven years captain of a packet-boat Gov. Sullivan.' That of course mainly ended in 1835 as the new railroad was beginning to come into its own. Meader then related Tyler's private opinion about the railroad and more significantly how he considered that the canal might have given it a run for its money. 'Mr. Tyler was of opinion that, with an enlargement of twenty feet in width and three in depth, this canal could have successfully competed with the railroad as one horse could then haul sixty tons of freight from Lowell to Boston.'

"Silas was also involved in the fisheries business. One account describes what it was like. 'The best haul of fish I ever knew was eleven hundred shad and eight to ten thousand alewives. This was in the Concord just below the Middlesex Mills. My uncle, Joe Tyler, once got so many alewives that he did not know what to do with them. The lass allowed us to fish two days in the week in the Concord and three in the Merrimack.'"[100]

A humorous article from a few years ago in "Towpath Topics," published by the Middlesex Canal Association, argued that Captain Tyler was a "scofflaw!" who routinely exceeded the speed limit for barges on the canal. By regulation, the speed limits on the Middlesex Canal were set at 1½ mph for rafts and bands of rafts, 2½ mph for luggage (freight) boats, and 3½ mph for Packet boats, with the practical speed of most boats governed by the walking speed of oxen. The author used an advertisement from the period indicating Captain Tyler's boat, the "Governor

Sullivan," could leave Middlesex Village at 8:00am and arrived back by 3:00pm. After calculating the time needed to go through twenty locks, the author showed Tyler must have been traveling over five miles per hour to make that time. Although it may not seem fast today, then such a speed could cause a problematic wake along the canal walls. It seems the captain could have been accused of speeding, but for our purposes no record of a speeding ticket has ever been found.[101]

The Other Comfort Tyler (1801–1873)

Comfort Tyler (#1799; Tyler-3736) was the son of Samuel Tyler (#637; Tyler-3738), who was a brother of Colonel Comfort Tyler (#639; Tyler-6346), described previously. Significantly, this Comfort was also political and was present at the organization of the Republican Party. His biography is taken from *The History of St. Joseph County, Michigan* (1877).

"Among the honored names of St. Joseph County, that of Comfort Tyler stands prominently out, as one who has done much to give the old county its proud position in the Peninsular State. His parents, Samuel and Deliverance (Whiting) Tyler, were natives of Connecticut, and removed therefrom in 1788 to Onondaga County, New York, where Mrs. Tyler lived nine months before seeing another white woman beside herself, and there months longer before she saw a second one. One of Mr. Samuel Tyler's brothers [Comfort] preceded him to Onondaga a short time before. They were of the very best and foremost of the families of that region, and gained a most enviable reputation as men of ability and straightforward business character.

"Comfort Tyler was born in the town of Marcellus, in the above-named county, on the 7th day of March, 1801, where he received a limited education in the common schools of the county, and assisted his father in the business of farming, milling and carding wool and dressing cloth, until he was twenty-four years of age, when he began life for himself in the business of his father before him.

"In the year 1833 he traveled through Michigan and northern Indiana and returned to Marcellus, and in the spring of 1834 removed with his family to the west, thinking to locate in Indiana; but on arriving at White Pigeon, those of the residents of St. Joseph County who had met him in the previous summer were so favorably impressed with his bearing they persuaded him to look further for a location in the county, and on doing so he made his selection for a home in the southwest corner of the township of Colon, buying three hundred and thirty-three acres on sections nineteen and thirty-one, with the intention of making further purchases on the Nottawa prairie, when the Indian reservation would come into the market, but did not do so by reason of the particular tract he wanted being located by another party.

"The people of the township found in him an able and careful counsellor, and guardian of their public trusts, and they gave those trusts into his hands in the fullest measure. He was the supervisor of the township to twenty-five years, his last term ending in the year when his health would not permit further service. He was also appreciated in the councils of the

State, representing St. Joseph County in the lower house of the general assembly in 1841 and in the upper house, as senator, in the year 1859. He was also a member of the constitutional convention of 1867 from St. Joseph County. In politics Mr. Tyler was originally a member of the Whig party, joining the Republican party at its organization, of which he remained a staunch advocate till his death."[102]

Comfort Tyler played a significant and once-in-a-lifetime role by participating in the first organizing convention to establish the Republican Party. The first statewide convention that formed a platform and nominated candidates under the name Republican was held near Jackson, Michigan on July 6, 1854. Due to the extreme heat and discomfort coupled with the large crowd that showed up, the convention was forced "Under the Oaks," where the location is now signified with a historical marker. It was a convention of anti-slavery advocates, including Whigs and southern Democrats. The participants declared their new party opposed to the expansion of slavery into new territories and selected a statewide slate of candidates. The Midwest took the lead in forming state party tickets while the eastern states lagged behind a year or so. There were no efforts to organize the party in the South, apart from St. Louis and a few areas adjacent to free states.

"Under the Oaks," Jackson, Michigan, 1854

"Mr. Comfort Tyler was broad in his views, and liberal and enterprising in schemes for the public good. Though not particularly to be benefited by his act, he nevertheless aided generously in the construction of the railroad through Colon, believing it to be of general value to the people of the township.

95

"He united with the Methodist Episcopal Church at Centreville in 1841, and was its recording steward for twenty-five years, and died on its communion. In all matters of the public entrusted to his care he was scrupulously exact to see that his duties were promptly and fully performed, and he had left behind him a record as his monument, upon which his children may look with pride, and his fellow citizens with admiration. His hospitality was unbounded, and he was generous to a fault."[103]

Sergeant Daniel Tyler (1819–??)

One of the Tyler family's most illustrious Mormon ancestors is Daniel Tyler (#2300; Tyler-6414). He was born in 1819 and was introduced to the Book of Mormon through a meeting he attended at his neighbor's house. Mormon missionaries were there and Daniel, aged fifteen at the time, picked up the book and began to read. It took only a few pages in order for him to feel a strong desire to be baptized into the church.

The Book of Mormon was a work accepted as holy scripture, in addition to the Bible, in the Church of Jesus Christ of Latter-day Saints and other Mormon churches. First published in 1830, its followers hold that it is a divinely inspired work revealed to and translated by the founder of their religion, Joseph Smith. It relates the history of a group of Hebrews who migrated from Jerusalem to America about 600 BC, led by a prophet, Lehi. One group, the Lamanites, forgot their beliefs, became heathens, and were the ancestors of native Americans.

Daniel Tyler served as the sergeant of Company C of the Mormon Battalion, the only religion-based unit in United States military history. Daniel kept a vivid account of all their doings. He is best known for his book, *A Concise History of the Mormon Battalion in the Mexican War: 1846–1847*, a 386-page documentation of the efforts of a Mormon Battalion to be involved in the Mexican War.[104]

How did the Mormon Battalion become part of the United States Army? The story of the Battalion began in early 1846 as members of The Church of Jesus Christ of Latter-day Saints prepared to abandon their city of Nauvoo, Illinois. Persecution and mob violence had made it impossible for them to stay. Under the direction of Brigham Young, President of the Quorum of the Twelve Apostles, they would leave their homes and most of their belongings behind. They would eventually establish a new community in the Salt Lake Valley.

Before the Saints left Nauvoo, President Young assigned Jesse C. Little to ask the United States government for help with the emigration. Little sent a letter to President James Polk. The letter detailed the Mormons' plan to travel over the Rocky Mountains and settle in Mexican territory. The letter also contained a warning: If they did not receive help from the U.S. government, they would be willing to accept assistance from rival governments.

At that time, the United States was engaged in the Mexican-American War, a battle for land that was then Mexican territory. Concerned about thousands of Mormons heading into enemy territory, President Polk ordered United States Army officials to recruit a few hundred Mormons to enlist in the army. President Polk said he hoped "to conciliate [the Mormons], attach them to our country, & prevent them from taking part against us."[105]

Why did five hundred volunteers agree to join the army? They joined because they listened to the Mormon's president, President Brigham Young, considered a living prophet. Their military leader never would have been able to persuade them to enlist. But President Young knew that their service would provide funds to help the Latter Day Saints reach Salt Lake Valley, allowing them to gather as a covenant people.

The Mormon Battalion never had to fight in the Mexican-American War. They did, however, face hardships, including fatigue, hunger, and sickness. Their most severe challenges were lack of water and harsh terrain. After their discharge, the members of the Battalion continued to make history as they made their way from the coast easterly by establishing wagon routes connecting California, Nevada, and Utah.

The following autobiographical sketch describes some of the conditions faced by the battalion and his role in its campaign:

"I then went to Ioway [Iowa] City Ioway [Iowa] Territory and joined the Camp of the Saints who were preparing to cross the plains to Utah with hand Carts. I was called and Set apart as Bishop of the Camp where I remained until the last Company started. Elder Edward Martin was appointed Captain and I his Counseler and Chaplain. My health was poor, but when I saw the Suffering of my brethren and Sisters in consequence of the cold[,] Storms and Scarcity of provisions I plead might[i]ly with the Lord and I was heald and became healthier than I had been for Several years[.] Elder Martin requested me to See every one out of Camp in the morning and in Camp at night, which I did, he going a head and looking out Camping places &c. I also had to See to burying the dead which in our Company amounted to Some thing over ninety during our over three month travel, out of our Six hundred, Souls! The heavy Snows Set in at the upper Crossing of the Plat[te] about the the first of Oct. and continued during the rest of the Journey at intervals the rest of the way. Many was the night after Camping as we some times must in a Scattered Condition that I have taken Small children in my arms from the wagons and hunted the mothers who had pulled the cart, for over an hour before finding her Camp fire, where She would be Cooking her Scanty allowance of food So Stupified that She was oblivious to every thing else—even the tender child of two or three years. But these scenes are too painful a detailed account would melt a heart of Stone. We done our best, and many to day congratulate us on Saving their lives while others whom by the utmost exertion we Succeeded in Saving can Scarcely think of any thing too wicked and false to Say about us."[106]

"Theirs was unlike any other unit ever formed in the history of the United States Army—a battalion of Saints. This band of 500 men and a few women and children fired not a shot in anger, except at a herd of rampaging bulls. True to the prophetic promise made to them by President Brigham Young, not one of them was lost to hostile action, although 20 lost their lives due to the privations they suffered. But their work in carving out a wagon road with picks, shovels, and even their bare hands across the barren deserts of the American Southwest—a road which thousands would later follow en route to the fabled riches of California—did as much to secure these vast territories to the United States as all the storied military deeds of the war with Mexico."[107]

Toward the end of the battalion's journey they first sighted the Pacific Ocean. Daniel recorded his thoughts on that very special day: "The joy, the cheer that filled our souls, none but worn-out pilgrims nearing a haven of rest can imagine. Prior to leaving Nauvoo, we had talked about and sung about "the great Pacific Sea," and we were now upon its very borders, and its beauty far exceeded our most sanguine expectations. . . . The next thought was, where, oh where were our fathers, mothers, brothers, sisters, wives and children."[108]

Daniel Tyler also was instrumental in the building up of the church in Europe. He was called to serve as a mission president of the Italian/Swiss/German/French Mission in 1854. While there, he received a letter from Professor Karl G. Maeser, a German citizen who was interested in the church. Professor Maeser was subsequently baptized a member of the Church, emigrated to Utah, and was one of the founding fathers of Brigham Young Academy, now known as Brigham Young University. Despite a stony expression and military stance, Daniel Tyler was a kind man who loved to share his testimony with others.

In 1861 Daniel and his wife of many years, Ruth, were called to Southern Utah to help strengthen a weak settlement. Their family accompanied them. Daniel taught school here for three years, then was called to Beaver City for the same purpose. He taught there one year. They resided in Beaver the remainder of their lives.

In the year 1873 Daniel was ordained patriarch by George Albert Smith under Brigham Young's direction. Saints throughout the southern boundaries came to Daniel for blessings. He was blessed with miraculous spiritual powers of healing the sick, casting out evil spirits, and was recognized as an authority on Church doctrine.[109]

Charles Marion Tyler (1829–1884)

Charles Marion Tyler (#4070; Tyler-3450) was born in Danville, Kentucky, in 1829 as his family moved from New Hampshire to Kentucky to Texas. As an adult, he married fourteen-year-old Mary Longley in Texas in 1854. Before Mary Catherine's father would give them permission to be married, he made Charles promise not to leave Texas for 15 years. (He hoped by extracting this promise from Charles that he would give up his notion of moving to the west.) True to his word Charles stayed in Texas for this period of time. In 1869 they moved west. Their journey represents well the life journey of a nineteenth century family who settled in different regions of the United States.

"Charles and Mary lived just outside of Evergreen, Texas, about fifteen years. Their first seven children were born there. Charles made their house from timber close at hand. He hewed out the weather boards with his board and drawing knife. The floor of one room was white cedar, and the other red cedar. He made all of his own furniture, with rawhide woven for springs in the beds and chair seats. The chairs were slat back. A big trundle bed rolled out from under the large bed on four little wooden wheels hand-turned. The bed was made of Oak which grew on their land. It had big blue chambray foot curtains, with white fringe and insertion on them. Blue chanbray window curtains had a valence of white linen or lawn.

"Charles was a farmer but freighted during the Civil War. He took supplies to the Confederate Army. This freighting was done by ox teams, drawing heavily loaded, over-sized wagons with beds 120 feet long and four feet long and four feet high. Shortly after the close of the war Charles bought some of these wagons with emigration to Utah in mind. He had joined The Church of Jesus Christ of Latter-day Saints several years before. He sold his farm and grazing land and invested part of his money in Texas cattle, about 500 head. His intention was to drive them to Utah, where three of his brothers had already gone.

"Charles made yokes and bows for the seven yoke of oxen, which were to pull the wagons. Mary made wagon covers out of 8 oz. duck, all by hand. She also made two tents by hand. They were sewn with #8 thread, each seam overcast twice. She made all of the children's clothes by hand as well, weaving the clothe from which they were made.

"The night before they left Evergreen, they stayed at the home of Mary's parents, the Longleys (From memories of Mary's brother, James). I remember way back yonder, 10 May 1869, I have a picture in my mind which will never fade—the day Mary and Charles left for Utah. They had three big scoop bed wagons loaded. One wagon had a six-mule team, two wagons had six oxen each (three teams each). The prairie was all covered with green grass and wild flowers and big butterflies were flying around. John, age 11-1/2, and I were running and catching butterflies and gathering wild flowers. Mary got onto the mule team wagon, took little Annie on her lap (she was six weeks old) and picked up the lines and said, 'Come on John. It is time to go.' So they left with Mary driving that six mule team. It was a beautiful Spring morning, dew was glistening on the flowers and grass. We children were all happy; we could not realize the awfulness of that separation for so long. But mother was crying and wiping her eyes on her apron and stood watching that caravan wind slowly out of sight, going Northward to the Austin Road; it was five miles. We watched until the wagons and cattle drifted dimly out of sight. My heart ached, and mother kept crying for days, and never did quit grieving. Every letter she would get she would wear it under her apron strings until they almost wore out. And when Tom Scott built that T and P Railroad, mother would pray for God to bless Tom Scott so that he could build that road then she could see 'My Mary Tyler.'"[110]

From there they went on to Kansas City arriving on 1 July 1870. From there they went by steamboat to Omaha, Nebraska having sold their cattle. In Omaha, Charles chartered a fully enclosed train boxcar which accommodated all their farm implements and the rest of their supplies and luggage. The family boarded the train in Omaha. They arrived in Ogden, Utah on 15 July 1870. The trip had only taken them 12 days from Omaha to Ogden compared to the many weeks or months it would have taken by wagon.[111]

Civil War Period (1850s–1860s)

Slavery was the law of the land, north and south, until the early nineteenth century, although it was concentrated in the southern states, where slaves were used as farm laborers and formed the backbone of the southern economy. In northern states, where industry drove the economy, many people believed that slavery was immoral and wrong. Southerners felt threatened by these northern "abolitionists" and claimed that the common government had no power to end slavery against the wishes of the states.

In the 1860 presidential election, Republicans, led by Abraham Lincoln, supported banning slavery in all the territories of the United States. The Southern states viewed this as a violation of their constitutional rights and as the first step in a grander Republican plan to eventually abolish slavery everywhere. Seven slave states with cotton-based economies declared secession and formed the Confederacy, leading to the country's brutal Civil War. At the beginning of the war twenty-two million people lived in the North and nine million people (four million of whom were slaves) lived in the South. The North also had more money, more factories, more horses, more railroads, and more food.

Many men in the Job Tyler family line served in the military during the Civil War, most for the Union Army, but a few for the Confederate Army. Although there are many stories of bravery and depredation, two soldiers were selected for this section of the narrative, one a successful and proud Union commander who celebrated victory by traveling to India after the war, the other a proud, but not-so-successful, Confederate commander who was the last general to be killed in the war.

Major General Robert Ogden Tyler (1831–1874)

Robert Ogden Tyler (#3383; Tyler-6426) was born in the tiny hamlet of Hunter, New York, in 1831. Brigham discussed some of his biography in Volume II of *The Tyler Genealogy.* The following supplement presents additional information on his very interesting life as both a soldier and a traveler.

In 1853 Robert graduated from the United States Military Academy at West Point, New York, and received an appointment as a second lieutenant. At the breakout of the Civil War, Tyler joined a Union Army force and was sent to Fort Sumter. The resupply of Fort Sumter became the first crisis of the administration of the newly inaugurated President Abraham Lincoln following his victory in the 1860 election. Lincoln's immediate call for 75,000 volunteers to suppress the rebellion resulted in an additional four southern states also declaring their secession and joining the Confederacy. The Battle of Fort Sumter is usually recognized as the conflict that opened the Civil War.

Tyler was appointed as a colonel and trained artillerymen for the 1st Connecticut Heavy Artillery regiment. Under Major General George McClellan he commanded a siege train and fought in the Battle of Fredericksburg, Virginia. This battle was part of the Union Army's futile frontal attacks against entrenched Confederate defenders on the heights behind the city. It is remembered as one of the most one-sided battles of the war, with Union casualties more than twice as heavy as those suffered by the Confederates. A visitor to the battlefield described the battle to President Lincoln as a "butchery."[112]

Tyler was promoted to brigadier general and next commanded an artillery reserve force during the battles of Chancellorsville and Gettysburg. Some nineteen batteries including 110 cannons and hundreds of attendant vehicles made up the Artillery Reserve during the Gettysburg campaign. On July 3rd of the battle, a Confederate cannonade began at 1:00 p.m. Tyler rode the lines on his horse overseeing the artillery and double-checking the location of ammunition wagons. According to one account, "A hissing shell, one of hundreds that sailed over

Cemetery Ridge and exploded in the rear among the parked guns, killed his horse. Tyler spent the next hour or so supervising the movement of the Reserve's guns further to the rear, out of danger. Working in the extreme heat and humidity of July weather, Tyler became prostrated by sunstroke. He was forced to leave his command, though he recovered and returned to duty by dusk."[113]

Portrait of General Robert Ogden Tyler

A quote from the "History of the Army of the Potomac" describes General Tyler's effectiveness: "As the batteries exhausted their ammunition it was replaced by the 'Artillery Reserve' sent forward by its efficient chief, General Robert O. Tyler."[114] A historical marker recognizing his contributions in these battles is located in Frederick, Maryland, as part of the Maryland Civil War Trails marker series.

By 1864, Tyler was assigned command of a division of heavy artillery regiments, where he led in other battles. He fought at the Battle of Cold Harbor near Mechanicsville, Virginia, remembered as one of American history's bloodiest, most lopsided battles. Thousands of Union soldiers were killed or wounded in a hopeless frontal assault against the fortified positions of the army led by Confederate General Robert E. Lee. It was an impressive defensive victory for Lee, but it was one of his last in the war. During the twelve days of fighting, Tyler was badly wounded in his foot and he could no longer lead any field duty during the rest of the war.

After the war, and just before he died at the early age of forty-two, he made a two-month trip to "British and farther India." He kept a journal of his travels through letters home to his family. The following excerpts from these letters give not only a better description of the man, but also chronicle the nature of overseas "exotic" travel in the year of 1873. This journal was written for the eyes of his immediate family, and he had no idea it would ever appear in print, but it makes interesting reading even today. (All the excerpts of the 99-page travel journal are taken from his Memoir; page numbers indicated after each excerpt.)

"My dear sister, We have avoided rather than sought colonial society, knowing that when dinners and junketings commence, sightseeing is at an end. We have tried to see something of the people and of their habits." (pp. 23-24)

"As soon as the arrival of a stranger is known at the hotel, he is besieged by a swarm of guides, body-servants, barbers, tailors, washermen (dhobes), cane-dealers, and peddlers, seeking the patronage of the newcomer. The first thing to be done is to employ a servant. Without this appendage a gentleman loses caste at Singapore. He who runs his own errands, carries his own bundles, packs his own luggage, and brushes his own clothes, shall remain unattended at breakfast, neglected at dinner, and from his apartment, without a bell, shall cry 'Boy!' unanswered, along the piazzas of the hotel. With a servant you are saluted by the title of 'master.'" (p. 25)

"I must here stop to pay a tribute to our boy Abdul. I find him about the best, most faithful and willing man I have ever seen in his position. My preconceived idea of Indian servants led me to suppose that we should require at least one for each of us; but Abdul goes against Scripture: he 'serves two Masters' and does it pretty well. He is our interpreter, guide, broker, courier, and body and table servant, all of which is, after all, more than any one man can do perfectly. . . He goes to sleep later and gets up earlier than ourselves, and is always good-natured and zealous. He travels and fares third-class, but will fight if anything less than first is attempted to be passed upon us. . . He tries his hand at supplying all our necessities; he mends clothes, sews on buttons, cobbles shoes, cooks, whips up a chutney or curry in ten minutes or spends a week in the composition of the former. He fears that greenhorns like ourselves may be robbed, and is always asking, 'Master, where is your watch?' and, if we are flush, insists on taking part of our money and putting it under lock and key. And all this for fifteen dollars per month!" (p. 81)

"My travel companions took an early walk this morning down to the burning ghat, where they saw the dead in all stages of increamation, and pariah dogs rugging at the remains of extinguished funeral-piles. . . I do not seriously object to the disposition of the dead by fire. The living are shocked by no grinning skull or other ghastly remnant of mortality. In over-crowded populations the dead may pollute the springs, or, as in China, rob labor of the soil which should support its share of life. . . By the alchemy of fire we are simply resolved into our original constituents, and after the elimination of the incorporal parts, our ashes returned to the earth may again become life in those who live after us." (p. 51)

In later years Tyler was honored with the rank of major general for his "great gallantry." The Grand Army of the Republic in Hartford, Connecticut, recognized him by naming their post, in his honor, the Robert O. Tyler Post #50. Perhaps the life of Robert Ogden Tyler can best be honored through the words of his sister, Mrs. S. S. Cowen, at his funeral: "So closed the earthly career of this gallant officer and true soldier. His record tells its own story, but it cannot speak of the high qualities which made up the finished character. His strict sense of justice; his perfect integrity and fine sense of honor; his devoted love of country and his loyalty to his friends; his scrupulous regard for the feelings of others; his cultivated and warm, affectionate heart,—who can justly estimate in words the value of all these characteristics?"[115]

Brigadier General Reuben Cutler (Robert Charles) Tyler (1832–1865)

Where the career of Robert Ogden Tyler (described above) as a soldier was honorable, the life of Reuben Cutler Tyler (#4329; Tyler-6453) (also known as Robert Charles Tyler) chronicled a very different adventurous saga. His story is especially intriguing because he could be seen as having both a seedy and a courageous character, perhaps at the same time.

Rueben Tyler was born in 1832 in Hartwick, Massachusetts, the son of a farmer and deacon of the local church. In 1852 he moved to California. By 1855 he was living in Sonoma County, California, being sued for debts. One can only speculate on why during the next year he changed his name to Robert Charles, but one could assume it ostensibly would be to evade his creditors.

In any case, he removed himself from his quandary by joining the army of William Walker, known as "The Most Notorious Soldier of Fortune of the Nineteenth Century."[116] William Walker was a Tennessee-born physician and journalist who became famous in the nineteenth century for funding and leading American mercenaries into Latin America for the purpose of establishing English-speaking colonies. Walker and his private army landed in Nicaragua at the behest of the embattled Liberals, who were then fighting Nicaraguan Conservatives and other right-wing factions from across Central America. Tyler came on as a first lieutenant in this "band of brothers," ending up fighting in the army's Nicaragua campaign of 1856-57. Ultimately, Walker staged a coup and named himself president of Nicaragua in 1856. President Walker's tenure, which saw the legalization of slavery and the establishment of English as the official language, was short, and a combined Liberal-Conservative army forced him to seek shelter with a U.S. Navy ship. A later expedition in 1860 resulted in the public execution of Walker by a Honduran firing squad.[117]

After Tyler's expedition with Walker's army in Central America he returned to the United States, working in Tennessee as a clerk. While there he helped organize the Knights of the Golden Table, a secret society that proposed a confederation of slave states—made up of southern states and annexed territories in Mexico, Central America, and the Caribbean—to be led by Maximilian I of Mexico. The goal was to increase the power of the Southern slave-holding upper class to such a degree that it could never be dislodged.[118]

When the Civil War erupted, Tyler joined a Tennessee infantry regiment as a private, soon being promoted to Quartermaster Sergeant, Regimental Quartermaster, and Quartermaster-General. He gained command of his own regiment at the Battle of Shiloh, where he was wounded while losing three horses from under him. He next became a Confederate Army Colonel and was given command of a consolidated regiment incorporating eight other brigades and regiments. At the Battle of Missionary Ridge, he was shot in his left leg and carried from the field. His leg was amputated, and he used crutches for the rest of his life. While recovering at a Georgia hospital he was promoted to the rank of Brigadier General. He then returned to action and his brigade was renamed Tyler's Brigade. Described by some historians as the most enigmatic Confederate general of the war, one commander described Tyler this way: "He was a stout, robust officer, and had firmness, determination, and courage written in every line of his face. . . I soon learned to look upon him as one of the bravest men I ever saw."[119]

In late 1864 Tyler was positioned as commander of Fort Tyler in West Point, Georgia. The fort was a small earthwork construction about thirty-five feet on a side, with two field guns and a large 32-pounder gun. He and his small residual detachment of convalescent soldiers, invalids, and young boys from town were responsible for guarding two strategic railroad bridges over the Chattahoochee River. The local community gave him a confederate flag, and he pledged to die beneath it rather than surrender to the enemy.

Fort Tyler, West Point, Georgia[120]

Early the next year the town was the scene of raids by Union cavalry. The most significant battle at Fort Tyler took place on Easter Sunday, April 16, 1865, a full week after Confederate General Robert E. Lee had surrendered to Union Army General Ulysses S. Grant at Appomattox, Virginia, and two days after Lincoln had been assassinated. Unfortunately, word of the surrender had not yet reached this part of Georgia, and Tyler and his 120 men tried to hold off 3,500 Union cavalrymen for a full day at Fort Tyler. Around noon, during a stalemate, Tyler, who was on crutches, hobbled outside the fort to get a better view of the Union positions. He looked out onto the battlefield and was shot twice by a sniper positioned in a nearby cottage—a structure Tyler had refused to burn earlier because he knew the owner and did not believe the person could afford the loss—with one bullet hitting him in the chest and the other splitting his crutches. He was borne back inside the fort and placed under the flag staff, where he died an hour later under the flag he swore to defend. Brigadier General Tyler, fighting his gallant but futile last-ditch defense, was the last general killed in the Civil War. He was buried at Fort Tyler Cemetery in West Point, Georgia.

Progressive Era (1880s–1910s)

In the late nineteenth century America was ready to take its place as a center of the world's economy and culture. Chicago stepped forward as the representative of a new time, and its very successful and popular Columbian Exposition of 1893 included many attractions never before viewed by Americans at that time, including idealistic classical architecture, examples of modern architecture, as well as engineering innovations such as electric lights, flush toilets, and a stunning 264-foot-high Ferris Wheel.

By 1900 the United States had established itself as a world power. The West was won; the frontier—the great fact of 300 years of American history—was no more, and the continent was settled from coast to coast. The nation was beginning a major industrial period, led by entrepreneurs who became incredibly wealthy. In the 1880s Andrew Carnegie had constructed the world's largest steel mill in Pittsburgh and by 1900 the United States was the largest steel producer in the world; John D. Rockefeller's Standard Oil Trust dominated the world's petroleum markets, controlling more than ninety percent of the nation's refinery capacity; and with the founding of the Ford Motor Company by Henry Ford in 1903 the age of the automobile was underway.

In this period of booming growth, the nation also experienced a dramatic presidential election. William McKinley, elected in 1896 and again in 1900, represented Eastern conservative mercantile and industrial interests. He was the last of the old-style, low-key presidents. After his assassination in 1901, vice-president Teddy Roosevelt ushered in a new age as a leader of the Progressive movement. Roosevelt believed that strong corporations were good for America, but he also believed that corporate behavior must be watched to ensure that corporate greed did not get out of hand.

Progressivism represented responses to the economic and social problems of rapid industrialization in the United States. Progressives, who lived mainly in the cities, were college educated and believed that government could be a tool for change. They believed the problems society faced (poverty, violence, greed, racism, class warfare) could best be addressed by providing good education, a safe environment, and an efficient workplace. They concentrated on exposing the evils of corporate greed, combating fear of immigrants, and urging Americans to think hard about what democracy meant.

The biographies that follow, selected as representative of this period, encompass individuals who were products of this complex period of growth and change. They include successful entrepreneurs, both men and one woman, but the section begins with an influential historian who gave perspective to the country's increasingly significant history.

Moses Coit Tyler (1835–1900)

Moses Coit Tyler (#5952; Tyler-6463) was a very well-respected early professor at the University of Michigan, where he was Chairman of the English Department for fifteen years. He was also recognized as one of the most extraordinary orators of his time. At Cornell University, he became the first recognized professor of American History in the United States and was a founder of the American Historical Society. When he died in 1900, the Literary Digest called him "the leading historian in American literature." There is much about his career that is worth the telling.

Portrait of Moses Coit Tyler

As a young man, Moses became quite involved in the temperance movement, described in this excerpt:

"Temperance was in fact the battle cry of the times. There had been a long campaign against licensing liquor dealers in Detroit, and during the struggle John B. Gough had been imported to thunder for ten consecutive nights in June, 1850, against the saloon keepers. The young were enlisted under the benevolent patronage of the ministers, divisions of the "Sons" of Temperance and the 'Cadets' of Temperance being promptly formed. Under the compelling personality of Mr. Kitchel, Moses joined not one, but both, rising rapidly in the ranks, for in July, 1851, he took his seat as 'Worthy Archon of Chrystal Fount Section No. 5, Cadets of Temperance,' and a year later became 'G[rand] W[orthy] Archon of the Sons of Temperance.' As Worthy Archon of the 'Chrystal Fount' section, and with Kitchel's sermons ringing in his ears, Moses delivered an 'Address' typical of earnest adolescence in the middle of the last century. He thought that the order of the Cadets of Temperance was of immense importance to 'every true Patriot and Philanthropist,' composed though it was of mere boys, since the 'Philanthropical Politician revolving in his mind the *present* condition of the Nation,' asks whether the next generation shall be '—a race of *dunces!*' The common schools, Moses hoped, 'on every bleak hill-top and in every fruitful valley' ought to help, provided that 'the tide of intemperance which has bourne so many of the past generation into a drunkard's grave and a drunkard's eternity' be checked. For intemperance, it seems, exercises a 'viscious influence' on youth, 'the seed time of life.' And Moses went on to picture 'the number of inebriates' who would be 'daily wallowing in our gutters, and staggering through our streets, and staggering from our docks, and *staggering into eternity*,' were it not for the Cadets. In fact, he used words with 'meaning, force and proper use'; he drew a lurid picture of 'Demon Alcohol,' of delirium tremens with it 'ten thousand clammy serpents' and 'horrid monsters' glistening from the wall. Alas, however, for human frailty! Cadets of Temperance, he said are sometimes seen 'standing around the great fountains of crime, which are pouring forth their incessant stream of corruption, into the community.' Slightly confusing his figures, Moses went on to describe the 'dazzling paintings within' which 'Adorn the view,' the 'gilded tapestry' that 'bedecks the walls,' and just as the reader is about to wonder how so luxurious a gambling den came to be built in simple Detroit, one learns that 'this they call the theatre.' And with some ringing temperance poetry the address concludes."[121]

In the fall of 1852 Moses was admitted to the University of Michigan for classical studies. To meet the requirements, he passed the entrance exams for the following studies: English Grammar, Geography, Arithmetic and Algebra, Latin Grammar, Caesar's Commentaries, Cicero's Select Orations, six books of Virgil's Aeneid, Greek Grammar, and Greek and Roman Geography.

Before graduating, and with support from his relative Samuel Coit, he transferred to Yale, where he could study to become a minister. His studies in Michigan were not accepted at Yale, and he began again as a freshman. During his studies he read widely and became more liberalized in his thinking. As the Civil War approached, almost everywhere in the North anti-slavery sentiment went hand-in-hand with liberalism. Church denominations began to split between southern and northern organizations.

In 1856 Moses attended a meeting in New Haven of the Free-Soil cause, a short-lived political party opposing slavery in the new western territories. As he explained in a letter to his father, the speaker challenged members of the audience to donate twenty-five dollars for purchase of one rifle to support their cause, and various men gave for this purpose. As described in Moses' letter: "The number of donations rose to 20, when there was a halt. At this point a Student rose in the gallery (which was crowded with men of that kind) and said, 'I will pledge myself to raise the amount of $25 for 1 Sharpe's Rifle from the Junior Class in Yale College.' The move was so unusual and so unexpected that it took the folks by storm and the way they cheered was perfectly frightful. When the noise which followed this remark had subsided, Capt. Lines looking toward the gallery shouted, 'What name?' Reply was made, 'Moses Tyler.' Then Beecher bellowed out 'Moses was a meek man, but he had wherewithal to stand up!' This brought the house down again."

Moses continues in the letter to his father:

"Before I left the Church numbers of my classmates swarmed around and expressed their gratification at my act and their willingness to back me up. Before I went to bed nearly the whole sum was raised. But the most ludicrous portion of the performance was to witness the effect it had on the Southerners. They stormed, they swore, they tore! That a class in Yale College should be committed to an Abolition Emigrant Co. for a rifle seemed 'infernal,' 'damnable,' and a sufficient ground for dissolving the Union. Accordingly, at all the tables and in every knot of students, for three days, the topic of debate and profanity has been your humble servant. There is one consolation, however, that while my name is damned in the most brimstone fashion by the segment of Southerners, it is defended with equal pertinacity, tho' with less swearing by the great body of back-bone Northerners. In view of the whole, I am seated, quietly grinning at the tempest which one short sentence can start up. The most grinding part of the whole performance is that the business has got into the N. Y. Papers, and thus it will go through the Nation that a Class in Yale College has given a Sharpe's Rifle. Rich fun!

"Truly yours,

"Moses"[122]

Moses became conflicted about whether he should continue on a tract to become a Calvinist-based clergy or whether he should have the freedom to express liberalism in pursuit of social causes. Even as a young man he had become a brilliant orator, and in 1856 became involved in the political campaign for the Republican Party. He supported Fremont over Buchanan for the presidential campaign and wrote a fiery opinion: "We shall wage the war of Fremont and Liberty, unmoved and unappalled by the stale and ragged threats, which Senators of weak nerves and small souls and streaked livers have always raised to scare us."[123]

When he was twenty-four, he was married and also invited to serve as pastor at a small church in Oswego, New York. He was ordained and served for one year, when he was solicited to serve as pastor for the First Congregational Church of Poughkeepsie. Because it had a larger congregation and better pay at $1,200 per year, so he accepted their invitation. In those years leading to the Civil War, Moses was deeply conflicted about the growing divide in the nation, and in 1862, after the war led to the bloodshed on the battlefield of Bull Run, Moses wondered what good it did to preach sermons while the world was on fire. After serving only two years in his pastorate, Moses was depressed and in poor health and decided to move with his family to Boston. As he wrote, "my whole state seemed so weak, incapable of work and perpetually shivering on the brink of good-for-nothingness. . . I was thoroughly disgusted and discouraged."[124]

He made a decision that his future lay with literature rather than with theology. He became separated from his wife and young child, who moved to Illinois to live with relatives. Moses began to feel more spirited by staying in Boston and benefited from contact with notable figures of the time, including Ralph Waldo Emerson, Henry Wadsworth Longfellow, John Greenleaf Whittier, Wendell Phillips, Frederick Douglass, Elizabeth Peabody, and others. It was a place he considered "the brain of this continent, the great idea-builder and thought-radiator."[125]

In the 1860s Moses Coit Tyler traveled to England, where he lived for a few years. He was exploring what it was like to be literary and wrote articles and lectured whenever he was able. Eventually it had a huge impact on him, and he was looking at ". . . the difference between the introspective Christianity of Andover [*Massachusetts*] and the possibility of living actively in the world; and the controversy in England over the American war and the second reform bill had shaped and strengthened his nascent[126] political philosophy. Before the English voyage, Tyler had been an amateur fumbling after values. But in London he had won status by his own exertions; he had learned that he could write; . . . The seal of maturity was upon him."[127]

While in London, he felt compelled to explain the differing perspectives of the British and Americans regarding American history. In 1865, he took on as a goal "to write six or eight elaborate lectures on 'The History of American Literature.'" This was a defining moment for him, for the decision was to have a career as a historian.

Moses returned to the United States, where he was offered a faculty position at his first college, The University of Michigan. He accepted a permanent appointment as professor of rhetoric and English literature at a salary of $1,500 per year. He studied hard in preparation for his courses and expected the same of his students. And he was always thinking of new ways to improve the pedagogy of the English Department. At one point, he made a request of the Regents to add a course in

American literature, at the time considered a revolutionary idea, since no important school offered such a course. He studied diligently; his "commonplace book" (diary) for one year indicates he read 166 books on English, Italian, and Greek literature, and moreover, if he read an English author, he would read that author's complete works. During breaks he traveled on a lecture circuit, from New York to St. Louis, where he acquired a commendable reputation.

He considered seriously the lack of depth on writings on American history. As he stated, "If early American history has seemed dry and provincial, and its social life helplessly petty, it must also be owned that a considerable part of this impression has been due, in the main, to the imperfect art of the American writers who have hitherto handled these topics. . . . American history still reserves its charms for the presence of a genius corresponding in that sphere to the greatness of Longfellow and Hawthorne in poetry and romance."[128] He had been preparing over many years to present himself as that historian?

Professor Tyler was a very popular professor at the university. It was noted,

> "There is no member of the faculty more popular and highly esteemed by all the students and citizens, and whose loss would be more felt." He was much in demand by students but limited his classes to afternoons so he could spend mornings working diligently on his new American history. The two volumes of *A History of American Literature During the Colonial Time, 1607–1765*, (622 pages in all) were published in 1878. When it first became available, the campus newspaper gave it high praise: "It is one of the great achievements which add to the permanent glory of a college. We ask nothing better for our University than that it may continue to be remembered as long as 'American Literature,' and be held in equal estimation with it. . . we think that it will stand the hundred years' test of a masterpiece." As a classic piece of literature, a contemporary reviewer gave it a 5-star Amazon review with the following statement: "Tyler's work is the foundation for everything else written on colonial literature since. Tyler is not only well read, but he reads well, and so does this book. His insights into the styles of the various authors is remarkable."[129]

At this point in time he was already considered the first great historian of the national mind as expressed through its literature. As a result of his newly minted reputation, he was elected as a member of a number of significant organizations of the time—the New England Historical and Genealogical Society, the Massachusetts Historical Society, the American Antiquarian Society, and the Rhode Island historical Society.

During the following years Tyler moved to teach at Cornell, and with five other scholars he became a founding member of the American Historical Association. Moses reflected on this period and what it meant to him: ". . . never before have I been so happy—so deeply, soundly, solidly happy. The great fermentations of existence are done. I have found my niche, my sphere, my vocation, my horizon, even my burial place."[130]

His next important project was to write the biography of a true patriot, *Patrick Henry* (1887). Its reception at the time was highly favorable. One reviewer noted, "It is not too much to say that the real Patrick Henry for the first time stands before us." The book's significance may be best represented by the fact that it is his only book still in publication. Near the end of the narrative, he describes Henry's death; it has been considered perhaps the finest single paragraph he ever wrote:

"Then Patrick Henry said, 'Excuse me, doctor, for a few minutes'; and drawing down over his eyes a silken cap which he usually wore, he prayed, in clear words, a simple childlike prayer, for his family, for his county, and for his own soul then in the presence of death. Afterward, in perfect calmness, he swallowed the medicine. Meanwhile, Dr. Cabell, who greatly loved him, went out upon the lawn, and in his grief threw himself down upon the earth under one of the trees, weeping bitterly. Soon, when he had sufficiently mastered himself, the doctor came back to his patient, whom he found calmly watching the congealing of the blood under his finder-nails, and speaking words of love and peace to his family, who were weeping around his chair. Among other things, he told them that he was thankful for that goodness of God, which, having blessed him through all his life, was then permitting him to die without any pain. Finally, fixing his eyes with much tenderness on his dear friend, Dr. Cabell, with whom he had formerly held many arguments respecting the Christian religion, he asked the doctor to observe how great a reality and benefit that religion was to a man about to die. And after Patrick Henry had spoken to his bellowed physician these few words, in praise of something which, having never failed him in all his life before, did not then fail him in his very last need of it, he continued to breathe very softly for some moments; after which they who were looking upon him saw that his life had departed."[131]

His next important book was *The Literary History of the American Revolution*, published in 1897. His scholarly approach for this book was to represent fairly both sides of the revolution—the Revolutionists and the Loyalists—without questioning the sincerity, magnanimity, patriotism, and courage of each. Each side was treated the same, without discrimination. It was referred to as "a necessary, a sympathetic, and a solid achievement in historical reconstruction." The book has been described as "a monument to American scholarship."

During the same year he also wrote the Introduction for a mammoth eight-volume set titled, *The World's History, Illuminated*, a definitive world history of the time (title page shown below). The first paragraph of his Introduction, titled, "The Educational Value of the Study of History," reads as follows:

"In order to do justice to the claims of historical study, it can never be necessary for us to depreciate those of any other branch of learning. Properly considered, there is no such thing as rivalry between different spheres of knowledge; only emulation, a novel and helpful emulation. All real knowledge is good, being in one way or another a world of power and happiness. The various realms of things known or knowable are but co-equal and fraternal states in that vast confederation which we may call the republic of science No single member of this confederation is strong, none is sufficient, standing alone. Each is necessary to all, all are necessary to each."[132]

Late in his career, Moses Coit was working on a number of works; they included *Glimpses of England*, revisions to *Patrick Henry*, and the *Literary History of the American Revolution*. One of the chapters in the latter was to be on John Tyler, a descendant of one of the three original Tyler brothers from whom it was assumed he himself had sprung. When he wrote the Virginia Tylers for material, the Southerners did not respond as he had hoped they would. It was too bad; had he been permitted to complete his book, had he given to the south the same sympathetic interpretation he had given the loyalists in the Revolution, he would have been again a pioneer. As he reflected on this, "As to our once-erring brethren of the South, I have long since come to see that, great as was their mistake in opinion, they were as sincere and as honorable as ourselves; and I am sure that I could never again bring myself to apply to them to them the great practical wrong they did, the harsh expressions which, in the heat of these angry days, so easily leaped from our pens and our tongues."[133]

Professor Moses Coit Tyler led a rich, full life, which included in 1896 serving a term as president of the American Tyler Family Association. At sixty-five years of age his life ended in 1900, at the dawn of a new century. The members of the American Historical Foundation felt as if a great tree had fallen amid a forest of younger trees, sprouting new branches. He moved slowly in old age, but had much to look back on, including the many honors that had been bestowed on him.

Charles Mellen Tyler (1831–1918)

Reverend Charles Mellen Tyler (#3221; Tyler-926) was born in 1832 in Maine. He was educated at the notable Phillips Academy in Andover, Massachusetts, and graduated from Yale College in 1855. Two years later he married Ellen Davis, a professor of music at Syracuse University. In 1857, he was ordained as a minister and ministered to congregations in Massachusetts, Chicago, and Ithaca, New York for thirty-four years. From 1861 to 1862 he also was a member of the Massachusetts House of Representatives. To portray his diversity of thought, during his life he was a member of the Loyal Legion, the Grand Army of the Republic, the American Oriental Society, and the Society for Psychical Research.

In 1891, he left the ministry to be appointed as the first professor of history and philosophy of religions at the Sage School of Philosophy at Cornell University. Professor Tyler was referred to as "a voluminous literary contributor." His publications include *Bases of Religious Belief Historic and Ideal: An Outline of Religious Study*. In its Preface he wrote: "Every serious mind has a philosophy of religion. In our modern thinking, we find the basis of our religious belief in the study of the facts of the world and of human nature. The latter force us to believe in a Being, above the course of the world which is developed in time—a Being of Goodness who is the cause of all that is include in the world."[134] Professor Tyler's view of the genesis of religion as defined in this book is described with the following excerpt from a 1898 review in *The American Journal of Theology*: "Our author in a very interesting way sets forth his own theory, in which those others blend and become stages in a prolonged process. He calls it the 'psychological genesis' of religion. 'Naturism' is the first stage, when primitive man, looking around upon all external activities, attributes to them such a causality as he himself possesses. Here is found the worship of great nature powers. The next stage is animism, which is marked by 'the discovery of soul as distinct from body.' The third stage is found in polytheism and henotheism. In Israel we find monotheism attained only after a prolonged discipline; that race 'possess and cherish a greater receptivity of the divine influence which is active in all history.'"[135]

Reverend Charles Mellen Tyler

He was described in *A History of Cornell* as a very popular professor, and in fact also the faculty dandy, whose elegances, such as necktie rings, set campus fashions. He was further described as a genial literate, well-liked minister, though there were some who thought him extremely lazy, and so eager to be popular that he agreed with everyone.[136]

Reverend Tyler died in 1918. In his honor Cornell University recognized his contributions with a Memorial Statement. It read as follows:

"The University Faculty of Cornell University desire to express their deep sorrow at the death of their honored and beloved colleague, the Reverend Charles Mellen Tyler, D.D., Professor Emeritus of the History and Philosophy of Religion and of Christian Ethics, and to record their appreciation of him as a scholar and as a man.

"After distinguished service in the church, in the General Court of Massachusetts, and as chaplain in the field in the arduous campaign of the Wilderness, Dr. Tyler came in 1872 to Ithaca, where his unusual gifts of mind and character made him a valued member of the community, in his office of clergyman and in civic and social life. After serving the University for five years as Trustee, he became in 1891 a member of the original faculty of the Sage School of Philosophy. He served for twelve years as professor, until his retirement in 1903, when he became Professor Emeritus and Lecturer. Since 1907 he has continued with Cornell University as a member of the Board of Trustees.

"As Professor, Dr. Tyler is remembered with affection and gratitude alike by his colleagues and by his students. His personal charm and his unfailing courtesy endeared him not only to his friends of long standing, but to the latest comers and the most diffident, while his openness of mind and aptness for lucid exposition made the work of his class-room attractive and stimulating. No one did more to make us realize that, as members of the University, in spite of all differences in our methods of approaching the truth, we are spiritually one body, and that our interests are not confined to the material and to the temporal. At a time of thoroughgoing and even radical reconstruction in many fields of investigation and speculation, Dr.

Tyler was never unprogressive or intolerant, for he never forsook the essentially humane point of view. Always ready to welcome the accredited results of modern scientific thought, his faith was even more in the future than in the past. More than usually endowed with sympathy and imagination, Dr. Tyler was not only keenly susceptible to all suggestions of beauty in nature and art, but in his daily walk and conversation he unconsciously exemplified the beautiful as well as the fearlessly true and the humanely good. And his military figure, erect to the last, looked always forward.

"We hereby express our sorrow and extend our sympathy to the family of our late colleague and friend.[137]

He died at Scranton, Pennsylvania, in 1918.

Polly Tyler Young (1839–1896)

Family histories tend to be the histories of prominent men. Occasionally, however, a woman takes on a noteworthy role. Polly Tyler (#4667; Tyler-6532) married Hamilton Young in 1858, when she was nineteen years old. They had three children, all who died young. Captain Hamilton died in the Civil War in 1863, and Polly was left to make her own way. Because of her unique and largely unknown story as the last of a family line, we have included this excerpt taken from Volume II of Brigham's *The Tyler Genealogy*.

Photograph of Polly Tyler

Polly, known for having a sweet and sympathetic disposition and a tender heart, went to the war front after the death of her husband and rendered aid to sick and wounded soldiers. "Some stories are told of her beautiful heroism that should give her a lasting place in the history of the war. In 1872 she settled on a claim in the west and began pioneer life. From farming she went to speculating and everything she touched turned into money. She built houses in Wichita, Kansas, in the early seventies, which paid her well; she went to Wellington, Kansas, with the railroad and erected houses there which she rented well, and from there she went to Caldwell, a wild cowboy town just north of the Oklahoma border, where her success was phenomenal. As the cowboys began to drive the cattle up the Chisholm Trail to Caldwell, the town took on all of the elements of a lawless frontier settlement. Being the first town north of Indian territory, it provided a place where the cowboys could go wild after months on the dusty and treacherous trail. Gunfights, showdowns, general hell-raising and hangings soon became commonplace. When Kiowa, Kansas, was started, Polly arrived on an early train and began to put up business buildings which paid for themselves in a short time. In other western Kansas towns, she was a leader in building up the places. She was looked upon as a 'mascot' in western Kansas, and people invested where she did because they believed in her 'luck.' She then went to Colorado, where her rare success attended her operations. When she entered a new town, she was soon surrounded by a swarm of carpenters and builders. In Oklahoma she went to El Reno, which benefited from the Oklahoma Land Rush that took place on April 22, 1889, when new cities were established by the end of the day. Land was open to settlement, and the Unassigned Lands were considered some of the best unoccupied public land in the United States. She set many builders at work there."[138]

Frank P. Tyler (1853–??)

Joyce G. Tyler did extensive research on Tyler settlers in Iowa. Royall Tyler (#3410; Tyler-6484) was born in 1815 in Vermont and moved as far west as Wisconsin, where he was sheriff of Jefferson County. His son, Frank Tyler (#5931; Tyler-6494), moved further west to Villisca, Iowa, where he established a significant number of early businesses. Frank Tyler serves as a good representative of the spirit of Midwestern businessmen in the late nineteenth century. The following story picks up where Brigham's *The Tyler Genealogy* leaves off and includes many details from Joyce Tyler's family research.

Frank Pierce Tyler was a very interesting local figure and represents well the entrepreneurial spirit found among early settlers. He arrived in Villisca in 1877, buying a forty-acre farm. Both he and his new wife, Flora, were teachers. They decided to trade their farm for some city property. It was a significant decision, since Frank eventually owned a number of the town's early businesses.

Frank began by establishing a barbed wire factory, having a machine which placed barbs on smooth wire, which was all that had been available to that time. He then began a dray business (a low, heavy cart without sides) and hauled freight from the depot to area businesses. During the winter of 1882 he began a new enterprise, cutting his first crop of ice off the Middle Nodaway River, storing it in a small ice house in back of his residence. Kids would push the floating ice blocks to a conveyor, which then transferred them up into the ice house. They would then be sold during the warmer months for refrigeration.

Frank also peddled the first gas and oil in Villisca, carrying the gas and oil about town in two large tin cans set in the front of his ice wagon. He also drove the first oil wagon, delivering for Standard Oil Company. Around 1882 he started a retail coal business, continuing it for 42 years, when he sold it to his brothers. Frank also pumped the city water under contract for several years.

In 1890 he began manufacturing brick, at first molding each brick by hand, but then purchased a molding machine. Most likely the house he and his wife lived in from 1913 on was constructed using his own bricks, heated with his own coal and oil, cooled with his own ice, and connected to water through his city contract. He also was contractor for the construction of several concrete bridges for the county.

With all that activity at home and in town, it was only natural for Frank to try to find a place to get away once in a while. But in his entrepreneurial spirit, he decided to buy property and make a business of it. In 1900 he purchased the fairgrounds nearby and built an artificial lake (from which the ice was cut each winter). On the property he built a concrete pool, diving boards, and a large toboggan slide, establishing the first amusement park in the region, known as "Tyler's Park," which became a popular and successful endeavor. To go along with the amusement park, the food of choice for visitors was ice cream, so Frank began manufacturing the dreamy delight in 1905, selling the business a few years later to the Tyler brothers.

In 1905 Frank Tyler wrote the following article for the Villisca Review, encouraging ladies to share in the use of the bathing pond. The article reads:

> "To the Ladies of Villisca!!!!! Do you know that Villisca has the finest bathing pond in Southwestern Iowa? Do you know there is nothing immoral in bathing in a bathing resort? Do you know that nothing that would shock the most modest lady is allowed at Tyler's Park? Do you know that ladies in towns both larger and smaller than Villisca go bathing in these ponds? Do you know that Villisca ladies go bathing in these ponds in other towns? Do you know that you will feel a whole lot better after bathing in this pond and chuting the chutes than bathing in a bath tub? Once you go into this pond, with a cement bottom and water changed every week, all well water, you could not be kept out. We know you want to come in, so don't be like a bashful boy sucking his thumb. BRING YOUR HUSBAND. BRING YOUR FELLOW. BRING YOUR PREACHER. BRING YOUR GRANDMOTHER. BRING the whole family and you will have the time of your life. Open day and night. We use our own electric light system. Ice cream at the park at all hours.
>
> "Yours truly, F. P. Tyler"[139]

Known as "Perk" Tyler for his effervescent personality, Frank enjoyed every minute of life. Villisca's "Grand Old Man" was a popular figure to all, especially to the children for whom he always had a piece of candy.

Abel Dudley Tyler, Jr. (1852–1902)

Abel Tyler, Jr. (#4799; Tyler-6506) was born in Camden, Maine, in 1817. He was the model-maker and superintendent of the largest shoe-tree manufacturing company in the country when, in 1884, he invented and patented a shoe-treeing machine. He sold the company two years later and next invented the "Tyler Hinged Last," which allowed shoes to keep their shape while not being worn. This largely revolutionized the shoe business at the turn of the century, and he had to protect his patent to retain profits from the business over the years.

As an interesting digression from the typical biographies in this family history, the following excerpts describe the interesting story of this enterprise as a "lasting memory."

"On the Subject of Hinged Lasts

> "It is well known that economy in shoe manufacture is secured by the use of hinged lasts. The recent granting of patents to the Tyler Hinged Last Co., of this city, on the Tyler hinged last is of great importance to last

makers as well as shoe manufacturers everywhere. The patentees of the Tyler hinged last claim that this is the only one which has stood the test of years. It has been in constant use since May 1893. Sales to date amount to over 500,000 pairs.

"A.D. Tyler, Jr., president and general manager of the Tyler Hinged Last Co., states that the patents granted in 1898 cover all practical hinged lasts in use today. He adds that no hinged lasts can legally be manufactured or used without licenses from his company. He therefore cautions shoe manufacturers to order all hinged lasts of the Tyler Hinged Last Co. or their licensees."[140]

Patent Case in Circuit Court, March 1898

This is a suit for infringement of the Tyler patent, No. 601, 622, dated March 29, 1898, for an improvement in shoe lasts. In describing the invention, the specification says:

"My invention relates to that class of lasts which are divided transversely into two sections, so as it allows the last to be contracted in length and withdrawn from the boot or shoe without exerting any strain upon the upper by the removal of the last; and the object of my invention is to increase the strength and rigidity of the last when in use and to so shape and arrange the sections of the last as to facilitate its removal and increase its efficiency."

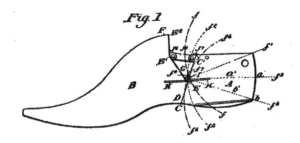

Patent Sketch of Tyler Hinged Last

"After a careful examination of the case at bar upon the record now before the court, I fully agree with the opinion off the Court of Appeals in Arnold v. Tyler. The Tyler invention represents a distinct advance in the shoe last art, and the evidence shows that this last has gone into extensive commercial use among shoe manufacturers. There is nothing in the prior art as exhibited in the record which is an anticipation of the Tyler device. On the contrary, the Tyler last possesses both novelty and great utility as compared with any of the lasts then in use or described in any of the prior patents."[141]

Franklin Tyler Wood (1877–1945)

Franklin Tyler Wood (#4654; Wood-31897) was the only boy of four children born to Captain Enoch Franklin Wood and Louise F. Monroe, whose families had been living in New England since the mid-seventeenth century. His Aunt Rebecca

Wood lived unmarried in the Tyler Homestead in West Boxford until she died in 1918. One can only imagine that Enoch, a lifelong professional educator, stressed excellence and achievement in his family. Unfortunately, he died in 1882, when Franklin was only four years old. Nonetheless, Enoch's pursuit for perfection seems to have manifested itself in the art of his prodigiously talented only son.

After two years of education under some of Boston's best art instructors, Franklin was determined to expand his skills and knowledge of art. To this end, he set off for New York City, where in 1897 he enrolled in the Art Students League. At this time New York City was the nucleus of American art. Like Paris, it was the American city in which an artist could make or break his career. Studying in the midst of unprecedented cultural activity, Wood was undoubtedly inspired by the art around him, but not by the loud and crowded urban conditions.

Determined to succeed as a professional, Franklin hoped to make graphic arts his specialty. In continued pursuit of his dream, he sailed to Europe in 1903. During this time, Franklin traveled widely through western Europe, including Italy, Sicily, and Spain. Numerous singular images and etchings derive from that period of Wood's "wanderjahre" on the European continent.

A year later he returned to Hyde Park to continue work in his studio. Apparently Wood was sought out by editors for his ability to depict or illustrate special glimpses in poems and stories that reflected the lingering influences of the genteel tradition in literature. He began his career as an illustrator for *The Youth's Companion*, *Boston Home Journal*, and *Frank Leslie's American Illustration*. The illustrations generally reveal his interest in themes of morality, religion, history, and patriotism.

An officer of the Chicago Society of Etchers wrote about Wood, "For sincerity of treatment, and delicacy of perception and good taste, I think we have no one in our list of 115 active members—practically from all over the world—who surpasses him." A well-known art critic of the time called Wood "an artist who stands among the leading portraitists in contemporary graphic art."

In 1915 Franklin moved to Rutland, Vermont, where, he stated, "if seems, one is closer to the infinite. The boundaries are the wide sky and the rolling hills, . . .the yesterdays and tomorrows are of small moment. The vague fears and worries of life lose shape in this restful beauty spot of nature."[142]

Wood exhibited at the Chicago Society of Etchers, the Panama-Pacific International Exposition, Doll and Richards Gallery, Goodspeed's Bookshop, and at the Bibliotheque Nationale in Paris. He had his last one-artist exhibition at the Grand Central Art Galleries.

He felt that "public interest was centered on color." A true conservative, Franklin was appalled as some contemporary use of color: "But what atrocious color has been used in some of the current radical exhibitions." Franklin was a traditional artist of some repute in the early part of the twentieth century and became well known for his etchings and drawings. He was the artist for a wonderful drawing of women moving a headboard into the Tyler Homestead.[143]

Franklin Tyler Wood drawing of Tyler Homestead

After a long illness, Franklin Tyler Wood died at the age of sixty-seven in 1945. He belonged to an older generation of artists who believed in working diligently every day. . . Undoubtedly, Wood's small editions and lack of self-promotional skills prevented his exceedingly accomplished images from being better known in recent decades.

Twentieth Century (1920s–1960s)

After World War I ended in 1918, the United States began to take its prominent role in world affairs. During this "American Century" the country became dominant in political, economic, and cultural terms. It was an era of industrial growth and progressive reform, shifting the country from Victorian affectations to more modern behavioral norms. America represented to the world the advantages of a constitutional republic based on a capitalist economy, with its cultural influence prominent in terms of music, film, art, and fashion.

The Twentieth Century had technological inventions that radically transformed the lives of people around the globe, with many changes originating in the United States. The Roaring '20s were a time of a booming stock market, speakeasies, short skirts, the Charleston, and jazz. The 1920s also showed great strides in women's suffrage—women got the vote in 1920. The 1930s brought The Great Depression, which hit the entire world very hard. The depression was followed by World War II, which tore apart and divided the world's great nations. However, the war was followed by decades of relative peace and prosperity and the growth of America's middle class.

In these more recent decades, the history of the extended Job Tyler family has separated into many branches—so many, it is virtually impossible to bring representation to all of them. Instead, a few biographies are included of individuals who portray some of the interesting traits of our more contemporary relatives.

George Frederick Tyler (1883–1947)

George Frederick Tyler (#7572; Tyler-6521) became a successful businessman as a Philadelphia banker and married into considerable wealth. He appreciated his fortune while he was alive and shared it after his passing. He could be considered as having lived the American dream.

George was born in 1883, and following his mother's early death in 1888 his father, Sidney Frederick Tyler, married Ida Elkins, a daughter of streetcar magnate William Lukens Elkins. Seventeen years later, George married his stepmother's niece, Stella Elkins, a budding sculptor. George, as scion to a banking and investment family of Mayflower descendants, was a prominent banker, progressive farmer, and avid sportsman whose leisure activities included safari hunting, mountain climbing, and yacht sailing.

Just after World War I, George and Stella, who lived on Philadelphia's Main Line at Georgian Terrace in Chestnut Hill, bought a Bucks County farm on the west bank of the Neshaminy Creek for a country retreat. Known as Indian Council Rock, the two-thousand-acre property included a cliff overlooking the creek reputed to have been a meeting place for the Lenni Lenape tribe.

In 1928, the Tylers decided to build a very large mansion on the property, measuring approximately three hundred feet from end to end, with approximately sixty rooms. Its construction occupied 128 stone masons for a year. Henry Slepper of Boston was hired to oversee the mansion's interior decorating, which included fine detailing incorporating specially made roof tiles and copper gutters on the exterior and Goya prints, antique frescoes and wallpapers, as well as many elaborate features such as gold fixtures in every bathroom and twenty different styles of fireplaces. The mansion also included a ten-car turntable garage, enabling each car to be cranked to its own spot. Forty servants staffed the Tyler residence in its heyday, and they lived either in the east wing of the house or in the small cottages situated on the estate.

Its architectural character was unique in the context of early twentieth century Bucks County. Financial records show the cost of the project was $1,361,000 in 1931 (comparable to a 2019 value of twenty-two million dollars).[144]

In 1932, the Tylers permanently moved to Indian Council Rock. George Tyler established a stable of about twenty-five fine horses and restarted a dairy that had been abandoned in 1925. The new dairy was in operation for the next forty years, and the Tylers had one of the leading Ayrshire herds in the country. They also raised grain, poultry, sheep, and pigs and owned the Spring Garden Mill. In addition, the Tylers often purchased rare birds, exotic plants, flowers, and trees that had never previously been grown in Bucks County. Many species of wild fowl were bred at Indian Council Rock, and at one time it was possible to find trees and flowers growing on the grounds that were found nowhere else in North America.

George F. Tyler Mansion, Bucks County, Pennsylvania, 1930

The mansion and gardens still afford a view that "is one never to be forgotten." The Tyler mansion is arguably the grandest home ever built in Bucks County and believed to be the last of the "great estates" ever constructed in the United States. Upon George Tyler's death, the Bucks County estate was bequeathed to his wife, who lived there until 1962 when she moved back to Chestnut Hill until her death one year later. Stella Tyler's will stipulated that two hundred acres of her Newtown property, including the buildings, be donated to Temple University. The remainder of the property was sold to the Commonwealth of Pennsylvania to become Tyler State Park. Park roads, trails, and facilities are carefully nestled within the original farm and woodland setting. Neshaminy Creek meanders through the park, dividing the land into several sections.

Chaplin Tyler (ca. 1897–2004)

Chaplin Tyler (#7861; Fuwa-2) is listed as Hamao Fuwa in Brigham's Volume II of *The Tyler Genealogy*. Born the son of Irene Chaplin Tyler (#7232; Tyler-6525) and Japanese diplomat Tamotsu Fuwa (fuwa-1), he changed his name as an adult. He had a long and productive life and career and is especially remembered for his significant financial contributions.[145]

Chaplin Tyler's mother, Irene Chaplin Tyler, was the daughter of George Prescott Tyler (#5149; Tyler-6524) and Irene Spofford (spofford-410) of Georgetown, Massachusetts. In 1897, Irene Chaplin married a Japanese man, Tamotsu Fuwa. As described in Brigham's Volume II, Fuwa was educated in the Buddhist faith and in the Confucian schools and when sixteen years old he entered Chinzai Seminary, Nagasaki, mainly for the study of English, this being a Methodist Episcopal mission school. In 1896, he graduated with a law degree from Howard University. He then married Irene Chaplin Tyler, who at the time was working in Washington, D. C. They soon had a son named Hamao Fuwa, and in 1899 they returned to Japan.

The marriage did not work out, so the mother and son returned to the United States, where Hamao changed his name to Chaplin Tyler. Chaplin tried to enter the Massachusetts Institute of Technology (MIT) but failed the history portion of the entrance exam. Instead, he entered a new school, Northeastern College, located in a few upper rooms of the city's YMCA. When he first went to visit, someone told him, "Take that staircase, and when the smell of chemicals becomes intolerable, that's Northeastern." He graduated in 1920 with a degree in Chemical Engineering. The school's youth worked to his advantage, since one of his chemical engineering instructors, an MIT moonlighter, offered him an assistantship at that school. He was told MIT had too many ingrown assistants and needed new blood. "I think you'd do all right on the job," the instructor told Tyler. "It pays $1,200 a year for eleven months work." Tyler was speechless, since that was a very respectable wage. "Maybe you'd like a few days to think it over," the teacher said. Tyler found his voice. "Sir, I would like fifteen seconds to think it over."[146]

Two years later he added a Business Administration degree from Boston College. For two years during World War I, he served overseas as a medic with Harvard Medical School in U. S. Hospital No. 5. After graduation he served in the position of second lieutenant in the Chemical Service Reserve for five years. He also received a master's degree in Chemical Engineering from the Massachusetts Institute of Technology.

Using his training in chemical engineering, he worked at DuPont Corporation for thirty-five years, eventually becoming a senior member of the DuPont Development Department. After retiring in 1962, he was appointed as a financial analyst for the University of Delaware, and also became executive director of the Higher Educational Advisory Committee for the State of Delaware, providing construction funding for institutions of higher learning. He wrote two books published by the University of Delaware on Chemical Engineering Economics that quickly became best-sellers in the field, with four more editions coming out over forty years, leading to an honorary doctorate degree.

Tyler then served as a corporate consultant for Coca-Cola Company for fifteen years, finally retiring at the age of eighty-two. At this point in his life, he decided to make other types of contributions to society. He donated three million dollars to the University of Delaware's College of Business and Economics, leading to the establishment of four named professorships in his name, as well as fellowships for graduate students. In announcing one of his gifts, Tyler said, "I was prompted to offer these gifts because of my great confidence in the people at the University of Delaware. Some people talk about 'giving until it hurts.' I think you should give until it feels good, and it makes me feel very good indeed to support business students at the University of Delaware."[147]

In 1992, the university awarded him a Medal of Distinction for professional achievement. People at the university described him as an important contributor in a number of ways. Kenneth Biederman said of him, "Chap was one of the most extraordinary people you could ever hope to meet. . . He was so well read, always current yet uniquely able to add a perspective that others could not." Michael Ginzberg said of him, "His support was much more than the financial support he provided. He drew from his wealth of experience to provide ideas about management education."

Chaplin Tyler continued to be productive well into old age. At the age of ninety-nine, he wrote, *Building for Success in Business: Your Mid-Career Years*. When he was 103, he published, "The View from Age 100," which shared some of his experiences and life lessons. He died in 2004 at the age of 105.

Vernon Lynn Tyler (1929–2008)

Vernon Lynn Tyler (#9018; Tyler-6531) was born in 1929 in Phoenix, Arizona, and married Arlean Kerby in 1952 at Salt Lake City Temple of the Mormon. In his early years Vernon spent time at an Argentine mission. After marrying Arlean, he took up the craft of painting along with Arlean's father and returned to California for two years doing service on Los Angeles Stake High Council "which set my professional life into a meaningful course of events."

Vernon and Arlean spent 22 months at Builder missionaries in Tonga Islands. He then followed further religious educational work on Samoa, Hawaii, and back in Tonga. He and Arlean enjoyed the challenges of extensive world service in the South Pacific, India, and elsewhere.

Church President Harvey Taylor, "one of the most influential men in my life," asked him to return to Provo to work on curriculum development in church school in Provo, Utah. During this time his work took a new turn toward translation, and eventually transculturalization. He became Associate Director of the Brigham Young University Language Research Center and was a member of the Board of Directors of the American Translators Association. During his forty years at Brigham Young University he worked as a global educator, helping to create bridges of understanding between cultures as the Director of Intercultural Communications at the Kennedy Center. Two of his most notable contributions were the creation of "Culturegrams" and the development of an Outreach Program for which he was widely known.

Vernon felt strong obligations for other members of their extended families, with genealogy and temple work being significant factors in his family's time/talent/resource focus. He was a strong supporter of the Job Tyler Family Association, and in 1988 he was quite involved in the planning and facilitation of the first national reunion of the Association that took place in North Andover and West Boxford, Massachusetts. He passed away in Provo, Utah, in 2008.

Chapter 6: Job Tyler Family Lineage of Presidents

The Job Tyler family lineage has a variety of connections with United States presidents. The following section describes linkages, some direct and others more obscure, to Presidents Teddy Roosevelt (and thus Franklin D. Roosevelt), Herbert Hoover and Harry Truman. Yet to be conclusively documented is a connection to the family lineage of President John Tyler.

Gertrude Tyler (1834–1895) and Teddy Roosevelt

Although the Job Tyler lineage may or may not be directly related to that of President John Tyler, there is a well-documented relationship through marriage to another United States president. Gertrude Elizabeth Tyler (#3386; Tyler-852) in her book, *The Story of Gertrude Tyler and Her Family, 1660–1860*,[148] describes family relationships through many generations, from immigrant Job Tyler seven generations before through to her daughter, Edith Kermit Carow, who would marry President Teddy Roosevelt.[149]

Gertrude Elizabeth (Tyler) Carow[150]

Gertrude Tyler came from a distinguished line of Tyler men. From Job and Hopestill, her line included four Daniels, with her father the fourth Daniel [#462; Tyler-1038]. All four Daniels lived in Wyndham County, Connecticut, in the little town of Brooklyn.

Little is known of Gertrude's great-great-grandfather, the first Daniel. He inherited land in Groton, Connecticut, from his father, Hopestill, including the section referred to as "Tyler Hill." Gertrude's great-grandfather, Daniel II was a house builder and designer, what today would be an architect. The story is told of him that, when over eighty years old he walked the ridge-pole of a church still standing in Brooklyn, Connecticut, which he was constructing. He was born in 1699 and died in 1800. It is rumored that the revenues of worthy local citizens were largely augmented by participation in the slave-trade, which was then considered perfectly reputable and legitimate. In the days of Gertrude's great-grandfather, Daniel II, slavery flourished in Connecticut, and he once told her that he had often seen older slaves that once belonged to him.

Living in true patriarchal style, he had (in due succession!) three wives, twenty-one children, fifty grandchildren and one hundred and twenty great-grandchildren. The majority of this offspring was grouped around him when he died. On his tombstone he caused to be engraved:

Although a hundred years I've seen,
My life was short,
'Twas all a dream.

Gertrude's grandfather, Daniel Tyler III, (#462; Tyler-1039) was a graduate of Harvard College in 1771 and soon after that time married Mehitabel Putnam, the daughter of General Israel Putnam. It is said that Daniel III's father, hearing of his intention to join the army, presented him with a deed of a fine farm so he might provide home and maintenance for his young family. When the war of the revolution broke out, Daniel accompanied General Putnam to the field and was Adjutant of his regiment. After serving for two years with this regiment, Daniel III raised and equipped at his own expense an artillery company then known as "matrosses." He commanded it with the rank of Major, and was stationed at one time in Newport, Rhode Island, to assist in the defense of the city, which at that time was an important seaport and had more commerce than New York or Boston.

Gertrude's father, Daniel IV, was a successful soldier and industrialist with many credits to his name. His full biography was presented in a previous chapter.

In 1859 Gertrude married Charles Carow. Charles benefited greatly from the business success of his brother-in-law, Robert Kermit, who took the younger Charles as a partner and established the Kermit & Carow shipping company. After Kermit's death, Charles continued the business and the ships sailed under his name. Charles and Gertrude had one daughter, who was given the name Edith Kermit Carow to recognize their relationship with Robert.

Carow's ship, West Point, carried goods to Liverpool in England and returned with passengers. During the California Gold Rush in the 1840s and 50s Carow made his fortune. But in 1861 everything changed when the American Civil War began, which caused a drastic reduction in the number of emigrants. The American merchant fleet generally was badly affected by this war. A ruinous rise in prices caused significant business setbacks and Charles began to drink. Beset by severe alcoholism and a serious fall and concussion, his success began to rapidly fade. Not much is known of his later years.

Edith Kermit Carow (1861–1948)

Edith Kermit Carow (#5895; Carow-1), daughter of Gertrude and Charles Carow, was born in Norwich, Connecticut, in 1861. When the family was still relatively wealthy, they moved next to the home of Theodore Roosevelt. The two families became close friends. However, as Charles drinking continued and his business declined, his daughter Edith tried to distance herself from the family.

As a child, Edith and her sister Emily were raised by an Irish immigrant nursemaid who spoke frequently of the impoverished life she had left in Ireland. Similarly, it was through another woman mentor, the sister of Mrs. Theodore Roosevelt, Sr., that she learned how to read, along with the Roosevelt children (Elliott, Theodore, Corinne and Anna). Theodore Roosevelt, Sr. also taught Edith Carow and his own children natural studies with trips to the countryside, wrote plays for them to memorize lines and perform, and gave them topics to prepare oral recitations on. Early on, Edith evidenced a voracious appetite for reading and poetry. She also attended the Dodsworth School for Dancing and Deportment in New York City for three years beginning at age eight. Here she was taught not only how to formally dance, but to affect the social mannerisms which denoted the upper-class.

Edith Kermit (Carow) Roosevelt[151]

As a young girl, Edith had a teen romance with Teddy Roosevelt. Although Edith and Teddy may have had a teenage romance, the relationship faded when Teddy went to Harvard University. While at Harvard, Teddy met Alice Lee. Teddy and Alice married in 1880, and Edith was enough of a friend to attend the wedding.

Edith and Teddy were not reunited until after he became a widower. In 1886 he married Edith at St. George's Anglican Church in London, England. After their wedding ceremony, the Roosevelts took a honeymoon in France, visiting Paris, Lyons, Marseilles and Hyeres in the Provence region and then Florence, Rome, Venice, Pompeii, Naples, and Capri., joined by her mother and sister who settled in Rome to live.

The couple had five children, and also raised Teddy's daughter from his first marriage. When they moved into the White House in 1901, it wasn't quite big enough for a family of six children, so Edith had a new West Wing built. She also established many of the traditions of the First Lady that remain today.

Edith is believed to have exerted subtle influence over her husband in the White House. She and Teddy met privately every day from 8:00 to 9:00 a.m. Edith read several newspapers a day and forwarded clippings she considered important to her husband. A perceptive aide described the First Lady as "always the gentle, high-bred hostess; smiling often at what went on about her, yet never critical of the ignorant and tolerant always of the little insincerities of political life."

Edith insisted on a lack of personal publicity while serving as First Lady, which kept her a background figure, although a gracious and dignified one. She was once quoted as saying: "A woman's name should appear in print but twice—when she was married and when she is buried."

After her husband's death in 1919, Edith traveled abroad but always returned to her home at Sagamore Hill, New York, as her home. She also established a second residence in the Tyler family's ancestral hometown of Brooklyn, Connecticut.

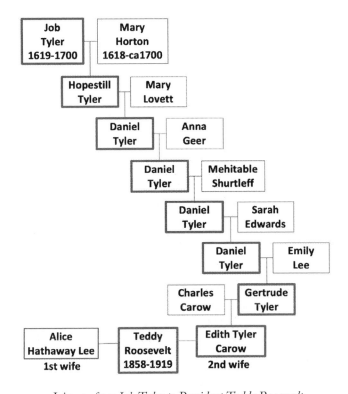

Lineage from Job Tyler to President Teddy Roosevelt

In 1889, Teddy Roosevelt wrote a letter to his mother-in-law, Gertrude, describing the activities of his two-year-old son, Theodore. The following is a section from that letter in Roosevelt's own hand and is one of a number of letters in the collection at the Theodore Roosevelt Center at Dickinson State University.

"Ted is just the dearest little two-year old boy that ever lived. I take him out to dig in the road, to see the chickens and horses and play in the barn; and he really loves me dearly. He is very much afraid now whenever I am dressed to go out that I am going away, and begs most piteously 'papa no leave Ted.' As soon as he sees me in the morning he begins to dance and clap his hands and then begs me to 'take Teddy climb in gun room,' or 'take Teddy see tiger book,' which is in the library. The little scamp picks up all kinds of sentences. New whenever he falls, which is very often, he says 'upon my word,' with the most roguish smile; and when I am carrying him off to do something he has requested he will keep repeating 'oh, what fun!' At night, when bed-time is impending, and he wishes a final play, he will beg 'papa, please; just one minnity!' (minute). The new heads and skins interest him greatly; he will inquire 'big bear no bite Teddy?' and then thrusts his little hand into its mouth. He is most active; and keeps on a chubby canter from morning to night. When I put cologne on his head he runs in to have his mama smell it. He is much interested in 'funny little baby brother Kermit,' and will imitate him when he cries; he says 'Kermit stay with dear mama' and when he finds him in the bassinet he usually begins an energetic burrowing down through the clothes to see what he looks like. Ted is now dancing about in front of me clamoring for me to get him 'little bit sugar.'"

"Aff. yours

Theodore Roosevelt"[152]

Teddy and Edith surrounded by children[153]

Hannah Tyler's Lineage to President Herbert Hoover

Hannah Tyler (#92; Tyler-116) was a daughter of Margaret Bradstreet, of the prominent Bradstreet family, and Job Tyler. The story of Margaret and Job was described earlier in this book.

Hannah's marriage to Captain John Spofford in 1728 took place in the Spofford House in Boxford, Massachusetts, which John had built the year before on "The Hill" in what was then known as Georgetown, part of Rowley and near Boxford. After moving to New Hampshire ten years later, John was captured and taken as a prisoner by Indians and carried to Canada. When he returned to Massachusetts a year later, the Spoffords found their house had been burned and their lands damaged. They petitioned Massachusetts for aid and reestablished themselves. Ultimately, "Captain Spofford was a most useful citizen, one of the ten male members who formed Rev. Bulkley Olcutt's church; twice elected to office of selectman."[154]

Hannah Tyler herself was a great-granddaughter of immigrant Job and granddaughter of Moses. She was also related as the fifth-generation great-grandmother to President Herbert Hoover. This lineage, shown below, is largely in the matriarchal line of descent, bringing in many other families.

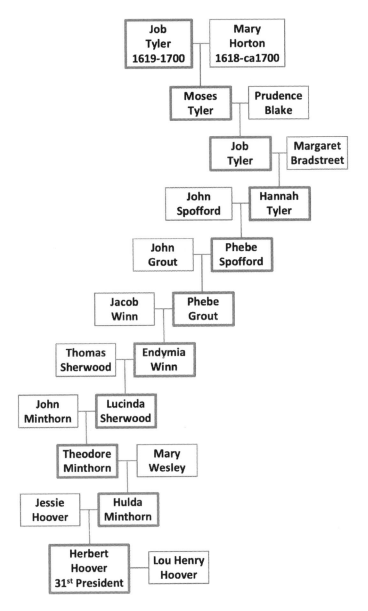

Line of descent of Job Tyler and Hannah Tyler to President Herbert Hoover

Ann Drusilla Tyler and her lineage to President Harry S. Truman[155]

Immigrant Job's father, Laurence, has a direct line of descent to President Harry S. Truman through Job's brother, Robert. There is some speculation as to whether Robert was a son of Laurence, since he was not included in Laurence's will, but he was included in his burial records. Our assumption is that the burial records should be taken as accurate as a historical document, giving credence to the lineage chart shown below.

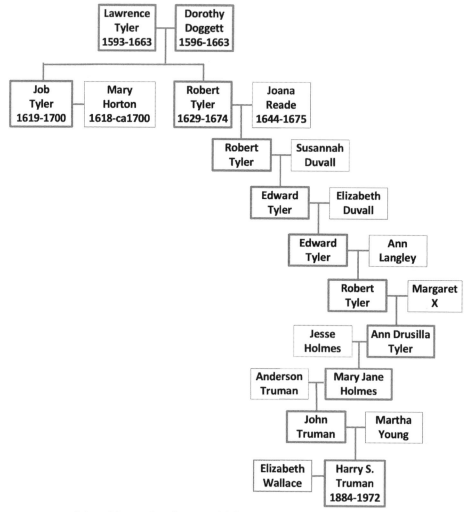

Line of descent from Laurence Tyler to President Harry S. Truman

The last Tyler in this Tyler line is Ann Drusilla Tyler (Tyler-9), born in Shelby County, Kentucky, who married Jesse Holmes, whose daughter married Anderson Truman, bringing the Tyler name into the Hoover genealogy. She married Holmes in 1803 and they moved to Missouri. As described in a Harry Truman biography, at that time Ann Drusilla "led her clan from Kentucky carrying a huge sack of teacakes and a gentleman's beaver hat in a leather hatbox." She had slaves to handle her luggage and they paid particular attention to the hatbox, saying, "Get Hannah a bonnet suitable to wear to church." The hat was not merely a relic of her husband, a remembrance of his passing years later, but of her "indestructible determination" to recognize her marriage. She held the strong view that any woman once a widow should always be a widow, and the hatbox went with her wherever she traveled during the next thirty-five years.

When Ann Drusilla's husband died in 1840, she remained well off with lands and slaves. "She saw no conflict between slavery and the Fourth of July freedoms." Indeed, some Truman family records show she may have had some objection to her daughter, Mary Jane, marrying into the Truman family, "because the Trumans were not slaveholders." In response, Mary Jane ran off with her new husband, Anderson Truman, and the groom's father did not give formal approval to the marriage until years later when the son brought back the old man's first grandchild to Missouri to see him. Sometimes old traditions die hard.

Chapter 7: Family Associations Over the Years

The Job Tyler line has been well researched for over a century. Although major work was completed by Willard I. Tyler Brigham, with his work, *The Tyler Genealogy, Volumes I and II,* significant work has also been completed of various family lines by many dedicated researchers and genealogist. Over the decades, communication among all the individuals and groups was largely done through genealogical and family history associations. This chapter describes the activities of some of the most prominent associations established to carry on the work of the immigrant Job Tyler lineage.

American Tyler Family Association

1896 Reunion in Andover, Massachusetts

The American Tyler Family Association was formed in 1896, the year it held its first reunion. The reunion was described in an article in the September 4, 1896, edition of the *Andover Townsman* newspaper.

"What more fitting than that the old North parish, Unitarian Church, in which last fall was observed the 250th Anniversary of the organization of the society, and about whose name clusters so much that is historic, should be selected as the roof tree beneath which should be held the first gathering of the Tyler family of America. Where also the history of the church is closely interwoven with that of this family represented by the names of Moses, Hopestill, and John, sons of the immigrant Job Tyler, whom all the kinsmen honor and cherish in memory.

"The name Tyler is honored in the nation, state, and in many a town, hamlet and village throughout this and other lands."

The reunion had a dinner program beginning at 1:00 pm on Wednesday, September 2, at the North Andover Center. The program listed the following topics:

The audience gave the "Tyler Yell." It goes as follows:

"Abram, Isaac, Jacob, Job,
William, Joseph, Parker, Cob:
T-Y-L-E-R! Rah! Rah! Rah!"

"Job Tyler: Our patient ancestor, first of the name in America. At last we greet you." Charles Edmund Bartlett Tyler, Boston

"My Grandfather: Dear old man; upright, honest and faithful; we all honor and love him." Hon. James M. Tyler, Brattleboro, Vermont (a Justice of the Vermont Supreme Court)

"A Pine Tree." The groves were God's first temples. Standing within our modern temples, we will strive to be worthy the sturdy oak, from whose primeval American trunk have sprung so many Tylers. Gen. Henry L. Mitchell, Esq., Bangor, Maine.

"Tyler Biology." We are of the stuff that dreams are made of, and our little life is rounded by a sleep. Prof. John M. Tyler, Amherst College, Massachusetts.

Song. "Mary Had a Little Lamb," (The *original* "Mary" was named *Tyler. Fact.*)

"Tyler Family History," by Willard I. Tyler Brigham, Esq. Response by the author.

"Philosophy of Intermarriage." "And Noah went forth, and his sons, and his wife, and his sons' wives with him." Wm. H. Tyler Phillips, Esq., Pittsfield, Massachusetts.

"A Taste of Nutmeg." (Being a family reunion, no "wooden" ones will pass.), Rollin U. Tyler, Esq., Middletown, Connecticut.

Benediction, Rev. George Leon Walker, Hartford, Connecticut.

After the dinner, attendees visited places of interest in North Andover and vicinity, including the Bradstreet House, Captain John Tyler's House, and Moses Tyler grave.

1898 Reunion in Boston[156]

"Reunion of the Tyler Family:
Tyler Brigham of Chicago Makes an Interesting History

"Boston, Mass., Sept. 7–Tremont Temple was this morning the scene of a gathering of representatives of the Tyler family, which not only had its prominent sons in pre-revolutionary times, but has given descendants to the number of 30,000.

"The family historian, Tyler Brigham of Chicago, contributes an interesting historical resume of the family. This paper showed that from very early times the Tylers have figured in the history of Boston in various capacities.

"There are three distinct branches which for generations have distinguished themselves almost side by side. The paper also dealt briefly with descriptions of historical houses with which the Tylers were connected. Among them was the Oshterlong, where it was said Paul Revere stopped on the night of his famous ride to beg 'mufflers' for his ears, and through a partially opened doorway was given hastily a petticoat of flannel.

"The first bell cast in Boston was by a Tyler and bore an inscription to the effect that it was the gift to a church of 'P. Revere.'"

1899 Reunion in Washington, D. C.[157]

"Session of the Tylers: An Elaborate Programme for the Family Reunion

"Two or Three Hundred Expected to Be in Attendance—Papers to Be Read at the Business Meeting—A Dinner Arranged at Willard's Hotel, with Many Toasts and Music.

"Tylers from all parts of the country will begin arriving in Washington this evening to attend the Fourth General American Tyler Reunion at Willard's Hotel tomorrow. It is expected that two or three hundred will be present. Lyon G. Tyler, President of William and Mary College, is president of the association and will preside at the meeting. William I. Tyler Brigham, of Chicago, is secretary and historian of the association, and has spent several years in gathering records of the Tyler family, and is aptly called the "mainspring" of the association.

"Mr. Brigham arrived in Washington several days ago, and has been actively at work getting ready for the meeting. He said this morning: 'We expect about 300 members of the Tyler family present and an unusually large number from the South and West. Previous to this time the family meetings have been held in the Northeast, and the impression is abroad that there is a difference between the Northern and Southern Tylers. but that is a mistake. There is no division in the family, but this is the first time the reunion has been held south of the Mason and Dixon line, and for that reason we expect an unusually large attendance.'"

"The Tyler Reunion: Virginia Most Largely Represented of All the States[158]

"Washington D. C., September 13–(Special)–The fourth annual reunion of the American branch of the Tyler family took place at Willard's Hall this morning, about 150 members (some say 200) being present, a majority of whom were ladies. The programme published in the Dispatch was carried out. It was stated that there were more members of the family from Virginia than from any other State. New York and Pennsylvania sent large delegations, and Maryland, Kentucky, Ohio, Illinois, and Louisiana were also represented. Among the distinguished persons present were Professor Lyon G. Tyler, president of William and Mary College, Virginia; Henry B. Brown, Associate Justice United States Supreme Court; W. I. Tyler Brigham, of Chicago, secretary of the Tyler Association, who is also the historian of the clan."

The Tylers, according to Mr. Brigham and other authorities, are principally descendants of Job Tyler, who settled near Amherst, Mass., in 1640; William Tyler, who came to Virginia in 1620; and Robert Tyler, who settled near Baltimore, Md., in 1660.

"The Tyler Reunion[159]

"The 4th reunion of the American Tyler association was held in Washington, D. C., September 13th. Mr. and Mrs. D. W. Tyler and Miss Wilmia of Junction City attended. A Washington paper of the 14th gave a column and a column and a half write-up, from which we clip: . . .

"Toasts had to be omitted at the dinner, as the time for the reception tendered by the President had arrived. Shortly before 2:30 o'clock nearly 200 Tylers proceeded to the Executive Mansion, where they were introduced to the President. Mr. Cadwell C. Tyler made the introductions. After this ceremony was concluded the body returned to Willard Hall and the annual group picture was taken on the steps.

"Miss Wilmia J. M. Tyler of Junction City, Kan., did effective execution on her harp."

"Each of the Tylers who were presented to the President were given a card bearing this wording: 'Please admit the bearer to the audience with President McKinley, at the Executive Mansion, on the occasion of the 4th reunion of the American Tyler Family Association, Wednesday, September 13, 1896, Washington, D. C.'

"It is needless to say that the meeting was one of the events of the season at the National capitol."

1900 Reunion in Philadelphia[160]

"Philadelphia, Sept. 13–Tylers from every section of the country are here attending the annual family reunion. Among the more prominent ones are Governor J. Hoge Tyler of Virginia, Professor Henry M. Tyler, of Smith College, Northampton, Mass., and Professor Charles M. Tyler, of Cornell University. This is the first reunion attended in numbers by the Southern Tylers, from which branch came President Tyler.

"A meeting was held, at which it developed that there were ten thousand descendants of the original Tyler, who landed in Virginia in 1638, and that there were three great branches, one in Massachusetts, one in New-Jersey and Pennsylvania and one in Virginia."

"Reunion of the Tylers: Plans for the Family Celebration in Philadelphia[161]

"Philadelphia, Sept 2.–The celebrated Tyler family, with branches all over the country, will assemble in Odd Fellows' Temple on Wednesday, September 12. This will be the fifth of the annual reunion of this family.

". . . At the conclusion of the session a historical article bearing upon the English origin of the Tyler race, will be read by the family historian, W. I. Tyler Brigham, of Chicago, Ill. Mr. Brigham has just returned from a trip abroad, and therefore an article of especial interest is anticipated."

1901 Reunion in North Andover, Massachusetts

At the 1901 Reunion, the sixth annual Tyler reunion, Job's descendants erected a monument next to the grave of his eldest son, Moses. It was a large granite boulder brought from a farm that had been owned by direct descendants and set on a cement base with a bronze plaque attached,

"IN MEMORIAM
JOB TYLER IMMIGRANT
FIRST ANDOVER SETTLER ABOUT MDCXXXIX
BORN MDCXIX DIED MDCC
DEDICATED BY THE WHOLE CLAN
SEPTEMBER 4TH 1901."

1904 Reunion in St. Louis, Missouri

"World's Fair News Notes[162]

"Several Numerous Families That Branch Out All Over the United States Will Hold Meetings in St. Louis.

"St. Louis Jan. 26.–A unique feature of the approaching World's Fair will be the nation family reunion. . . The idea, in fact, is international, for there are families which are reaching out all over the world for information as to relatives who may be induced to join the assemblage of kinsfolk at the exposition. Already several prominent American families have made arrangements for reunion. The Tyler family, which included a president of the United States, will meet at the World's Fair on Wednesday, August 31, that day having been assigned to the family by the committee on ceremonies. It is expected also that the Brigham family will meet on the same day. The Tylers and the Brighams are said to be closely related, and therefore their joint gathering will be in the nature of a double reunion."

"Family Reunions at St. Louis[163]

"St. Louis, Mo., Jan. 22–The committee on ceremonies of the world's fair has assigned September 7 to the Brigham families for a reunion. The Tyler family, which is closely related to the Brighams, is to have August 31. W. J.[sic] Tyler Brigham writes from Phoenix, Arizona, that he thinks a room seating 800 persons will be large enough for each family."

Tyler Kindred of America Reunion, 1921

In 1921 the "Tyler Kindred of America" held its first reunion. This organization was formed by members of the "Branford line," or the descendants of one of Roger Tyler, Sr.'s four sons: Roger, Jr.; Peter; Francis; and George, and the "Wallingford line," or the descendants of William Tyler, Sr.'s sons William, Jr. and John. Rollin U. Tyler of Tylersville, Connecticut, was President and F. (Fay) Webster Tyler of New York State was Secretary and Genealogist. Fay Webster collected genealogical data on the Branford and Wallingford lines with plans to update and publish Brigham's third volume. That result was finally accomplished in 1976 by Calvin C. Tyler of Grand Rapids, Michigan.

The Job Tyler Family Association

The Job Tyler Family Association was established by Charles and Norma Tyler in 1988 as a follow-up to the 1988 Tyler Family Reunion in North Andover and West Boxford, Massachusetts. Charles was first president of the Association, followed by his son, Norman, who had primary responsibility for the Association newsletter. The newsletter was generally printed and distributed twice a year to hundreds of members of the Association. The newsletter and activities of the Association continued through 2002, when there was no longer regular communication to members. Norman continues to be the informal archivist of many of the family's records and is the author of this book. The following are selected sections describing the activities of the Association over its fourteen years.

Introduction to the First Newsletter, February 1989

"Hello Tyler Cousins,
"Reunion '88 is now history. We have just gone through another holiday season and into a new year, and each new year demands new ideas and new goals.
"Our goal for this year is to organize the Tyler Association discussed and supported at the Reunion. Such an Association will be a way for us to communicate with each other between reunions—after all, it has been 85 years since the last general Job Tyler reunion and many new faces have come along since then.
"Those who volunteered at that time have been contacted and we have received their input and ideas on setting up the Association. It is now time to put these ideas out to all Tylers, for only with your support and encouragement will such an effort be a success.

"The name chosen by the organizing group is 'The Job Tyler Family Association.' This is not meant to exclude the membership and involvement of members of other Tyler families, but does indicate that the Association is especially interested in the Job Tyler line. We do not mean to discourage the involvement of anyone who feels the Association can be a help to them. All are welcome. And after a while maybe we'll be able to broaden its scope.

1988 Reunion in West Boxford

Reunion '88 Logo

Program for the Saturday Evening Banquet

Norman Tyler, Master of Ceremonies

Welcome, Charles R. Tyler

Recap of Day's Events

Tyler Hymn, sung from song sheet

Comments of *The Tyler Genealogy*, Volumes I, II, and III

Job's "Apology," a more-or-less true story

Story of the Pewter Cup

Song: "Mary Had a Little Lamb"
  Story behind the song
  Group sing by children

Anecdotes about the Homestead
  Audrey Ladd, "Witches, and Witch Hollow Farm"
  A reading from "Memory Hold the Door"

Comments on establishing a Tyler Family Association

Recognition of Special People

Toast

Hymn: from song sheet

Tyler Yell: from 1896 Reunion

Vernon Lynn Tyler of Provo, Utah, gave "A Memorium to Job and Mary Tyler, to Their Ancestors, to Their Descendants, and to their God, Our God." Excerpts from this presentation are included here:

"And thus was, at least in parts we do not yet understand, the life and lives of JOB and MARY—as well as of their contemporaries, and many joined as descendants. Exploring new lands with an ever-abounding progeny, they worked the land and the land worked them. They helped fight the local battles with oppressors and lifted up others oppressed. Slowly they learned wisdom by experience and faith. . . So we study, and learn, and become acquainted with the complexities they endured increasingly well, as too we are coming to understand.

". . . Before us, it was said and still holds: 'Many have been American Tylers in all stages and degrees—from common, honest laborers, up to the highest position, even President of the United States.' All are in their own ways great: to their children, often to their neighbors, and, hopefully, to those who bear their heritage.

"As we learn more of ourselves—as being of JOB and MARY and others who forged our birthings, we see ourselves newly (as they) 'possessing some of the graces of human nature' and of the divine . . . as our forebearers planted such seeds in us. Earlier tributest Henry M. Tyler (1901) painted a picture of JOB and his MARY as those who learned prudence at times slowly 'with more vigor than grace.' But they and their sons (and daughters) stood firm in trials and died for the right for generations by increasing hundreds and thousands in peace and in war as pioneers and as pilgrims, as planners and prospectors, as teachers and statesmen, as mothers and ministers. By the thousands they also have not had around them many 'saints to live with, were the truth to be known.'

". . . Henry and Moses had wished, 'May such men and women and their children and children's children ever be the strength and glory the Tyler family may enjoy in its part contributed to the salvation of our republic, our mother nations, and our world.' It can only be good to feel a humbling sense of pride in JOB and MARY and in each other TYLER and our myriad cousins—to feel strength from their past accomplishments and from the service we can better render because of them. They give us courage to face out own change and challenges, share with those greatly in need of our caring, who lay on the Samaritan paths before us. We can only honor these who made possible what becomes our blessing . . . as we bless others as well."

Attendees of 1988 Reunion from across the country

Norma Tyler was fully involved with all aspects of Reunion '88, from planning to volunteering to later giving review of the activities. She put her thoughts and memories down in the following paper:

"Memories of Reunion 88"

"Friday evening reception:—By 7:00 p.m. everyone had gathered in the meeting room for the evening program and Dr. Norman Tyler gave a welcome to all who had come from all over the U.S. to attend the reunion. He stated that Lynn Tyler from Provo, Utah, was to have charge of the evening program. The first thing Lynn did was to introduce Charles and myself. He then called us forward and asked the audience to imagine that it was Job and Mary standing in front of them. He wanted everyone to try and picture what kind of life Job and his family had led back in the 1600s. Picture what you could about hardships they had to endure, what kind of education their children received, how they made a livelihood, and also what the area must have looked like at the time they were living there. We all tried to feel the love that has been passed down through generation after generation and now we can pass these same thoughts down to our children and grandchildren. To me this made everything a little more personal, for it made Job and his family seem a little more familiar to each one of us. We have no pictures of Job or Mary, so really don't know if there is any resemblance to Charlie, but the Tyler nose, which is supposed to be a family trait, may be one area where he could have a resemblance. Norman was filming this program, and Lynn asked him to pan the audience and see if the Tyler nose was represented here. . .

"Saturday afternoon tour of Tyler Homestead:—Everyone was so pleased to think that this couple (Homestead owners Steve and Jean Rich) were willing to open their home to such a large group and greeting each one of us as we passed through. Barbara Tyler had made quite a study of the history of this home, when the different sections had been built, and who some of the previous owners had been. On our tour she spoke of the various doorways, and as to when they had been the main entrances to the home; they had been changed due to a different location of the road which passes the home. I was impressed by the varying sizes of the floor boards, which were the original ones. For the many years of use they were still in good shape. Just thinking about Moses and his children living in this first section of the house made my mind wander as to how they probably sat around their table to eat and where they all slept. The ceilings were low throughout most of the house. Barbara then took us outside to see the different chimneys and where the additions had been joined as they had been built.

"After our tour through the home we were taken outside to meet Walter Bryant, a former resident of the homestead. He took us out to the barn and explained where the horses had been stabled, how they brought in the hay to be stored for the winter, and also showed us the unusual design on the roof of the barn. It's hard to imagine that this building was in such good condition after so many hundreds of years of being used. Next to the barn was a carriage house.

"Sunday Morning:–Sunday morning had now rolled around and it was time to head back to the church at West Boxford for the Memorial Service. The attendance was very good and a worshipful atmosphere was felt by all, I'm sure. Anette Snyder gave a musical prelude prior to the service, and the invocation was given by Pastor Ed Remaly. The pastor said he felt very touched by this reunion and it brought out thoughts about his own family ties and how much they meant to him.

"... When we were again outside, goodbye's were given and many pictures were taken of the whole group. There were so many photographers and so many subjects that it took quite a while to accomplish this part of the reunion. One last remark was heard from Charles Tyler when he said, 'I've never had so many pictures taken in my whole life.'"

1990 Reunion in Watervliet, Michigan

A Tyler Family Association Picnic was held at the homestead of Warren and Barbara Tyler. The eighty-three attendees allowed ample time to meet and greet, with tables for books, literature, and photos. Calvin Cedric Tyler provided a wealth of material he had collected on the Branford, Connecticut line.

John Tyler of Muskegon entertained with bagpipe music, with the sound filling the country air. After dinner, a member of each attending family told a little about their family and its history. The day ended with a lively session of T-Y-L-E-R Bingo.

1993 Reunion in San Diego

Following is a smattering of excerpts from the "Recap of Reunion '93 written by Norma Tyler and included in the Association newsletter. This reunion brought together many Tylers from the western states:

"Joyce Tyler from Villisca, Iowa, stopped in our room to say Hi. She did more than say Hi, however, for she wheeled in a whole suitcase full of information on Tylers in Iowa. She certainly had done a lot of research, and had interesting stories to tell about the Royal Tyler family, and Frank P. Tyler, the entrepreneur of the family, who started up at least six businesses, from ice to barbed wire to an amusement park.

"... Don Rohrabacher offered to shoot videos of the entire weekend. Don's son, Dana, the Congressman who was to be featured speaker, was stuck in Washington on Friday night. It's just as well, for Friday evening's program extended well past dinner, with a series of stories, readings, songs, and ending with the traditional Tyler Yell. It would have been difficult even for a politician to keep people awake after all that. Dana did arrive for Saturday's luncheon and spoke briefly about what being a Tyler meant to him. Not to be let off easily, however, he was then peppered with a series of questions from the audience about various problems needing to be dealt with in Washington, including their current budget crisis. Oh... to come back to your constituents.

"Arriving late Friday night was Rodger Chartrand, our Hollywood connection, having acted in a number of TV productions, including *Bay Watch*. His claim to fame was having recently held Jane Seymour in his arms. Rodger brought a box of T-shirts that said 'Tyler Reunion '93' he had specially made and gave one to anyone wishing to have one.

"The last activity of the weekend was a Remembrance service held on Sunday morning at the Mormon Battalion Memorial Visitors Center. We toured the exhibits and heard the story of Daniel Tyler, the famous historian being in the Mormon regiment that first established a foothold at a site that was to become the city of San Diego."

1998 Reunion in West Boxford

The Job Tyler Family Association had Reunion '98 in West Boxford. The announcement for the reunion is shown as stated in the Association newsletter:

"The Job Tyler Family Association is announcing its national reunion to take place in North Andover, Massachusetts on July 3-5, 1998. The North Andover Marriott Hotel will be the base location, with local tours to the national landmark Tyler Homestead, West Boxford Documents Center, other family sites, and the North Andover Historical Museum.

"Activities include a tour of the 300-year-old homestead in West Boxford, other tours, a memorial service at the family's local church, genealogy workshops, and an ice cream social. A primary event will be the Saturday evening banquet, which will include brief presentations on early family history, the family involvement in the Salem witch trials, and various 'diversions.'"

Reunion 1998 Attendees at Tyler Homestead

<u>Presentation by Marvin Tyler in West Boxford Church</u>

On Sunday morning, the final event was the remembering service, which took place at the Second Congregational Church in West Boxford. Marvin Tyler, who came from Grand Rapids, Michigan, led the service, aided by his two young grandchildren, Brynn and Christian. Following is an abridged account of this service and Marvin's inspiring presentation:

"When we think of what has happened this weekend, we think of a time filled with "icons." What are icons? They are items that facilitate our remembering important things.

"And as we have seen, the Job Tyler family has many icons that we can use to remember. Two of the most significant icons for the family are Job and Moses. Both are biblical names, and it helps us to identify with stories from the Bible. Job of the Bible was severely tested and had many challenges, as was the young immigrant Job who arrived in the 1600s in Massachusetts. The biblical Moses led his people in a new land, as Moses Tyler provided important leadership for a new "people" here in Boxford and Andover.

"We also have the "icon" of the homestead and the barn. These are more than just old buildings, for they provided, in a very real way, the tie between us and our ancestors. As we walk the grounds and touch the beams and walls we are, in a way, communicating with the people that went before. The structures serve as icons, or important emblems, that help us remember so much more.

"There are many other icons that we have used this weekend. There is the church, where we are having this service this morning. We can sit in the pews that were one "purchased" by John Tyler and Bradstreet Tyler and others for whom we no longer have records. There are also the headstones on the graves of those who passed on many years ago. They remind us not only of the individuals, but of the fact that we will be tied to this land permanently, no matter where we live or where we die.

"One of the icons I feel is most strong is the rock wall in front of the barn, built three hundred years ago by Moses, probably with some help from elderly Job and some of Moses' siblings and offspring. This wall has been maintained over the centuries, and its continuing rebuilding can be seen as representative of the continuing rebuilding of the Tyler family through every generation. It was with a great feeling of pride that, at last night's banquet, my name was selected in the random lottery to receive the prize of a rock from the wall. This means it is a symbol that, in a small way, I will be able to take home with me.

Tyler Homestead Barn and Rock Wall

"In the Bible, twelve rocks were taken across a river and deposited on the opposite bank as a memorial to the twelve tribes of Israel. Because of the symbolism of rocks and their ability to serve as icons, I have brought with me this morning a number of rocks that I will ask my grandchildren, Brynn and Christian, to pass out to each of the families here today. After they have handed them out, I would like each of you to make a simple statement as a memory for this reunion of Tylers. It can be something about what has happened this weekend or it can be a remembrance for a special family member. As you return the rock, Brynn and Christian will return them to the front of the sanctuary, where they will form a memorial this morning and serve as an icon for the Tyler family."[164]

Many in the audience made statements of the meaningfulness of the weekend to them, and the importance of staying tied with other family members.

Chapter 8: Other Particulars

Origins of the Tyler Name

Surnames evolved over time based on what was important to a society at the time they were adopted. Before the Norman Conquest of Britain, people did not have hereditary surnames; each person was identifiable by a single name. Over time in early societies, further identification was given by adding a second name based on an individual's home town, their occupation, a personal characteristic, a religious connotation, or even a special event as an identifier. As populations increased, individuals took on these fuller identities, leading to names such as John the butcher, William the short, Henry from Sutton, Mary of the wood, Roger son of Richard. Over time, with a settled society, such a descriptive words or phrases became official surnames—Henry Sutton, Mary Wood, or Roger Richards.

It is most commonly assumed the surname Tyler originated is England. It was derived from the occupational name for a maker or layer of tiles, derived from the agent derivative of the Middle English word "tile," from the Old English word "tigele," from the Latin word "tegula," a derivative of "tegere" meaning to cover.[165]

In 1896 Willard I. Tyler Brigham wrote a lengthy speech on the origin of the Tyler name for the first national Tyler Family Reunion, which took place in Andover, Massachusetts. He explained to the attendees:

> "The name Tyler is usually considered English. But for all that, probably it was born 'on the Continent;' likely in France, which country especially felt the throes of expiring Roman Civilization, as well as awakening thrills of its surviving conqueror, Gothic. There is early record of an hereditary domain in France, called *'Castellum de Tillieres,'* a name suggesting that of our own family. And it has further been thought out, that some descendant of that house was with William the Conqueror when he went into England with his army in the year 1066; and that it is his name we see spelled *'Le Sire de Tilly,'* or Lord Tyler, as preserved on the Roll of Battle Abbey, that historic church founded after the Conqueror's decisive Battle of Hastings. Some persons in America have almost claimed to be descended from this person. It *may* be so; at present it is conjectural. 'Castles in Spain' may be maintained without expenditures for taxes and servants.
>
> "Howbeit, it is certain, from time immemorial, there have been in various parts of Great Britain families bearing the name Tyler, or its equivalent, spelled in a dozen different forms. In Burke's Armory are recorded no less than eight Tyler coats of arms, evidence seemingly conclusive that numerous branches became prominent and hobnobbed with nobility. Such aristocrats are, or have been, seated, among other places, at Monmouth, at Lynsted Lodge, Kent County, and at Pembridge, County Hereford, in England. Of this last line, probably, came the distinguished ecclesiast, John Tyler, Dean of Hereford in 1692, who was Bishop of Llandaff from 1704–24."[166]

In the 1920s, Charles Arthur Hoppin wrote a more detailed account of the origin of the name based on further research. As he wrote in the publication, *Tyler's Quarterly Historical and Genealogical Magazine*:

"By virtue of the fact that the British nation has so carefully preserved its early records and has made them accessible for examination, success in the discovery has been a simple matter. The first appearance of the name of Tyler is in the reign of Henry III (1216-1272). Thus, the surname originated almost with the Magna Carta, 'the Englishman's Declaration of Independence,' in 1215. . . It was the Seventh Crusade to the Holy Land that gave rise to the creation of the first record now extant of our surname. It was King Louis IX of France who directed this Seventh Crusade to 'rescue the Holy Land from the Infidels.' The absence of Prince Edward from England in 1270 gave rise to a certain event, in England, which now enables us to peep into the cottages of the very first Tylers, who certainly were at home in the years 1272 and 1273. This event was an official inquiry ordered by Edward I on his return from Palestine, after the death of his father, Henry III, in 1272. The nature of this inquiry was to ascertain the exact state of the royal demesnes [feudal land owned by a lord], and of the rights and revenues of the Crown, many of which, during the previous turbulent reign, had been usurped by the clergy and laity. A jury was summoned in each hundred of the realm to ascertain the facts and report thereon under oath. The fundamental title to land was vested in the king; much land was held in capite, by fealty only. This sweeping inquiry all over England into the minute particulars of the tenure of land, shows only five adult males surnamed Tyler then alive in England. Thus we are close to the very beginning of this family, as a family, with a distinct surname; so few were the members of it in the year 1272, and as three of the five were living together in the same district, probably in the same town, it is clear that these five first Tylers were exactly in the position to have been the children of the tile-maker, or tiler, the first man who, as a tiler, derived or was accorded his surname form his occupation."

Hoppin continued his detailed account of the first Tylers:

"Thus Galfridus (otherwise Geoffray) le Tylere and Radulphus (otherwise Ralph) de Tilere with another were cottars, tenants of three cottages each with a few acres of land rented to them by the Abbot of Sawtry who was the resident ecclesiastical lord of the district, and the representative of the monastery of Great Sawtry, in which was vested the actual ownership of the land; and for the use of the cottages and land they paid to the said abbot the same as did Ralph Vaccary, i.e., two shillings annually each, and each gave free to the abbot eight days of assistance upon the demesne lands of the abbot at the time of the harvest. . . Sawtry was upon the old Roman road from London to York, about eight miles north of the shire town of Huntingdon. The earth is flat in that region and clay abounds in vast quantities. Ely Cathedral was the mother church of the first Tylers."[167]

English Tyler or French Tillieres?

Tyler family researcher Larry Tyler of Missouri presented his extensive original research on the history of the Tyler name in his self-published book, *Tyler History* (1989). In its 321 pages he presents links to the Tyler name from throughout world history. His conclusions, sometimes with tenuous distant connections, have been seen as controversial by some family researchers. Included from his book is a section that represents the heart of his arguments:

"The first thing the student of Tyler History needs to know is that the Official Account concerning Tyler Origins is 100% completely WRONG! And in order to understand the facts as they really are, it is necessary to become familiar with the Official version of Tyler Origins with all its many contradictions, impossibilities, and basic untruths.

"When one looks inside almost any book on Surnames for the meaning of the name, 'TYLER,' one invariably finds the same definition: TYLER = 'tilemaker.' Thus, the Tyler families are (officially) universally held to originate with "VARIOUS UNRELATED PEASANT TILE-MAKERS" no earlier than 1272 (the date of the record of the "HUNTINGTON TYLERS" who are held to be the original Tyler clan).

". . . President John Tyler of Virginia (10th President of the United States), 1790–1862, was an avid student of TYLER history and called the tilemaker myth in still-classic words, 'SUPREMELY RIDICULOUS!' He had researched enough to know that the Tylers descend from Tillieres, France, as he wrote in 1859: 'The Tyler Family is reported to have sprung from <u>Gilbert</u>, who is mentioned as Gilbert de Tyler (Gilbert Tillieres II) and who accompanied William the Conqueror . . . (and) Wat Tyler's name (Tyler) was known in England from the time of the Conqueror.' (President Tyler, 1859)"

To lend support to these arguments from Larry Tyler, the web site, *houseofnames.com*, includes information on the evolution of the Tillieres name used for those who lived in and protected the Castle Tillieres in Normandy, France. It describes how the name became Anglicized to Tylor, Tiler, Tellier, and Tyler. The following is taken from that web site.

"Tillieres is a name that was carried to England in the great wave of migration from Normandy following the Norman Conquest of 1066. The surname Tillieres was first found in Glamorgan, Monmouthshire, and Herefordshire, where they were granted large estates after the Norman Conquest."[168]

The notion that the Tyler surname came from France is supported by the Falaise Roll, a record created in 1931 listing names of people who were companions of William, Duke of Normandy, at the conquest of England in 1066. Interestingly, one of the names on the Falaise Roll is Gilbert Crispin, 2nd Seigneur de Tillieres, whose family had control of the Castle Tillieres in Normandy. Their history is briefly described in the Falaise Roll in the following way: "Deep in the centre of France on the southern border of Normandy there lie the remains of the ancient castle of Tillieres-sur-Avre, in its day one of the strongest fortresses of the Norman dukes, built by them more than 900 years ago. . . The Crispin family acquired the hereditary guardianship of this fortress ca. 1030. They held Tillieres until the middle of the 14th century. They were known usually by the name de Tillieres, later sometimes corrupted into Tyler and Taylor."

A book published in 1874 called *The Norman People* included a further clarification (or confusion) about the origin of the name It also indicates the Tyler surname is based in Normandy: "Tyler, from the fief and Castle of Tilers or Tillers, Normandy. Gislebert de Teliers and Gillo (Gilbert), 1180-98 (MRS); Ralph de Tilere, Engl. c. 1272 (RH)."[169]

The reader can decide how much to rely on these historical tidbits to reconstruct the Tyler family legacy. Obviously, the family name extends a long time into the past and becomes documented in some form as a surname in early English history.

Other Tyler lines in America

Genealogist Willard I. Tyler Brigham had conducted significant research on Tyler lines other than that of immigrant Job Tyler. He included in his speech at the Tyler Family Reunion of 1896 a listing of Tyler immigrant families other than the Job Tyler line.

"More than a dozen *early* Tylers settled within the United States. Not all of them, however, have surviving descendants; from about half of the number most of the myriads have sprung. Of those whom we may at this time dismiss with shortest reference were:

"(1). Abraham Tyler, at Haverhill, Mass., about 1640; had three children, all of whom died young. He died in 1673, and his line became extinct.

"(2). Nathaniel Tyler was at Lynn, Mass., about 1640; he made his will (1652) before starting out on a long sea voyage, wherein is mentioned a son in Shrewsbury, England. There is present doubt about his destination. Some opine that he returned to England, while others think that the Branford, Conn., branch of Tylers are sprung from him, and that the voyage he took was either to Long Island or Connecticut.

"(3). Roger Tyler was in Connecticut by 1650; probably had a son Roger, Jr., who died at Wallingford, Conn., seemingly without issue, and *as far as known*, the family became extinct, though some claim him for progenitor of the Connecticut line.

"(4). John Tyler, shopkeeper, Charlestown, Mass., had a son John, born in 1696. The father died in Carolina; if there are latter-day descendants, they are thus far untraced.

"(5). Thomas Tyler, of Boston, Mass., had a son Samuel, born in 1657. No grandchildren have yet been found.

"(6). William Tyler, of Boston, Mass., came from London on the first vessel which sailed after the close of the American Revolution. He was a ropemaker; his descendants are believed to be not numerous.

"(7). William Tyler was at Salem, N. J., about 1688, a Quaker. His line seems not to be very distinguished or numerous, but a quiet, respectable class of citizens. His descendants are principally confined to the state of New Jersey and bordering Pennsylvania.

"(8). A Maryland *Tylor* family, Quakers, date from about 1750. They are probably a distinct race, for there are many English *Tylors*, which may be of anterior common origin with the *Tylers*.

"Of those lines having descendants known to have figured most conspicuously in the history of our country, are the following:

"(1). Job Tyler, the Andover, Mass., line.

"(2). Capt. Thomas Tyler, the Boston line.

"(3). The Branford and Wallingford, Connecticut lines.

"(4). The Virginia and Maryland lines.

"[Note] To these must be added John Tyler, at Gloucester, Mass,. 1719 (who turns out to be the founder of a distinct American branch)."

The section above gives the first instance of Tyler family lines in the seventeenth and eighteenth centuries. Brigham continued his exposition of Tyler lines by briefly introducing six other instances of Tyler family links as they were known at the time.

"*Second.* In Voluntown and Preston, Conn., and Portsmouth, R. I., we find record of an early John Tyler family. He died in 1700, leaving one son, Lazarus, who left sons. This family did not get well started before 1700 and is not believed to be very numerous. There are reasons why I am at present inclined to believe this John and Job of Andover were brothers.

"*Third.* Thomas Tyler, Sea Captain, from Budleigh, England, was at Boston about 1685. He and his eldest son, Thomas, Jr., were in 1703 taken by a Barbary pirate vessel. Large ransoms were offered but their fate remains a mystery. He left three sons, who had issue. While not so numerous as some of the other lines, taken altogether, it is usually thought the most aristocratic of our northern lines. Two of Thomas' sons had a coat of arms granted while we were under British rule. Nevertheless, these were loyal Americans. Royall Tyler, notwithstanding his given name, was one of Boston's most active agitators against the mother country, a worthy coadjutor of John Adams. Among his distinguished sons, Royall, Jr., has the unique honor or writing the first American comedy produced by an American company.

"*Fourth.* William Tyler took the oath of fidelity at New Haven, Conn., in 1657; removed to Milford, Conn., where he married and had three sons. One died unmarried at Derby. The other two, William, Jr., and John, early removed to Wallingford, Conn., where they had numerous descendants, and so I have very naturally fallen into the habit of calling this the Wallingford branch. The most conspicuous founder of a colony sent out by this line made history at Claremont, New Hampshire, where as inventors and mill-builders Tylers have been conspicuous for generations.

"*Fifth.* Branford, Conn., in point of numbers, will probably be found to follow Job's line most closely. Also, it may be discovered that it to the Wallingford line is very closely related. Four male Tylers were at Branford quite early: Charles, Peter, Francis, and George by name; all probably brothers, the last three are known to have been.

. . . "*Sixth.* The Maryland line seems to have started with Robert Tyler, whose will was probated in 1738. It would not be surprising to later learn, he was originally from Virginia.

"*Seventh.* The Virginia lines are four or more in number, as Lyon G. Tyler, President of William and Mary College, has within the past year informed us. Most conspicuous is the line of Henry Tyler, traditionally (like Job), from Shropshire, England, who had a large grant at Williamsburg, Va., as early as 1652. A part of this was later selected for the site of the Governor's Palace. This on one of the 'F. F. Vs.,' having won distinguished laurels in state and national sense; furnished conspicuous incumbents of state and federal courts, its own state governor and lieutenant-governor, as well as president of the United States."

Dispersion of the Tyler name

The Tyler name has been part of American history since its earliest settlement period. The Tyler family name has been found in the United States, the United Kingdom, Canada, and Scotland between 1840 and 1920. Generally, the most Tyler families were found in the United States. Over many decades, Tyler families moved from the eastern seaboard to the Western Territories. The greatest number lived in New York State. In 1840 there were 287 Tyler families living in New York; this was about twenty-four percent of all the recorded Tyler families in this country at the time.

The maps below illustrate the dispersion of the Tyler surname across the continent over eighty years of the nineteenth century. This information is taken from the genealogy web site "ancestry.com" and is based on data from the United States Census Bureau.

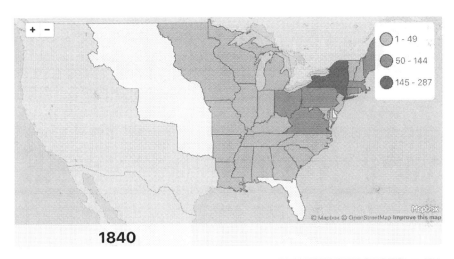

1840

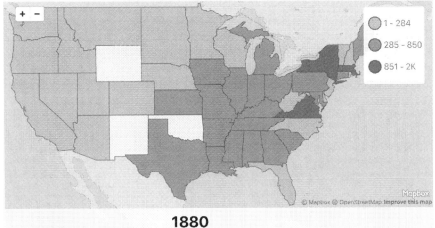

1880

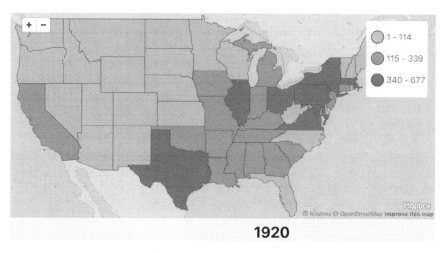

1920

Tyler surname dispersion map[170]

Ethnic distribution of the Tyler surname in the United States

Figures taken from the 2010 national census indicate the great majority of individuals with the Tyler surname are either Caucasian or African-American.[171]

Classification of the Tyler surname

TOTAL number, all Tylers	66,056
Percent	
White (Caucasian)	62
Black (African-American)	31
Mixed Race	3
White (Hispanic)	2
Native American/Alaskan	1
Asian/Pacific	1

The great majority of Caucasians have had the Tyler surname for many generations, as far back as the thirteenth century in early English history. In contrast, for most African-Americans the surname was taken by slaves when they gained their freedom in the nineteenth century. Most did not know their original African names, since they were renamed when brought to America, and after a number of generations they were not familiar with African names in general. They also were not given surnames as slaves, but only first names. Upon gaining freedom there were a number of logical reasons for selecting a surname—they may have adopted their former owners surname; taken on the name of someone they respected, such as Washington or Jefferson; they were a black woman who was partnered with a white man and took on his name; they selected a European name to have a better chance of being hired for work; or they simply took on a name they liked.

Tyler versus Taylor

A name often confused with Tyler is Taylor, which of course was typically adopted historically by a worker who was a tailor by trade. Since a town had a need for more tailors than tile-makers, it should not be surprising that Taylor is the more common surname. It is listed in the 2010 United States Census as the 20th most common surname in the United States, while Tyler is the 512th most common, making up just 0.02 percent of the population.[172] Although the number of Tylers is slowly increasing over time, it is becoming proportionally less common as the country gains large numbers of new immigrant families with Hispanic, Asian, and Middle Eastern names.

Popular Forenames

According to the genealogical web site WikiTree.com, the most popular forenames (first names) for the Tyler surname are the following:

Male: William, John, George, Thomas, James, Charles, Henry, Joseph, Alfred, Edward.

Female: Mary, Elizabeth, Sarah, Emma, Eliza, Ann, Alice, Jane, Emily, Annie.

It is interesting to include information on the use of "Tyler" as a first name, which is a relatively recent phenomenon. Tyler has become a popular first name, with its particular peak in the year of 1995.

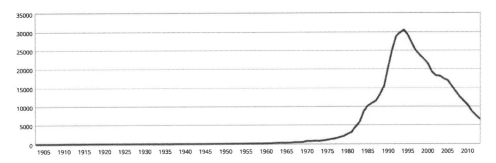

"Tyler" used as a first name, 1900–2015[173]

Tyler Coat of Arms (1774)

The American Tyler family does not have an official Coat of Arms, since they are not granted in America. However, a French-derived Coat of Arms has some validity as a representative image. In the *Rietstap Armorial General*, a Tyler Coat of Arms was officially documented. It was described in the following way: Blue; a silver horizontal band charged with a red Cross of Lorraine between two red crescents; the band accompanied by three gold leopards.

The Tyler Coats of Arms illustrated in documents such as Rietstap and Burke were never officially granted by kings, so the origin of the Coat of Arms remains a mystery, although it is commonly accepted by many Tyler genealogists.

In 1774, the descendants of Andrew Tyler of Boston and his brother William were issued a Coat of Arms by the College of Arms.

Below the illustration is an explanation of its creation and description of its symbols, which could be assumed to be representative of all American Tyler families.

Coat of Arms Illustration

"Armorial Ensigns, as here represented, were granted by the College of Arms, Nov. 21, 1774, to the descendants of Andrew Tyler of Boston in New England, Gent., and of William Tyler his brother:—Sabler, on a fess Erminois, between three mountain-cats passant guardant Ermine, a cross formy on either side a crescent gules. Crest, A demi-mountain-cat issuant guardant Erminois.

"This Coat Armor is emblazoned on the Chart containing the pedigree of Tyler of America, recorded at the College March 2, 1778, attested by Catherine, Lady Heard, a daughter of Andrew and Miriam (Pepperell) Tyler, and grand-daughter of Thomas Tyler from Budleigh in Devonshire, the immigrant ancestor of the family."[174]

Pewter Mug (1923)

There has been discussion for many years among Tyler family researchers regarding whether immigrant Job Tyler came to America from Shropshire County or Kent County, England. They are in different parts of the country, so this discrepancy is not simply a matter of slightly varying geographic areas.

Family researchers Charles and Norman Tyler visited one of their distant relatives, William Guerdon Tyler, in Baltimore in 1984 because they had heard about an heirloom pewter mug and they wanted to see it for themselves. William Guerdon showed them the pewter mug that had been in his family for many generations and was the mug immigrant Job Tyler likely brought with him from England in 1638. The mug is listed in the first will ever filed in Norwich, Connecticut. An expert indicated the mug had been made in 1533. On it was inscribed the names of its owners over many generations:

Job Tyler	Shropshire, England	1619
Hopestill Tyler	Andover, Massachusetts	1645
Hopestill Tyler, Jr.	Preston, Connecticut	1685
Joseph Tyler	Preston, Connecticut	1711

Joseph Tyler, Jr.	Preston, Connecticut	1766
Oliver S. Tyler	Preston, Connecticut	1798
Sarah L. Tyler	Norwich, Connecticut	1848
William G. Tyler	Baltimore, Maryland	1873
William G. Tyler, Jr.	Baltimore, Maryland	1911

Additional information on the pewter mug was described in the Prologue of Job Tyler gamily genealogy, Volume III, *The Descendants of Job Tyler Since 1619*. This excerpt is from the Prologue: "The following is a quote from a letter sent to William Guerdon Tyler I (#6101) from his second cousin, Sarah Lester Tyler (#3552). Dated 4 November, 1923, she states to "cousin Will"...

"'In each of the wills, mention is made of the pewter cup. Hopestill, Jr. (#35) gives the cup to his wife Anne and she gives it to her son Deacon Joseph (#140). He in turn gives it to his son Captain Joseph, Jr. (#528). Captain Joseph then gives everything to his oldest son Stephen (#1542) who is to take care of his wife, Lucy Kimball, and to bring up the children. Uncle Stephen gave the cup to my father and I now pass it on to you.'

"Because Stephen had no children the cup then passed on to a brother of Stephen, Oliver Spicer Tyler (#1549). From Oliver Spicer the cup passed on down to his daughter Sarah Lester Tyler (#3552), who in turn gives it to her second cousin William Guerdon Tyler I (#6101). This William Guerdon I passed the pewter mug on to his son William Guerdon II (#8417), who at the time of this printing has it in his possession."

Because there is ample evidence Job Tyler was born in Kent County, England (his father's will and burial records), the mystery of why Shropshire is inscribed on the pewter mug will remain. Perhaps there was confusion regarding his birthplace even centuries ago, or maybe Job really did come from Shropshire, as is written in a number of archival documents. The mystery will remain for future detectives to resolve.

Tyler Hymn (ca. 1900)

The Tyler Hymn likely was written by Grace Lord for one of the early Tyler Association reunions. It was included on the program for the 1900 meeting of the Tyler Family Association. Many years later, it was sung at the West Boxford Church during the Sunday morning remembrance service of the 1988 Reunion in West Boxford, Massachusetts. (Note: Copies are available from the author.)

Tyler Hymn

Words by Charles Tyler
Brooklyn, New York

Music by Grace Lord
Northampton, Massachusetts

O Thou whose hand is strong to save! Who bore our fathers from a- far. Thro' words of flame. O
Still from the past their voices call, In coun- sels wise and home and friends, We'll
The sim- ple faiths they suffered for, The love of coun- try,

rag- ing wind and beat- ing wave, To safe- ty un- der Free-dom's star. Lord,
may no mar- ring sha- dow fall A- thwart the lus- tre of that name! Be-
sa- cred keep for- ev- er- more, to learn to trea- sure and de- fend With

lead us with a glow- ing light, That we, like they, may walk a- right.
queathed by sires who kept it fair In time of woe and black des- pair.
faith in Him our sir- es knew, To keep us, strong and brave and true.

The Tyler Nose

From the Tyler Family Association Official Report of the 1st-5th American
Family Reunion . . . 1896-1899, by Willard I. Tyler Brigham comes this traditional
Tyler story by an unknown author:

"Several years ago, while traveling on the continent, I fell into
conversation with an English gentleman. He asked me if my name was not
Tyler. I answered, 'Yes, but I do not recollect your face, sir; and I am fairly
good at remembering faces.'

"'No,' he replied, 'I am sure I have never seen you before, sire; but what
county in England are you from, Mr. Tyler?'

"'I am American,' said I.

"'That is very strange,' he replied. 'But what county did your father
come from, to America?' I answered that my forefathers for many
generations were Americans.

"'Most extraordinary!' he exclaimed. 'You must think it strange that I
knew your name was Tyler, but the fact is you have THE TYLER NOSE!
We have a number of Tylers in my county and they all have the same nose.'

Of course, I immediately felt my nose, but I could not discover that it materially differed from other peoples' noses.

"I thanked him for telling me that I possessed this remarkable facial phenomenon, and assured him that it was the first time in my life that I fully realized that I have a nose; -- but now I know that I am really a Tyler. Indeed, I should be certain of it, even if some gipsy had stolen me from my cradle and named me Con Alonzo Nevarro; and I am so proud of it that I would rather die in the poorhouse than to live in luxury by selling my TYLER NOSE for a 'mess of pottage.'"

Cultural biases

The Sturdiest Race (1899)

In 1899, Penn Tyler wrote to his cousin describing common connections in their family. After listing many relatives and the family's lineage, Penn Tyler continued his correspondence with thoughts and attitudes more common in the nineteenth century, but that would not be acceptable or politically correct today. Following is an excerpt from the letter.

"Your genealogy is Job, Moses, John (the sea captain), Abner, John, Abner, Jane, Silas, and Hamilton. You are the 9th generation in this country.

"I take great satisfaction in thinking what a sturdy race I belong. I hope you do the same, the best race the world ever saw. Today, they are the leading race of the world, and in the future no doubt the English language is to be the language of the world.

"The English nation is made up of Britons, Danes, Anglos, Saxons, and Normans: all sturdy races never much subject to Kings or Priests. When the Laws are just, they obey; when unjust, they rebel. The Latin races have not the lofty manhood of the Anglo-Saxon. The Spanish, French and Italians. These show today, more than ever before, their weakness and superstition. If they, the Spanish and French, especially, if they keep in their old ruts, will be nations of the past.

"When I began this letter I did not think of writing to so young a boy as you; but hope it will lead you to think more of the race to which you belong; more of your ancestry; your nation and your flag.

"My best love to all the family and friends whom you may see—and especially to your Grandmother.

"Your cousin Penn Tyler"[175]

"A Greetin' frum Old Ferginny" (1900)

During the same time period, racism was a largely acceptable cultural norm. This is evidenced starkly in a brief passage from the program of the Fifth General American Tyler Family gathering held in Philadelphia in 1900. The following excerpt from the program describes "A Greetin' frum Ole Ferginny," a "humorous" portrayal of the demeanor of Negroes in Tyler family life. The description, as disturbing and shameful as it would seem today, was written as follows: "This last is in the raciest Negro gabble, evincing, indeed, a positive genius in dialect; and, while expressing the delicious complacency of the black servant in the family of his master, turns a compliment to the Tylers in such lines as these:—

> "Knowed 'em all 'f'um fust to las',
> Knowed they all 'us jes' fust class—
> Pes'dents, gubnors, big-bugs gin'ly,
> Way aheaid dish yer McKinley."

Tylers and the Ku Klux Klan (1924)

History of the Ku Klux Klan in Michigan

Founded in 1866, the Ku Klux Klan (KKK) extended into almost every southern state by 1870 and became a vehicle for white southern resistance to the Republican Party's Reconstruction-era policies aimed at establishing political and economic equality for blacks. Its members waged an underground campaign of intimidation and violence directed at white and black Republican leaders. Though Congress passed legislation designed to curb Klan terrorism, the organization saw its primary goal—the reestablishment of white supremacy—fulfilled through Democratic victories in state legislatures across the South in the 1870s.

After a period of decline, white Protestant nativist groups revived the Klan in the early twentieth century, burning crosses and staging rallies, parades and marches denouncing immigrants, Catholics, Jews, blacks, and organized labor. In 1915, white Protestant nativists organized a revival of the Ku Klux Klan near Atlanta, Georgia, inspired by their romantic view of the Old South as well as Thomas Dixon's 1905 book "The Clansman" and D.W. Griffith's 1915 film "Birth of a Nation."

Michigan was fertile ground for Klan recruiters in the early twentieth century. As the auto industry grew, white and black southerners traveled north for jobs. Immigrants also came into the state looking for jobs and most of them were Catholic. On July 4, 1924, in Jackson, Michigan, one hundred thousand Klan members marched in a two-mile-long procession. "It was a broadly-based organization, which was mostly anti-immigrant and anti-Catholic. A lot of people felt that way, and they were not perceived as fringe or kooks."[176]

Although Michigan membership is difficult to pinpoint, there were reports of between 265,000 to 875,000 total members. Members were not ashamed to be affiliated with the group, and many marched without their hoods. For a few years in the 1920s the Klan exerted a strong political influence on Michigan and was close to electing Klan members to the highest political offices. The Klan peaked in 1924 but was all but dead by 1926. Michigan's flirtation with it, whilst enthusiastic, was probably shorter than most.

Klan member Max E. Tyler

The Tyler family was not exempt from membership in the Klan. The 1924 photograph below shows a memorial parade for Max E. Tyler that took place in the small town of Hart, Michigan. The funeral procession was "In honor of one of our 100% Americans," as it says on the photo. Max was an electrician born in 1892, the son of Elmer, the son of Joseph, the son of Isaac, from Sturgis, Michigan.

Funeral procession for Max E. Tyler, Hart, Michigan

Max was obviously a respected member of the community, as is evidenced by the length of the procession. What is disturbing, from a more contemporary perspective, is that the procession is being led by dozens of members of the Ku Klux Klan. This brings up a thought-provoking question: How should this kind of story be included in a family history?

The photograph was found by an auctioneer who was preparing for the sale of a house. As he looked through the house, he discovered a false wall leading to a room in the attic. In the room were boxes holding fifty Klan uniforms and files with names of members from all over the country. This photo was found among the collection of records.

Chapter 9: Further Research

Boxford Historical Document Center

Boxford Historical Document Center, West Boxford, Massachusetts

The Boxford Historical Document Center is a modest one-story brick building situated next to the Second Congregational Church in the center of West Boxford, Massachusetts. It contains a wealth of historical records, photographs, maps, genealogies, microfilm, models and numerous artifacts that have meaningful connections to the history of the town. Built in 1930 as a library, the structure was transformed into a historical document center at the time of the country's Bicentennial in 1976. Since it opened there have been only two archivists in charge—Margaret Lane, who worked from July 4, 1976 until she retired in 1991 and the current part-time archivist Martha Clark, who has also worked as the curator for the Massachusetts State Archives in Boston.

The oldest document in the archives is the first Book of Records from the First Congregational Church of Boxford, dating back to 1702-1703. The original book lists names of the church's earliest members including Lt. John Peabody of Topsfield, Lt. Perley's wife of Rowley, and the widow Hannah Peabody. It also lists baptisms and Town Meeting notes from the early 1700s. The Center includes many documents on the Tyler family, which had a presence in the village from its earliest years.

Over the decades many have seen West Boxford as a bucolic summer place. Older homes were bought by people who summered here and restored them. Archivist Clark gave the example of Witch Hollow Farm {the Tyler Homestead] that was owned by the Tyler family for centuries and purchased by the wealthy Pinkham family of Salem in 1921, who occupied the property as a summer house.

Online genealogical sites

There are a number of increasingly sophisticated web sites providing information on family genealogies. The ones the author has found most useful for tracking Tyler family information are listed below in alphabetical order.

Ancestry.com

Ancestry.com is a membership site. Many how-tos in the Family History 101 section are free to use. Once you have a membership, you can search digitized records and indexes from around the world. Use the Family Tree tab if you're a member (but not if you're using Ancestry.com at a library) to create your family tree and post photos and stories, which you may share with others.

FamilySearch.org

This site, hosted through the resources of The Church of Jesus Christ of Latter-Day Saints (Mormons), is one of the best free online resources available. Search millions of digitized and indexed records and over a billion unique profiles from around the world. Some results point to offsite sources for digitized records. Don't ignore the Learn tab; it's packed with keyword-searchable articles and online courses. The Catalog tab takes you to the most extensive genealogy library catalog in the world. Microfilmed holdings can be rented for use at a FamilySearch Center near you (see the FamilySearch Centers tab). Share your family tree at the bottom of the home page; learn how you can contribute to online records access under the Indexing tab.

Geni.com

Geni.com is designed to host online family trees. Users add and invite their close relatives to join their family tree. All Geni users can share photos, videos, and documents with their families. In November 2012, Geni was acquired by MyHeritage Ltd.

Geneanet.org

En.Geneanet.org is a Europe-based genealogy research service headquartered in France. Launched in 1996 specifically to help family historians search for and share relevant information, the website has had over a decade to accumulate submitted data and add that to its small but formidable archive of records.

MyHeritage.com

Discover several innovative features tech-savvy genealogists like; many are free. Click on Genealogy for an overview of those features: build a family tree, run simultaneous searches across major genealogy databases, create a family website, find help on message boards and more. MyHeritage charges for some search results once your family tree reaches a certain size.

RootsWeb.com

RootsWeb is a free genealogy community that uses online forums, mailing lists, and other resources to help people research their family history. Founded in 1993 as the Roots Surname List, it is the oldest free online community genealogy research website. It is now partnered with Ancestry.com.

WikiTree.com

WikiTree is a free, shared social networking genealogy website that allows users individually to research and contribute to their own personal family trees, while building and collaborating on a singular worldwide family tree within the same system. Because of its ease of use, no cost, and ability to merge family trees, this is the site favored by this author. As an example, by finding Norman Raymond Tyler (my name) on WikiTree, one can trace over eleven generations the direct line back to immigrant Job Tyler.

WikiTree now includes over twenty million profiles, with more than five million including DNA test connections. Contributions have been included by over 600,000 genealogist volunteers. Information can be uploaded that either adds or revises existing biographies or creates new profiles not yet included.

Readers of this Tyler history are encouraged to sign up on the WikiTree site and contribute information, connecting their more immediate family to this world-wide family tree of Tylers.

Drawing Genealogy Family Charts

One of the most interesting parts of genealogy is when a researcher has enough information to chart a family tree and data can be described through use of a graphic illustration showing relationships over generations. There are many ways to create charts. Perhaps the simplest type of genealogical chart is the Lineage Chart, in which direct descent is shown. This type of chart does not get encumbered with siblings, aunts and uncles, or other marriages; it simply traces fathers and mothers through the paternal side of the family.

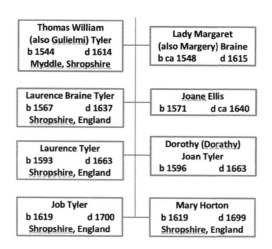

Example of Lineage Chart

An interesting variation on the Lineage Chart shows direct descent, but includes simply the number of siblings, illustrating how many in each generation and whether they are older or younger than the direct descendant. The author prepared such a chart for his direct line, from Job Tyler through to his grandchildren.

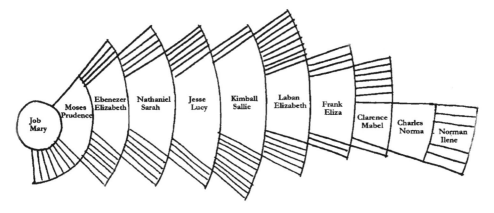

Norman Raymond Tyler Family Lineage Chart

The Skeletal Ancestral Chart is a common format, with the name of some family member on a single left line and listing previous generations in an expanding skeleton of names that includes birth, death, and marriage data. (Note: For any such charting of the Job Tyler line, it is useful to follow and adapt to the numbering system established in Brigham's Volumes I and II of *The Tyler Genealogy* and Tyler's Volume III, *The Descendants of Job Tyler Since 1619*.)

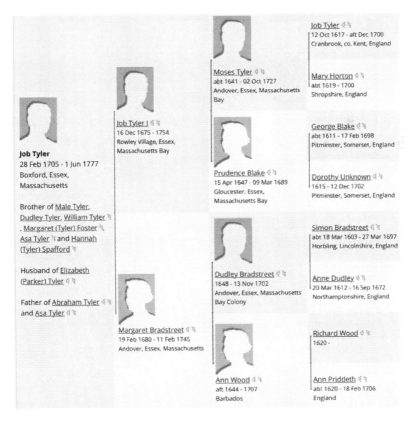

Example of Skeletal Ancestral Chart

A more schematic type of chart is the Radial Chart. Although it is more difficult to create and use because of the many angles, it clearly describes how a family breaks out over many generations. This chart, created by family historian Larry Tyler, uses Job II as the central ancestor and expands from there.

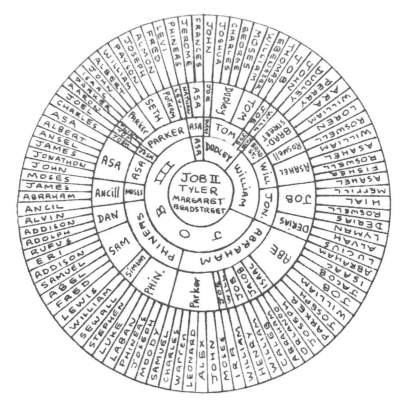

Radial Chart of Job Tyler II–Margaret Bradstreet[177]

One other type of genealogical chart was developed by researcher Audrey Ladd, a former owner of the Tyler Homestead. Her Double Fan Chart fans out from the current generation back and then fans back in to a prominent ancestor. For example, if you wanted to show family relationships from immigrant Job Tyler forward over ten generations, the chart would fan out from Job for five generations and then fan backward over five generations from the latest individual. This chart, although cumbersome, would allow a more inclusive, but manageable, record over generations. There is no example of this type of chart, but it could be a meaningful alternative.

Other general resources

Forrest Rickly

Forrest Rickly is a genealogist who has listed information on the Job Tyler line in England which takes the line back three generations from Job's father, Laurence. This opens significant information for further research. Rickly's page on the web site on Geneanet includes hundreds of names on the Job Tyler line. This document

lists the following genealogy prior to Job Tyler, taking the genealogy well back into the 16th Century. Forrest Rickly's web site is:
https://gw.geneanet.org/woodybillie?lang=en&m=N&v=TYLER

Resources available from the author

The author, Norman Raymond Tyler, has an extensive archive of resources on the Job Tyler family line. Items listed below are available by contacting Norman at: http://tylertopics.com (personal web site), ntyler_at_emich.edu (email), or 126 North Division Street, Ann Arbor, Michigan 48104.

The Descendants of Job Tyler Since 1619, Volume III, Charles R. Tyler, Norma L. Tyler, and Norman R. Tyler

This third volume of *The Descendants of Job Tyler Since 1619*, written by the author and his parents and self-published in paperback in 1985, is an update to the original two volumes written by Willard I. Tyler Brigham first published in 1912.

"Memory Hold the Door," by Arthur Pinkham

Arthur Pinkham, a Tyler descendant, first learned the Tyler Homestead in West Boxford was his ancestral home at a meeting of the Whiting Club, a social fraternity. Both Mr. Pinkham and his wife had ancestors in the family ten generations back. He then found out more about the homestead in Volumes I and II of *The Tyler Genealogy*.

Pinkham wrote an intriguing story for a 1944 meeting of the Whiting Club in which he remembers living in the house, describing the structure, the barn and farm, what memorabilia he found in the old house, the homestead's previous occupants, and "ghosts, witches, and buried treasure."

Historic photos of the Tyler Homestead and West Boxford

Historic and contemporary photos of the Tyler Homestead and property and the town of West Boxford are available for purchase. Ask the author for a listing of available reprints.

Other resources

Genealogy papers from other families and sources are list on the web site: http://tylertopics.com/job-Tyler-family-association/job-Tyler-association-genealogy/genealogy-papers-archives/

Epilogue

Charles and Norma Tyler

A primary inspiration for authoring this book was my parent's dedication to documenting and updating the genealogy of the Job Tyler line. As a child, my father, Charles Tyler (#8640; Tyler-6036), grew up in the 1930s in a totally dysfunctional family structure. He had been raised by his depression-poor grandparents, had little contact with his no-account father, and was in his teens before he was permitted to meet his mother for the first time. I saw the lifechanging impact on my dad when as an older adult he first came across Brigham's two volumes and in those 881 pages found thousands of relatives, many of great distinction. This discovery was a momentous day for him and gave him an entirely new perspective on his life and family heritage.

Known by everyone as Charlie, my dad's younger life had many aspects to it that were largely unknown even to his own five children, including myself. Just before his passing in 1989 he completed a personal memoir titled, *Memories: Charles R. Tyler.* The following excerpt is a revealing portrait of an important part of his early life. It also may be representative of the experiences of many families in the 1920s and 30s.

Riding the wagon

"My own personal life got off to a somewhat shaky start, having been born into a broken family relationship, which is never an asset to a new arrival into this problem-plagued world. I hold no resentment for my mother and father because I learned later in life it was for the better the way circumstances turned out.

"Grandpa Tyler was of the hardy new England stock and a stern, but very loving, gentleman. Remarks were made, as I was to remember, that 'Wherever Grandpa was, there was Charlie.' I remember many times riding beside him in the old spring wagon as he traveled through the countryside buying scrap metal, old rags, and bottles for resale to the Muskegon [Michigan] Rag & Metal Co.

"Yes, you could call him a junk man, but I think if you knew him better you would call him a country ambassador and redeemer of salvageable material. Nowhere would he go but someone would shout out 'Hi, Frank.' Of course, that would mean a stop and visit and maybe a little nip of that slightly fermented hard cider so abundant in the back-wood sheds of all these old farm homes. There were always children of all ages at the farms and often, as children do, I would strike up a brief acquaintance and while away the time until Grandpa said, 'Let's go.' And then we would head on with the horse and wagon.

"Many trips on the wagon with my Grandpa was my lot, and many times I would ride on the tailgate of his wagon, hopping off occasionally to stop by a frog pond near the road or stopping to pick up a special looking stone or flower, and then running behind to catch up and jump back on the tailgate. A familiar expression of Grandpa's, without looking back to see, was 'Are you still coming?' although he knew full well that I wasn't far behind.

Grandpa Frank Tyler with Charlie

"Another favorite time on the wagon was when we would take our load of 'salvageable materials' to the Rag & Metal Company. There were so many goodies in those scrap metal piles, like bicycles with only one wheel missing, toy dump trucks, etc. But it wasn't my lot to be able to take any of them home.

"After the unloading was completed and the finances of the deal taken care of, it was time to go over to an old boarding house for a family style dinner. It seemed that Grandpa would always set me down in that great big dining room with all those strangers and in a quiet, subtle way inform me that it would be a little while before we would eat. He had a little business to attend to and would be back soon. It was many years later that it came to my mind that Grandpa might just need a little liquid to freshen his lips a wee bit at this time.

"On the way home, we would stop along the way to pick up some grass that had been mowed at one of the city homes and throw it into the wagon for the horses to eat when we came back to the barn. It was not uncommon on the way home to stop along the shore of Mona Lake and let the horses drink. We might also splash a little water on the wagon wheels to keep them moist and relieve the squeaking sound of the worn wheel spokes.

"Grandpa's last ride on the wagon was a tragic memory for me, and was the beginning of a series of things that a twelve-year-old boy should not have had to be involved in. I recall so well to this day things about the tragedy.

"Grandpa had gone out with the wagon. I had not been along this time; I was in the yard playing. All of a sudden, the team of horses came down the road and into our yard at full gallop. They pulled up to the barn and stopped, all panting and breathing very hard. I looked, but Grandpa was not on the wagon. Grandma saw the horses, but of course didn't know what had happened or what to do. We were both very scared. She told me to go out to the road and look to see if Grandpa was in sight. I went out on our side road, looked down it, and saw something laying in the road. Expecting to find Grandpa lying there, and as scared as a young boy could be, I approached the object and found it was a blanket he had used on the seat of the wagon. Going further, to the main highway, I could see a large gathering of cars and people a short distance away. Not knowing what to do, and afraid to do anything, nevertheless I hurried over to the area. I saw Grandpa sitting by the roadside, bleeding and in much pain.

"This is an experience I cannot forget, even as I sit here writing about it many years later. I walked up to Grandpa, with more fear in my body than I had ever known. As soon as he saw me, he said, 'Go home and tell Grandma that I'm hurt.' Having been brought up knowing that when Grandpa said to do something I had better get moving, I quickly did as I was told and went to tell Grandma.

"Things that happened after that are completely lost to my memory. I later found out that an automobile had hit the rear of the wagon, causing the horses to bolt, and throwing Grandpa out of the back of the wagon onto the pavement.

"Things were never the same after that. Grandpa lost an ear in that accident and later developed cancer in the cheek on the side of his head. He suffered much pain before his God called him home. Grandma was very attentive to him during this tragic period of their life, and for this I trust she is now enjoying her reward in heaven.

Dad lived on his own for a number of years after the loss of his grandparents making a living as a house carpenter. He was a very shy young man, but eventually was encouraged by others to introduce himself to Norma. They were married and had two sons when he was enlisted in the infantry of the United States Army during World War II. After the war, they settled into a more typical postwar lifestyle, eventually growing into a family of three sons and two daughters.

Known by everyone as Charlie, he and my mother, Norma, made the decision to update Volumes I and II of Brigham's *The Tyler Genealogy* (1912), with an updated volume. The story behind this third volume speaks loudly of the power of genealogy. Together they spent years traveling across the country, finding and visiting Tyler relatives, and collecting information. After years of research, correspondence, cemetery stops, and home visits during the 1970s and 80s, in 1985 they published Volume III, titled *The Descendants of Job Tyler Since 1619*. This volume added more than two thousand names to the Job Tyler lineage.

Included in the following sections are excerpts from a personal paper written by Charles on how he and his wife, Norma, became involved with years of intensive genealogical research on the Job Tyler family, resulting in publication of Volume III of *The Descendants of Job Tyler Since 1619*.

"First interest in genealogy

"Just when and where the desire to locate and study the background of my family really started, I cannot remember. I do know that I have always been interested in listening to the older generations telling about their experiences, where they came from and some of the joys and heartbreaks they have encountered.

"One day I asked a student in a course I was teaching named Richard Tyler if we could possibly be related. He said his great aunt, Mrs. Breusch, would know much more about the family. I met with her and found that her grandfather came from the area of Paw Paw, Michigan, from where my grandfather and great-grandfather had also come. Each family had come to Michigan from Massachusetts in the 1800s. Mrs. Breusch brought out an old family Bible in which she had death announcements, pictures, and articles pertaining to the Tyler family. Sure enough, her grandfather Samuel G. Tyler and my grandfather were cousins. This was just the information I needed in order to whet my appetite for getting deeper into the study of the Tyler family.

"Norma and I were spending our winters in Florida, and we heard the Tampa library had a good genealogy department. This is where we really began digging for family files. We would often spend eight hours a day there going through family histories, historical references, and other resources looking for the name of Laban Tyler, who was my great-grandfather. One day we discovered that name in an index reference book and questioned the librarian as to where this material was located. She checked and found that the University of Virginia had it, and she said she would send for it, but did not know if it would be just a paragraph, leaflet, or what have you. We anxiously waited for it to arrive. To our surprise, two volumes called *The Tyler Genealogy* arrived. On page 683 was listed my father, aunts, uncles, and grandfather. To me this was the most exciting find. We realized that in the 1800s someone had made a thorough search of my family tree. Now I could take my family roots back well beyond Laban, all the way to Job Tyler, who came to America in 1638 and settled in the Massachusetts Bay Colony area.

"In 1976, we traveled to Massachusetts, having a desire to see the memorial grave in Andover that had been erected in memory of Job, right next to the gravestone of his son, Moses. On our way, we went through the very small town of West Boxford and happened to see a road sign called the Tyler-Kimball Road. There was a small building there which was the town gas station, post office, grocery, and even had four stools for its snack bar. The people inside were very congenial. We questioned them as to what Tyler the road had been named after, and they sent us to see a couple of people who could tell us more about the history of the area. One was the township clerk; she was very helpful in taking us to the cemetery, locating the graves of Tylers. She also told us about the church that stood at the corner. There had been a John Tyler who lived in the area, a bachelor, and when he died he left the sum of $30,000 to the church. Up to this day, this full amount was still in the bank; they had only used the interest all these many years. Just think of the amount of interest that had been drawn over more than two hundred years.

"During our travel that day we had gone past a large Old New England-style house a number of times. The local historian asked us if we knew that was the home that had been built by Moses, son of Job? The name on a sign in front of the home was Witch Hollow Farm. Our curiosity got the best of us, so we stopped to see if the present occupants would talk with us. We were welcomed into the house. They were in the process of renovation to bring it back to the original details as much as possible. The interesting thing is the farm got its name from history, for just beyond the residence in the farm field is where hangings took place for the Salem witch trials. Yes, some of the Tylers were from that period and had been accused, but they had all been acquitted. Take time to read about this period and you will find how small facts can sometimes be blown way out of proportion."

Charles and Norma Tyler, 1976

Copying Volumes I and II

Charles and Norma were able to find Volumes I and II by Brigham in the Tampa library. They were doing extensive research for their new volume but recognized anyone who purchased a Volume III would likely also be interested in owning Volumes I and II, which were not readily available. They decided that since there was no longer a copyright on the first volumes, it would be necessary to make a photocopy of the complete works of these volumes and have them printed, bound, published and made available for sale with Volume III. The library was not willing to release the two volumes to have them copied professionally and did not have the resources to copy them in-house. However, the library did have a copy machine available for public use. Providing themselves with a bag-full of nickels, they began to copy each page on a less-than-adequate-quality copier. Fortunately, it was located away from the library's main desk, so they made as many copies as feasible on the first day. They came back on the following days until the librarians began to realize they had commandeered the copier for a project much too big for its capabilities.

They were in a quandary as what to do, so laid low for a few days, then returned and made fewer copies each time. As the ink level changed over time, some pages were quite readable, and others were not. However, they were stubborn enough to eventually get all 881 pages copied. They were able to prepare the sheets for a printing company and printed a good number of both hardbound and softbound copies. Although the work they put into making a hand-done reprint of Volumes I and II was appreciated by many in the family who bought these copies, it was not too many years when high quality reprints became readily available, making their version obsolete.

Writing and Printing Volume III

In 1985, Charles and Norma were ready to take all of their research that updated the thousands of names in the Brigham volumes and write Volume III. The work became much easier because of the availability of the earliest personal computers. At the time I was a graduate student at the University of Michigan and was willing to do the typing of the content on two conditions: first, they needed to purchase the newest Macintosh 512K computer with word processing software and second, they needed to stay at our home in Ann Arbor long enough for me to complete the typing with them feeding me the information one name at a time. Volume III added another 393 pages to the Brigham genealogy, including the updating or adding of about two thousand names to the 7,724 names in the first two volumes. This was a project that probably could not have been done even a year or two earlier, since it relied heavily on the formatting capabilities of a computer and Microsoft Word software. Volume III was printed and ready for sale in 1985. It was a huge burden taken off their shoulders and mine.

Over the course of their research the Tylers had developed an extensive list of near and distant relatives across the country. To provide coordination with all the resources available, both theirs and that of other Tyler families, they decided to establish a new membership organization, the Job Tyler Family Association. Although there were smaller family organizations scattered across the country, this was the first national organization representing the Job Tyler family heritage since the American Tyler Family Association and its large reunions that were regular events at the turn of the 20th Century. Membership in the Job Tyler Family Association quickly grew to over 230 families. It also led in 1988 to the first of a number of national family reunions—in Massachusetts, Michigan, and California—described in the chapter on family reunions.

Continuing the History: Norman Tyler

With my father's passing in 1989, my mother and I (Norman Raymond Tyler: #9114; Tyler-5642) continued the genealogy activities that had been the focus of my dad's life for many years. We kept up correspondence with hundreds of families that had been connected with us, primarily through the Job Tyler Family Association, an organization that was active in the 1980s and 90s sponsoring a series of reunions in various states, publishing a regular Association newsletter for its hundreds of member families, and serving as a clearing-house for information from families across the country. For another fourteen years, we published articles on a diversity of topics in the Association newsletter and mailed it to the membership. It was quite rewarding to receive letters, queries, and general support from so many individuals who were doing their own family's research, some in considerable depth and some researching only a few generations of their close family members. With changing times, we tried publishing an online edition of the newsletter to save on copy and mailing costs and to give my mother freedom from addressing so many labels by hand. But at that time many of our members could not accept the online format, leaving a gap in the quality of communication.

Eventually, we realized our period of intense involvement was coming to a close and it was time to archive all of the genealogy files and folders by storing them in my attic. This is where they are stored today, along with dozens of paperback copies of our self-published Volume III. Although we would have loved to have transferred all the information to another resource, none was available. I visited the Family History Library of the Latter-Day Saints in Salt Lake City to see if they would accept our collection of Job Tyler Family files. They indicated they would be willing to accept them, but only if we took all the data, with its thousands of names, and put them in the LDS format ourselves. This was too onerous a burden to consider seriously, so the files and folders still sit in multiple file cabinets in my attic, bearing their burden of waiting for a younger researcher to discover them.

Norman Tyler

During this period, I came to the realization I was not as interested in being a genealogist searching for dates of births, marriages, and deaths as I was in exploring information as a family historian. My interest in history has always been strong; I had already written and published a number of books on topics such as historic preservation, Greek Revival architecture, and the history of transcontinental travel.

I became quite intrigued with the idea of researching and writing a narrative history of the family. It would be a gratifying challenge that would utilize the many thoughts, memories, and pieces of information gleaned from working with my parents and communicating with others for so many years. The research and writing became a labor of love, both because it was fascinating to uncover information describing my relatives, but also because so many of them had curious biographies with unique stories to tell. The process of pruning the wealth of available information to actualize a readable document representing the history of the family from its earliest generations to the present was an undertaking I deemed well worth the effort.

I hope you have enjoyed reading about the history of the extended family of immigrant Job Tyler as much as I have enjoyed relating these many stories. The spirit of the family is still strong after all these generations, and it remains our responsibility to convey this knowledge to new generations.

Appendix

During the research and writing of this manuscript many other sources were considered and for various reasons were not directly quoted or used in the narrative. Although the reliability of some of the information could be questioned, the reader should find them curious nonetheless, and to that end they are included in this appendix.

Excerpt from Tyler's Quarterly Historical and Genealogical Magazine, *Volume III, Genealogical Publishing Co., Inc. (1981) p. 770.*

"Doubtless it is well known to many who bear this most ancient surname that, as Mark Antony Lower stated in his 'Patronymica Brittannica,' the surname of Tyler or Tiler was derived from the occupation of the first man in England to whom this surname became applied. The learned etymologists, however, tell us neither when nor where in England the surname originated, nor who were the first to be known by that surname. These points are determinable. One may note that Lower declares that the surname of Tileman (Tillman) originated from exactly the same causes as did the surname of Tyler; also, that he described 'Tylor' as a 'genteel form of Tyler.' Bardsley, the more recent etymologist, agrees with Lower that the first Tyler was a tiler, a maker or layer of tiles, 'one who bakes clay into tiles,' he further avers. Also, he agrees with Skeats, author of an etymological dictionary, that the word tiler is from the Anglo-Saxon tigele, which antedates all British surnames. The Latin form is tegula, from tegere, meaning to cover. Henry Harrison, the most scholarly of the etymologists, agrees with those predecessors, and adds that a 'tylee' or 'tiley' was a dweller at a tile field, and derived from the Old English tigel leah.
An effort has been made to find the actual records of the first Tylers in human history."

Halbert's Family Heritage publishes custom books with immigrant information for the Tyler family in general, based on resources available to them. The World Book of Tylers *includes the bulk of its pages filled with generic information on genealogical research. One section includes a long listing of early immigrants with the surname, Tyler. Although the listing includes many individuals who arrived in places such as Virginia, Maryland, Rhode Island, San Francisco, even Barbados, the following list shows early immigrants who arrived in New England, including sources for this information.*

Nathaniel Tyler arrived in Lynn, Massachusetts, in 1620. Charles Edward Banks. *Topographical Dictionary of 2,885 English Immigrants.* (Baltimore: Genealogical Publishing Company, 1957) 137.

Nathaniel Tyler arrived in Lynn, Massachusetts, in 1642. *Genealogical Register of First Settlers of New England,* Reprint (Baltimore: Genealogical Publishing Company, 1976)) 294.

Abraham Tyler arrived in New England in 1650. John Farmer, "Familles Acadiennes Qui Sont," 294.

Roger Tyler arrived in New Haven, Connecticut, in 1650. Meredith B. Colket, Jr. "Surname Index." *Founders of Early American Families: Emigrants . . .* (Cleveland: General Court of Order, 1975) 299.

Job Tyler arrived in New England in 1653 (Ibid) 294.

Andries Tyler arrived in New York in 1664. John Romeyn Brodhead. "Names of the Dutch Who Swore Allegiance." *Documents Relative to the Colonial History* (Albany, New York: Weed, Parsons & Company, 1853) 77.

William Tyler arrived in New York in 1664 (Ibid) 77.

William Tyler arrived in Connecticut. "English and Welsh Emigrant Index." *The English Genealogist.* volume 4:2 (1981) 371.

The following extended description of the life and personality of immigrant Job is from "Who Was This Jobe Tyler We Read About In Our Annals?", compiled by Alice Pickering Palladini, 1994, for the Mendon Historical Society. Her information comes from the following sources: The Tyler Genealogy by Willard Tyler Brigham; "The Annals of Mendon" by John G. Metcalf; an unpublished manuscript by Gordon Norton; and excerpts from the address given by Rev. Carlton A. Staples on the occasion of the 200th anniversary of Mendon, Massachusetts.[178]

"One of Mendon's early settlers, Jobe Tyler, is found in many places in Ma. & R.I.; Rowley, Andover, Roxbury, Dedham, Newport, Providence & Mendon. As you look at the photograph of this monument, we've all heard about or seen in the woods behind the old Trask property ... and the photo of the grave stones in the Old Cemetery ... for John Tyler and his father Deacon John Tyler, we wonder! Who were these John Tyler's? Were they descendants of one of the first settlers of Mendon, Jobe Tyler, we read about in the Annals? Was the early settler Jobe Tyler their ancestor? After searching several files and sources, I found there was very little written material here in Mendon about this Tyler Family, except what we read in the Annals.

"The first we hear of Jobe in the *Annals of Mendon*, is July 14, 1669. At this time according to other records he was about 50 years old, although a deposition was made in 1659 and his age is stated as 'about 40 yrs.' Reading pg. 43 of the Annals would certainly raise anyone's interest to learn more about this Job Tyler.

"As stated in the *Annals*, 'The Selectmen, it seems, were as careful to look after the spiritual as well as the temporal welfare of their constituents in the olden time, and it is believed it would be of some service, in the present day and generation, if 'the enforcement of the laws' were more punctually executed now. To this end the Selectmen issued the following order: 'Ordered by us to Reade the law to ye youth to exhorte them to the due & carefull observation of the Lord's Day, and that theire parents be desired to doe theire duty herein for the promotinge God's glory theres and theire children's good.'

"Job obviously had different feelings about such obligations, leading to his reprimand. 'One Job Tyler, it seems, had 'carried himself so unworthily' that the Selectmen felt bound to notice the matter, and in order that the authority of the magistrate should be sustained and the laws enforced, on July 14th, 1669, the Selectman met and ordered to send the Constable to summon before us Job Tyler the next fryday at one of the clock at Gregory Cook's house to answer his contempt of our orders and alsoe why he refuses to worke aboute the Selor at the Minister's house, at y^t tyme ye Constable Retourne his answer to us.'[179] When the Constable returned, Job's answer to the Selectman was 'he could not or would not come, but if the Selectman had more to say to him, than he had to say to them, they might come to him!' The Townsmen, upon receiving this answer made a complaint to the Magistrates of Job Tyler's contempt of the Selectman's orders and of his miscarriages of the Lord's Day & at public assemblies, which he does not submit, which he did not. (seems Job Tyler did not attend church nor Town Meetings).

"On Dec. 1st, 1669, Job's shortcomings were condoned as he is on the list, helping to confirm (in his humble way) Rev. Joseph Emerson, the first settled Minister of Mendon. Then later comes an entry in our Annals, 'whereas there has been complaint against Job Tyler heretofore recorded, he has given satisfaction for that offense.' It was said, by Rev. Carlton Staples, 'In the book of Job, that on a certain day when the sons of God came to present themselves before the Lord, Satan came with them.' 'and so it was here, (in Mendon) so it is everywhere.'

"How Jobe Tyler got here, in a territory where 'only honest men and of good report' were permitted to settle is hard to understand (records already showed he had stolen hay from the Indians). Probably he came as Satan usually does 'in the guise of an Angel of Light.' Jobe Tyler was considered by many here in Mendon to be 'Satan's especial representative. Stubborn, Irreverent, Job Tyler!!! Good blood in thee never-the-less! For John, Deacon of the Church was thy Son: and a long line of useful, brave men came of thee.' (Rev. C. Staples. Add.) . . .

"Jobe's Church-goings were not only questioned in Mendon, we find another record in 1680 in Rowley Village, Ma. Jobe, Moses Tyler and many other 'Good-Kickers' against taxes, were duly inspected 'to see if they go to Church.' ('Annals of Andover') Jobe was probably in Andover again in 1681 and then it is found HE was PAYING Minister's rates in Mendon—1688, 1689, 1691, & 1695. It has been said, 'He was a rude, self-asserting, striking personality.' There are but a few highlights in the picture, presented in this report , the shadows are all there. 'He did not learn prudence very fast, but he was himself, . . . he had a good deal of individuality and gave utterance to it at times with more vigor than grace.' (Brigham, _The Tyler Genealogy_)

"He did not shape his words to suit sensitive ears. He resented dictation and found it hard to restrain himself from what he wanted to do in any prudent way. The very first record of Jobe is in 1638 in the R.I. Colony. He was admitted to the town of Newport. A widow Joan Tyler in the R.I. at the same time, has been thought to possibly be Jobe's mother or a widow of a brother John. This John was the progenitor of the R.I. line of Tylers. In 1639, we find Job, in Andover, Ma., a soldiery Squatter (believed to be about 20 yrs. old). A few years later, he was in Roxbury, but he soon returned to Andover: In 1650: In Andover, Job put up his house, land & 3 cows, and other merchantables, such as wheat, rye, etc. for a debt due to John Godfrey. In 1662 in Andover Job Tyler turns his house, in which he lives, barn, land containing 25 acres, 9-acre meadow, for 3 separate bonds he owed said John Godfrey, and if paid the sale would be void.

"Job had many legal problems in Andover, also: 1658, a charge against John Godfrey of witch-craft, and the accuser was Mary wife of Jobe Tyler. John Godfrey was said by historians to be a 'hard-bitted money lender' and hints that they may have had some cause for the bitterness shown by the Tyler family against him. The deposition although sworn in 1659, was brought forward in 1665. Claiming Job abt. age 40. wife Mary and son Moses between 17 & 18 yrs. and a Mary abt. 15 yrs. They witness they saw a thing like a bird to come in at the door of their house, with John Godfrey, in the night. It was about the bigness of a Blackbird, or rather bigger, to wit, as a big Pigeon and did fly about. John Godfrey labouring to catch it and the bird vanished as they said through a chinck of joined board ... This as they remember was 5 or 6 years ago. The Annals of Andover state ... 'this charge was too ridiculous a character to be seriously considered and was discharged.'

". . . Job probably returned to Roxbury, as a birth of a grandson is recorded there in 1676. In 1680, he is again living in Rowley Village, but was back in Mendon prior to 1688, as he was paying Minister rates. Job was now probably about 69 years old. His son Hopestill also was in Mendon, in 1669, and probably remained here, only leaving the 5/6 years of the War.

"1700- The last entry for Job is a deed to his son Moses, for 60 lbs. for land in Mendon. This lot was 15 acres in Ye Township with 5 acres of it, the doubling lot in the 2nd division, 20 acres or more bounded north by Ebenezer Road, South by Samuel Tyler, easterly upon the brook known as Muddy Brook, & west upon the house lot of John Moore, now deceased, and in the possession of Samuel Moore. This land was later granted to John Farnum of Andover (Hopestill's son-in-law) who afterwards settled in Mendon, by Moses Tyler for 61 pounds, in 1701. *The Tyler Genealogy* sums Jobe Tyler up as 'hardly ever has any other immigrant American had such a word picture as this.' Superstitious, willful, hot-tempered, independent and self-reliant. However, he did not have saints to live with; were all the truths known, it would be seen he was on par with a large proportion of his neighbors. The puritan iron rule, which made no allowance for any man, met a sturdy opposition in this possible descendant of Wat Tyler of England, and it is too late to determine if he was always justified.

"From this story there gazes not an ideal but a very real personage, an out & out Yankee Type. He is the progenitor of thousands of descendants, that came down through the years, that were honored, useful in both private & public life, served their country in war & peace, dwellers of city & rural areas, and as you read about his descendants you can't help but believe the old man came from good stock."

- - - - -

"So this importance of the privileged few, helped raise a class of bold, defiant, reckless men, who had no particular interest in the affairs of church, state, or little or nothing to do with the government of the Community. These pioneers considered Church, ministers and its members as linked together to keep them down. At the same time the Church drew a class of men whom religion was only a stepping stone to privilege, and place, and these men were continually bringing it into contempt among honest men. (Rev. C. Staples. Address)

"Was it not these 12 privilege men who in '1672' petitioned the General Court 'to take this poor place' under their immediate care and heal it if possible of the dissentions of its people????? Which brings us back to our subject Jobe Tyler: Questions have arose through the years whether there was one Jobe Tyler or two (could one Jobe Tyler be in so many places causing strife everywhere he went????) Research shows there was only one Jobe Tyler. He had a wife Mary. . . it is said she was the 'widow Horton,' but no proof has been found. No record of his death or her death has been found although all records point to the fact that he died and was buried in Mendon, Ma.

"A Memorial Plaque was dedicated in his honor at the 6th Annual Reunion, by his thousands of descendants. The Memorial was erected Sept. 4, 1901, in Andover, Ma., beside the grave of his eldest son Moses. Upon a boulder, securely riveted, bears the following legend:

"In Memoriam
"Job Tyler
"Immigrant First settler
"Andover about 1639
"Born 1619 : died 1700

"(This is called legend because no records of dates can be found on this couple.)

. . .

"Other legal problems, arose with Thomas Chandler of Andover to whom Job had apprenticed his son Hopestill and which bargain, Job wished to dissolve. Job stole the written signed document, thus giving rise to much criticism, and for 10 years this case was carried from court to court. Finally Job lost the suit and the decision was that Job was "POOR" and should not be fined the 6 pounds, but a penalty was imposed.

"Job had to nail up and fasten upon posts in Andover & Roxbury Meeting Houses for 14 days a confession and acknowledgement as follows. "In brief Job, admitted to have shamefully reproached Thomas Chandler, by saying he was a base, lying, Cozening, cheating knave, that hath got his estate by cozening in a base (cowardly) reviling (abusing) manner & that he was recorded for a liar & that he was cheating, lying whoring knave fit for all manner of bawdery wishing that the devil had him. Job admitted he had been most wicked in this slander and said he was sorry, and that no person should think the worst of Chandler for this sinful expressions. Shortly before this in 1662 Job sold 3 parcels of land, his house and etc. in Andover and removed to Rowley, possibly with a horse he had bargained 12 acres for, leaving it seems like he never was going to return to Andover. Little did he know years later a Memorial would be placed in that town, by his descendants.

"Again we find Job in trouble, this time with the Indians, near Marlborough, they complain the said Jobe Tyler of Roxbury was cutting and carrying hay from their meadows. He was fined with cost, 10 shillings. His wife Mary was dismissed from the Roxbury Church to Mendon, on the 28th day of May 1665. This was probably about the time they came to Mendon. Although none of the Mendon Records show Jobe in this area till 1669. In June 1671 he was among those who drew lots in Mendon 'for doubling of their houselots.' In 1675, and the outbreak of King Philip's War, Job along with the other families, must have buried his pewter, plates and brass kettles in the swamps, loaded the wagons with precious feather beds and children and fled (Tyler Gen.).

"… He had 8 children. The eldest child was born in Roxbury or Andover as probably was the 3rd, 5th, and 6th in Roxbury...other birth places are uncertain: Moses, b. 1641-42 - d. 2 Oct. 1727; Mary Tyler, b. about 1644; Hopestill, b. 1645-1646; Child who died Jan. 28, 1646 (which says a twin child); Hannah; John, b. ca. 1650, Andover - died 28 Sept. 1652; John, b. 16 Apr. 1653 - d. 1742, 90 yrs. (settled Mendon, from him come the better known Tyler line in Mendon and area); and

Samuel, b. May 24, 1655."

Volume I of Brigham's The Tyler Genealogy *includes many stories of Job's colorful years as a young man. One story not included in that narrative is found in the paper, "Early Records of the Tyler Family of Andover," compiled by Charlotte Helen Abbott many years ago.*

"Job left town in 1662, but held Proprietors' rights. He sold 12 acres to Thomas Abbott, possibly the site of the Kittredge place in No. Andover centre. He was in Roxbury, 1665, and there brought suit against Thos. Chandler and John Godfrey.

"On the lands in Roxbury and Natick, the Indians held rights to the graves of their people, and just to get into more trouble, apparently, our Job removed the graves, and was promptly sued for the outrage.

"In 1671 he left for Mendon, and quarreled there with his neighbors, but not so extensively as in Andover. He did a lot of neighborly stunts—helped fix up the meeting house, etc. He helped 'set up' the Rev. John Emerson, 1st pastor at Mendon. He is recorded as giving satisfaction for some offense for which he was overhauled, though it is also noted that when the Selectmen sent for him he sent word that they could come to him if they had any business.

"There were no more controversies, so he must have turned over a new leaf. He is supposed to have skedaddled with the rest in the Indian raid in 1678. The people hid their plate and brass kettles in a swamp, loaded the children and feather beds in carts and on horseback. In 1680 he was in Rowley Village with his son Moses, and both are on the Tax List. He was taxed there from 1688 to 1695, for land in Mendon, which he gave to Moses (#2) in 1700, as recorded in Boston Court.

"The old enmity against John Godfrey again flared in the Witch trials when old Job and Mary, with Moses and daughter Mary, testified that when Jn. Godfrey entered their door a bird flew in—which later disappeared. This was a ridiculous charge and Godfrey was set free."

The following is an excerpt from a recollection of life in the Tyler Homestead written by Arthur Pinkham, who lived there for many years beginning in 1929. He wrote the paper "Memory Hold the Door" for a presentation he gave in 1944 to the Whiting Club. Excerpts from this account give information on Mary Tyler.

"Ghosts, Witches, and Buried Treasure"

"Quartermaster Moses Tyler had a sister Mary, who, it is alleged, has been a frequent visitor in this household during these last three hundred years. Oh, not in the daytime, but in the small hours of the night when the fog blows in from the meadow and when the master is alone in the house.

"He hears her first in the attic opening an old trunk full of papers, yellow with age. He hears her coming down the back stairs. His bedroom door is closed but she doesn't stop to open it. She comes right through the pine panels. As she approaches, he sits right up in bed and holds out his arms to receive her. Why not? She's young and attractive. Did you ever try to hug a ghost? Don't do it! It's not worthwhile.

"Now away back there in 1692, there was a young man named Timothy Swan who came a-courting Mary, but she didn't care for his attentions and every time he came around to call, she refused to see him or to let him in. This was adding insult to injury and he couldn't stand it, so he had her arrested. They took her by oxcart to Salem where she was accused of witchcraft. At her trial she was indicted on two counts:

"First, because she had wickedly made a covenant with the Devil, had signed his book, was baptized by him and had renounced her former Christian baptism, she had become a detestable witch.

"Second, because she practiced certain detestable acts called Witchcraft on one Timothy Swan, he was tortured and afflicted and pined and wasted away.

"The jury found her guilty and sentenced her to death. She languished in jail all summer, but in September she was granted a reprieve, awarded damages of 8 pounds, 14 shillings, and sent back to Boxford.

"According to Charles B. Rice, minister of the First Parish of Salem Village, now Danvers, as many as three or four hundred persons were imprisoned for a space of several months during the Witchcraft Delusion. The first arrests were made in February 1692 and all were finally released by the Governor's Proclamation in May 1693. During those sixteen months of panic, fear and hysteria, nineteen were hanged and one old man was pressed to death.

"The trouble really began in the home of Samuel Parris, pastor of the First Parish. He had been a student at Harvard and later a trader in the West Indies. When, in 1689, he was elected to be the minister, he had in his household a daughter aged nine, a niece aged eleven, also certain servants or slaves of Indian or mixed extraction. The latter he had brought from the West Indies and, as Mr. Rice says, he might better have left them behind. Their heads were full of barbarian beliefs and they were most unfit to be companions of children.

"After a while, a group was formed consisting of these servants, the children of the household and those in the neighborhood. They met evenings in the church and their topics for discussion were murders and darkness and devils and the dead that could not rest in their graves.

"Here was the breeding place of the whole plague. Had the minister given these slaves their freedom and sent them away with his blessing, and had the parents kept their children at home, the Salem Witchcraft would never have been heard of. Instead, the children began to act strangely; they got into an utterly morbid state of mind and body. They were bewitched all right, but not by the people whom they accused. Those poor souls had never claimed preternatural powers or to have any particular acquaintance with the Devil or his works. Furthermore, most of those who suffered death exhibited throughout their trial and imprisonment a genuinely Christian combination of meekness and courage. Their conduct, in most cases, was honorable and blameless."

Taken from Witchcraft in Salem Village, the following is a brief account of the start of "The Witchcraft Delusion."

"In early 1692, Rev. [Samuel] Parris's 9-year-old daughter Elizabeth, 12-year-old niece Abigail Williams, as well as other neighborhood girls began to fall into horrid fits. Their parents tried to discover what was causing their distress, and village doctor William Griggs gave his opinion that the girls were the victims of witchcraft. Put upon to tell who was causing their afflictions, the girls finally accused three village women, and warrants were sworn out for the arrest of Sarah Osburn, Sarah Good and Parris's slave, Tituba.

"On March 1, 1692, magistrates John Hathorne and Jonathan Corwin conducted an examination at the Meeting House. Sarah Good and Sarah Osburn were separately examined and as they answered the questions put to them, the 'afflicted' girls went into horrific fits. To all present, the girls were obviously victims of these women's witchcraft. Though the two protested their own innocence, Tituba unraveled a confession of meeting with the devil and stating there were still other witches in the neighborhood. This evidence was sufficient for the magistrates, and the three women were jailed. The girls' afflictions did not abate, however, and still more villagers became 'afflicted.'

"Soon more accusations were made, and by the end of March Church members Martha Cory and Rebecca Nurse were also arrested, examined and jailed. No longer were just the lowly being accused, but people formerly in good standing in the community. By May, scores of 'witches,' both men and women, had been examined in Salem Village, and jails were being filled with up to 150 accused persons from many towns including Salem, Topsfield and Andover. Dozens of people under excruciating religious, civil and family pressures found themselves confessing to being witches.

"In May, Governor William Phips called a special court to try the cases of those accused witches who had not confessed. Convening in Salem in June 1692, the court quickly condemned Bridget Bishop to death. During July, August and September 18 people, including Nurse, Good and Cory were hanged. In addition, one man, Giles Cory of Salem Farms, died under torture. At least 5 others including Sarah Osburn died in jail. By the new year the colony was becoming exhausted with the witchcraft frenzy, and learned persons were speaking against the validity of 'spectral evidence' being used in court. When the trials resumed, this former evidence was disallowed and proof was insufficient to condemn any other accused. The witch horror was over. Of the 19 people who were executed during this tragic yet heroic period, 12 came from the Salem Village area, dying rather than confessing to what they had not done."

The book, History of Rowley, *Massachusetts, includes a chapter on witchcraft.*[180] *It concludes with the story of the jury trial of Mary Tyler Post Bridges, daughter of Job and Mary Tyler. She was accused of being a witch. An excerpt from this chapter is included here because it describes how the witch trials came to an end.*

"Upon the aforesaid indictments, and each of them, the said Mary [Tyler] Post (#3; Tyler-179) was, then and there, before the Justices of our Lord and Lady, the King and Queen aforesaid, arraigned, and, upon her arraignment, did, then and there, the day and year aforesaid, plead to them and each of them, not guilty, and put herself upon trial by God and her country.

"A jury being called, . . . and accordingly sworn, no exception being made by the prisoner, the said indictments, and each of them, being read, together with evidences and examinations and the prisoner's defence being heard, the jury went out to agree on their verdict, who, returning, did then and there, in open Court, deliver their verdict, that the said Mary Post was guilty of covenanting with the Devill, for which she stood indicted in the second indictment.

"The Court ordered the keeper of the Goale to take care of the prisoner according to law. She soon after this received sentence of death, but was finally reprieved.

"On the second Tuesday of May, 1693, the Court sits at Ipswich. They try and clear several persons accused of witchcraft. Soon after this, the Governor ordered all others accused of witchcraft, and not tried, to be discharged. And here ended the dreadful infatuations, which had possessed the minds of many in the county of Essex. Twenty had been put to death, eleven others condemned for witchcraft, and more than fifty had confessed themselves guilty, most of whom made recantations Over the years there were some challenges to get to this point. The Daughters of the American Revolution dedicated the original plaque in 1941 honoring Tyler and detailing his life in 1941. As time passed, the park fell into disuse and neglect. By the early 1990s, the plaque had disappeared from the concrete base and there was only a small piece of monument left where the flagpole had been."

This section of the Appendix continues with articles about the ghost of Witch Hollow Farm (the Tyler Homestead). It continues here with an account from a book on haunted dwellings and active spirits published in 1986[181]

"The Ghost of the Salem 'Witch': Boxford, Massachusetts"
   Arthur Myers (1986)

"Location: The address of Witch Hollow Farm in 474 Ipswich Road, Boxford.
"Description of place: A beautifully maintained Colonial farmhouse in northeastern Massachusetts built in 1666.
"Ghostly manifestations: The house has been known as a haunted place for many generations. The chief ghost is believed to be Mary Tyler, who was condemned as a witch in Salem in 1693 and had lived in the house as a young woman. The most enthusiastic observer of Mary in recent times has been the late Arthur Pinkham, who lived in the house in the mid-twentieth century. He spoke and wrote extensively in his memoirs of continually seeing the ghost Mary. Pinkham was the grandson of Lydia Pinkham, the inventor of the famed women's tonic. He was president of the Lydia Pinkham Company, based in Lynn, not far from Boxford, for thirty years.

"From 1958, the place was owned by Ed French for twelve years. The Frenches moved to New Hampshire when living in this chic pocket of northeastern Massachusetts got too expensive. French says he saw Mary 'a couple of times' walking from the carriage house toward the main house. This was by night, by the light of the moon. He didn't try to speak to her. 'I was too dumbfounded,' he says. He says she appeared as a young woman.

"Currently living in the house are Steve and Jean Rich and three of their children. The children are in their early twenties. The elder Riches have not seen any ghosts, although they feel presences and hear unexplained noises. Their daughter, Sarah, however, a college student, has had more explicit experiences. At night in her bedroom she would hear rustling. When she turned the light on, nobody would be there. Once she heard a voice whisper her name. 'One night,' she says, 'I turned the light out and felt something come down on top of me. I couldn't move my arms or legs, as though somebody was holding them down. I tried to speak, but something came down over my mouth. I just prayed that it would go away, and after about ten minutes it did.' Another time while lying in bed she felt as though somebody were poking her, but when she turned the light on no one was there. Sometimes she would see a green light as she approached her bedroom, but when she opened the door it would go away. The Frenches also spoke of seeing green light in that room. The elder Riches and Sarah and her brother Bill sometimes would hear a bang in the attic. Sarah says she feels cold spots in the house. On one occasion, she and a friend heard unexplained noises in the kitchen, as though the cupboard doors were being opened and banged shut. The noises stopped when they went into the room. When they returned to the living room, the fire in the huge fireplace had inexplicably blazed up, and the room was full of smoke.

"History: The house was built in 1666 by Moses Tyler. Mary, his sister, lived there until she married Richard Post. She later was accused during the witchcraft hysteria in nearby Salem, but she confessed and was not hanged.

"Identity of ghost(s): Mary Tyler seems the most likely ghostly occupant, but psychics have said there are other ghosts in residence. Sarah Rich feels some of the manifestations of which she has been aware were caused by a male ghost.

"Personalities of ghosts: The current owners feel very much at home in the house, ghosts and all. They feel they are welcomed by the ghosts, although some of Sarah's experiences seem rather negative. There is no record of anyone ever having been hurt by a ghost in the house; however, some visitors to the house have felt they were unwanted, that there were presences that were unfriendly to them. One visitor said she felt ghostly hands pushing her out the door.

"Witnesses: The Riches, Arthur Pinkham, Ed French, and various visitors.

"Best time to witness: The Riches say the ghosts walk by night, when the lights go out.

"Still haunted? Seems to be.

"Investigations: Various professional psychics have felt presences in the house, as have other people who claim psychic sensitivities.

"Data submitted by: The Riches; Ed French; Charles Pinkham, son of Arthur Pinkham; the Essex Institute, a historical museum in Salem; and various others who desire to remain anonymous."

Sometimes the story of an ordinary individual overcoming struggles to make a difference with their life can be as edifying as someone being born into wealth and privilege and making a difference using those resources. The simple story of Inez Melissa Tyler (no number) reminds us we can all make a difference.

"Inez was born in 1897 on the Winnebago Indian Reservation in Nebraska on land her father had leased. Her parents, Edward Stephen Tyler and Ella May Snyder Tyler, brought their eleven children to Oregon in 1900 and homesteaded in Heppner. After her father's untimely death from pneumonia in 1903, the family moved to Salem so the children could go to school. Young Inez lived in a tent with her family for three summers picking fruit to earn money for food, books, and clothing.

"Inez earned a B.A. degree from the University of Oregon and a Master of Arts degree from the University of Chicago's School of Social Service Administration. She worked in programs helping the poor and sick in New York, the Northwest, and Arizona. She taught courses in social work at the University of Hawaii and the University of Washington.

"In 1955, she became the first medical social worker to the Navajo Indian Nation. In 1964, he received a Superior Service medal for her work there from the U.S. Department of Health, Education, and Welfare. She died in 1977 at 99 years old after giving a life of service."

There have been many researchers who suggest a link between the lineage of President John Tyler and immigrant Job Tyler. At this time, it is not clear whether any of those linkages have stood the test of time and review by other researchers.

One argument showing such a connection has been submitted by Debbie Parsons on the Worldconnect Project.182 She has represented Job having two brothers, Henry and William. According to this source, it is Job's brother Henry (Worldconnect ID: 121087) who settled in Virginia and is the forebear of the President. Henry was born ca. 1620 in Shropshire, England, and died ca. 1672 in York County, Virginia. In Volume III of the Virginia Land Register is the record of a Patent in Henry Tyler's name dated January 7, 1652, locating 254 acres in Middle Plantation, Virginia, due to him by and for transporting to this colony six persons. Henry is a descendant of Wat Tyler, according to G. C. Greer in his "Early Virginia Immigrants." Henry Tyler lived in the outskirts of what is now the city of Williamsburg, Virginia. The three children of Henry and Anne went on to have many descendants.

There is perhaps a stronger argument against any definable connection based on the genealogy of Henry Tyler of Shropshire, England. As portrayed on geni.com,

"Henry was NOT the son of Laurence and Dorothy Joan Tyler. DNA has proven they were not connected by blood.183

"Henry Tyler lived in the outskirts of what is now the city of Williamsburg, Virginia.

"At June Court 1672, Ann Tyler his relic [widow], (Henry), entered a record of Deed of Gift disposing of her separate estate among her three sons, Henry, John and Daniel. There were no heirs by his first wife Mary. Two children of Henry and Anne went on to have many descendants: His oldest son, Henry Tyler stayed in VA and his line is the 10th President John Tyler's line. This line of John Tyler's can be considered "The Southern Tylers". The Tylers migrated heavily after the Revolutionary War, to Texas, Missouri, Mississippi and Louisiana.

"In 1-7-1652 Henry was granted 254 Acres of land for importing himself and wife Mary and 4 other persons to Middle Plantation, VA. He was the original grantee of land upon which the Governor's palace was erected, where it now stands. He was also a sheriff, coroner and Justice of the Peace in 1658. He was a churchman of Bruton parish, an architect, aristocrat, wealthy and educated man. See the Letters and Times of Tylers, Vol. 36-37.

"In 1658 he married Ann ORCHARD, in York Co., VA" "Henry Tyler, a descendant of Wat Tyler, came to VA before 1645. He was "patented" 254 acres of land at Middle Plantation, which is today's Williamsburg. In 1653 he was a Justice of the Peace in York Co."[184]

The evidence of no documented connection is further shown through a listing of John Tyler's ancestors going back eight generations. This ancestry can be found at the web site, famouskin.com, "Ancestry of John Tyler: 10th U.S. President."

Endnotes

[1] Referring to Jack Lindsay, *Nine Days' Hero: Wat Tyler* (London: Dennis Dobson, 1964).

[2] Walter G. Davis. *The New England Historical and Genealogical Register*" (Portland, Maine, January 1961). This will is also found in the Hartford Times, D-561-(1) D. K. M. Ref.,: N. E. H. and G. Reg. Vol CXV.

[3] "England Births and Christenings, 1538-1975," database, FamilySearch (https://familysearch.org/ark:/61903/1:1:NJRJ-B36 : 11 February 2018, John Tyler,); citing Cranbrook, Kent, England, index based upon data collected by the Genealogical Society of Utah, Salt Lake City; FHL microfilm 2,228,373.

[4] "England Births and Christenings, 1538-1975," database, FamilySearch (https://familysearch.org/ark:/61903/1:1:N1N2-H48 : 11 February 2018, Joab Tyler,); citing Cranbrook, Kent, England, index based upon data collected by the Genealogical Society of Utah, Salt Lake City; FHL microfilm 2,228,373.

[5] "England Births and Christenings, 1538-1975," database, FamilySearch (https://familysearch.org/ark:/61903/1:1:J7GQ-YTT : 11 February 2018, Moses Tyler,); citing Cranbrook, Kent, England, index based upon data collected by the Genealogical Society of Utah, Salt Lake City; FHL microfilm 1,751,814.

[6] "England Births and Christenings, 1538-1975," database, FamilySearch (https://familysearch.org/ark:/61903/1:1:NJRJ-16P : 11 February 2018, Mary Tyler,); citing Cranbrook, Kent, England, index based upon data collected by the Genealogical Society of Utah, Salt Lake City; FHL microfilm 2,228,373.

[7] Family History Library microfilm 1866585

[8] https://gw.geneanet.org/woodybillie?lang=en&v=TYLER&m=N

[9] Lois Kimball Mathews. *The Expansion of New England: The Spread of New England Settlement and Institutions to the Mississippi River, 1620-1865* (New York: Russell & Russell, Inc., 1962) 22a.

[10] John C. Hotten. *The Original Lists of Persons of Quality ... 1600-1700* (Baltimore, 1980) reprinted from 1874, pp. 119-21.

[11] Research and compilation of transport information was by Anne Stevens and found at packrat-pro.com/ships/globe.htm

[12] From "Ancestors of David Lee Archibald" (Accessed: https://www.genealogy.com/ftm/a/r/c/David-Lee-Archibald/GENE1-0018.html, 12 April 2019).

[13] Casady, Thomas Edgar. *Moses Coit Tyler: A Critical Biography* (Ann Arbor, Michigan: University of Michigan, 1929)

[14] Bill Dalton, "Dalton Column: Job Tyler, Andover's original pioneer?" Andover Townsman, 24 January 2013 (Accessed: *https://www.andovertownsman.com/community/dalton-column-job-tyler-andover-s-original-pioneer/article_dfbac6c4-c015-5a36-b85e-057bfd8845a8.html*, 15 December 2018).

[15] Photo of old Abbot homestead, built in 1600s, from "Early Settlers of Andover, Massachusetts" project (accessed: https://www.geni.com/photo/view?album_type=project&photo_id=6000000041809100857&project_id=33999, 5 May 2019). (Permission needed ??)

[16] (Accessed: https://www.mhl.org/sites/default/files/files/Abbott/Tyler%20Family.pdf, 15 December 2018).

[17] *Register of the New England Historic Genealogical Society*, Volume 115 (January 1961).

[18] From a letter sent by Edward M. Tyler (#7720-2) in 1976 from Baldwin, New York. He talks about a letter written sometime before 1924 by Ann M. Tyler (#7719).

[19] "52 Ancestors 2015 #13 Job Tyler—Described as 'evil incarnate'" (Accessed: https://kessgen.wordpress.com/2015/03/28/52-ancestors-2015-13-job-tyler-described-as-evil-incarnate/, posteed 28 March, 2015).

[20] Bill Dalton, "Dalton Column: Job Tyler, Andover's original pioneer?" Andover Townsman, 24 January 2013 (Accessed: *https://www.andovertownsman.com/community/dalton-column-job-tyler-andover-s-original-pioneer/article_dfbac6c4-c015-5a36-b85e-057bfd8845a8.html*, 15 December 2018).

[21] www.genealogy.com/ftm/m/a/c/Dana-Duff/WEBSITE-0001/UHP-0197.html. (Note: No name to ask for permission.)

[22] Sidney Perley. *The History of Boxford, Essex County, Massachusetts, from the Earliest Settlement Known to the Present Time: A Period of About Two Hundred and Thirty Years* (Boxford, Massachusetts: Published by the author, 1880).

[23] Sidney Perley. *The History of Boxford, Essex County, Massachusetts, from the earliest settlement known to the present time: a period of about two hundred and thirty years* (Boxford, Massachusetts: Published by author, 1880). 108.

[24] Sidney Perley. *History of Boxford* (Boxford, Massachusetts: Published by author, 1880). 110.

[25] Ibid. 111.

[26] From Elizabeth Sanborn Pearl, *Memories of West Boxford.* 5-6.

[27] Sidney Perley. *History of Boxford* (Boxford, Massachusetts: Published by author, 1880). 337-8.

[28] Willard Tyler Brigham. Excerpt from a presentation on the history of the Tyler Homestead given at the Tyler Family Association Reunion of 1896 that took place in North Andover, Massachusetts.

[29] Williard Tyler Brigham. Excerpt from a presentation on the history of the Tyler Homestead given at the Tyler Family Association Reunion of 1897 in New Haven, Connecticut.

[30] "52 Ancestors 2015 #13 Job Tyler." (28 March 2015) (Accessed: https://kessgen.wordpress.com/2015/03/28/52-ancestors-2015-13-job-tyler-described-as-evil-incarnate/).

[31] Taken from the article, "Colonial houses of Boxford," on the "Historic Ipswich" web site, (Accessed: https://historicipswich.org/2017/03/23/colonial-houses-of-boxford/).

[32] Willard Tyler Brigham. Excerpt from a presentation on the history of the Tyler Homestead given at the Tyler Family Association Reunion of 1897 in New Haven, Connecticut. p. 47.

[33] Willard Tyler Brigham. Excerpt from a presentation on the history of the Tyler Homestead given at the Tyler Family Association Reunion of 1897 in New Haven, Connecticut. p. 47.

[34] Norman Tyler. *Job Tyler Family Association Newsletter.* September, 1994.

[35] Excerpts are from a two-page personal paper describing aspects of the Tyler family heritage in West Boxford written by Mrs. Charles Austin, 1971.

[36] From Proprietors' Records, Mendon, Massachusetts.

[37] Brigham, Willard I. Tyler. *The Tyler Genealogy: The Descendants of Job Tyler of Andover, Massachusetts, 1619–1700.* (Publishers: Cornelius B. Tyler of Plainsfield, New Jersey, and Bollin U. Tyler of Tylerville, Connecticut, 1912)

[38] W. I. Tyler Brigham, Emma E. Brigham, William E. Brigham. *The History of the Brigham Family: Descendants of Thomas Brigham,* a Continuation of the 1907 and 1927 Volumes by W. I. Tyler Brigham and Emma Elisabeth Brigham (Boston: Newberry Street Press, 2010).

[39] Excerpt from a speech given by Willard I. Tyler Brigham at the Fifth Annual American Tyler Family Reunion, Philadelphia, Pennsylvania, 1900.

[40] Emma Elizabeth Brigham. "Willard Irving Tyler Brigham." *The Grafton Magazine of History and Genealogy,* Volume 1 (New York: The Grafton Press, 1908-9) 29.

[41] *The Houston Post.* 30 December 1906 (page 34).

[42] Source unknown.

[43] Both volumes are available for free online through Google books. They are found at: https://books.google.com/books/about/The_Tyler_Genealogy.html?id=WhQfAAAAMAAJ and https://books.google.com/books/about/The_Tyler_Genealogy.html?id=Jx4bAAAAYAAJ

[44] Source: Justin H. Petrosek. Wikimedia Commons. File: Boxforde ma highlight.png (Accessed: https://commons.wikimedia.org/wiki/File:Boxford_ma_highlight.png, 10 October, 2019).

[45] Photo courtesy of Barbara Poole, FindAGrave (Accessed: https://www.findagrave.com/memorial/7868366/moses-tyler, 10 October 2019).

[46] Excerpt from the program of the American Tyler Family Reunion of 1896, held in Andover, Massachusetts.

[47] Colonel O. S. Tyler. *Sweet Land of Liberty: One Family's Saga in Colonial America* (Pompano Beach, Florida: Exposition Press of Florida, Inc., 1987) 80–97 (permission to use excerpts given by Col. Tyler).

[48] From the American Tyler Family Association Reunion of 1896, p. 5.

[49] Gretchen Gibbs. *The Book of Maggie Bradstreet* (Warwick, New York: Glenmere Press, 2012).

[50] "Witchcraft at Salem Village.jpg" William A. Crafts (1876), Published by Samuel Walker and Company (Public domain).

[51] Accessed: http://whitsettandwall.com/Tyler/Tyler_Salem_Witch_Trials.htm, 12 April 2019.

[52] Wesley Tyler. "Job Tyler instigator, Mary Tyler a Witch, let the witch hunts begin." (Accessed: http://wesleytyler.com/2013/11/job-tyler-instagator-mary-tyler-witch.html, 11 April 2019).

[53] The digest of the "recantation" obtained from Hopestill Tyler's wife by the Rev. Increase Mather, the same being followed by *Bailey's Sketches of Andover* Sarah Loring Bailey. *Historical Sketches of Andover, (Comprising the present towns of North Andover and Andover, Massachusetts)* (Boston: Houghton, Mifflin and Company, 1880) 222-223.

[54] Wesley Tyler. "Job Tyler instigator, Mary Tyler a Witch, let the witch hunts begin." (Accessed: http://wesleytyler.com/2013/11/job-tyler-instagator-mary-tyler-witch.html, 11 April 2019).

[55] Source unknown.

[56] Samuel Adams Drake. *A Book of New England Legends and Folk Lore: In Prose and Poetry*, Revised edition (Rutland, Vermont: Charles E. Tuttle Company, 1884, revised 1906, 1985) 189.

[57] Wesley Tyler. "Job Tyler instigator, Mary Tyler a Witch, let the witch hunts begin." (Accessed: http://wesleytyler.com/2013/11/job-tyler-instagator-mary-tyler-witch.html, 11 April 2019).

[58] "Nathaniel and Abigail Andrews Tyler" found in "Aunt Roma's Family History. (Accessed: http://www.auntroma.com/nathaniel-tyler-and-abigail-andrews.html, 15 December 2018).

[59] Thomas Williams Bicknell. *A History of Barrington, Rhode Island* (Providence, Rhode Island: Snow & Farnum, printers, 1898) 584. (Accessed: http://dunhamwilcox.net/ri/barrington_ri_bios1.htm, 26 April 2019).

[60] Thomas Williams Bicknell. *A History of Barrington, Rhode Island* (Providence, Rhode Island: Snow & Farnum, printers, 1898) 396-97.

[61] Based on information from Edwin Tyler and written by Barbara F. Dyer in her history of "The Tyler Family." (Accessed: https://knox.villagesoup.com/p/the-tyler-family/824168, 15 December 2018).

[62] Carroll E. Smith and Charles Carroll Smith. *Pioneer Times* (Bibliobazaar, 1904, republished 2009).

[63] Hibernicus (DeWitt Clinton). "Letters on the Natural History and Internal Resources of the State of New York" (New York: E. Bliss & E. White, 1822) 123.

[64] Thomas Perkins Abernethy. *The Burr Conspiracy* (New York: Oxford University Press, 1954) 149.

[65] Ibid. 62.

[66] Ibid. 102-3.

[67] "To Dr. Joseph Priestley Washington, Jan. 29, 1804." University of Groningen, Humanities Computing (Accessed: http://www.let.rug.nl/usa/presidents/thomas-jefferson/letters-of-thomas-jefferson/jefl161.php, 10 September 2019).

[68] Photo courtesy of West Virginia State Parks.

[69] Walter Flavius McCaleb. *The Aaron Burr Conspiracy and a New Light on Aaron Burr* (New York: Argosy-Antiquarian Ltd, 1966) 205.

[70] Ibid. 207.

[71] Ibid. 217.

[72] Ibid. 218.

[73] Ibid. 220.

[74] Joseph P. Brady. *The Trial of Aaron Burr* (New York: The Neale Publishing Company, 1913) 10-11.

[75] Ibid. 43.

[76] James E. Lewis, Jr. *The Burr Conspiracy: Uncovering the Story of an Early American Crisis* (Princeton, New Jersey: Princeton University Press, 2017) 161.

[77] Ibid. 390.

[78] Hibernicus (DeWitt Clinton). "Letters on the Natural History and Internal Resources of the State of New York" (New York: E. Bliss & E. White, 1822) 7.

[79] Excerpts from a brochure written by Richard N. Wright, with assistance from the Onondaga Historical Association

[80] Mrs. Theodore Roosevelt and Kermit Roosevelt. *The Story of Gertrude Tyler and Her Family, 1660–1860* (New York: Charles Scribner's Sons, 1928), 30-32.

[81] Ibid. 32-34.

[82] Ibid. 34-35.

[83] Ibid. 34.

[84] Ibid. 36-37.

[85] Ibid. 38.

[86] Sidney Perley. *The Dwellings of Boxford: Essex County, Massachusetts* (Salem, Massachusetts: The Essex Institute, 1893) 37-38.

[87] Brigham, Willard I. Tyler. *The Tyler Genealogy: The Descendants of Job Tyler of Andover, Massachusetts, 1619–1700.* (Publishers: Cornelius B. Tyler of Plainsfield, New Jersey, and Bollin U. Tyler of Tylerville, Connecticut, 1912) 193-4.

[88] Photo attribution to Dudesleeper at English Wikipedia.

[89] "The Story of Mary and Her Little Lamb: As told by Mary and Her Neighbors and Friends, to which is added a critical analysis of the poem." (Dearborn, Michigan: published by Mr. and Mrs. Henry Ford, 1928).

[90] John Cunningham Wood and Michael C. Wood (editors). *Henry Ford: Critical Evaluations in Business and Management,* Volume 1 (New York: Routledge, Taylor and Francis Group, 2003) 120.

[91] Music cover, "The Village Blacksmith" (1848) (Library of Congress, Reproduction Number LC-USZ62-8299).

[92] "The Village Blacksmith." Gulf Coast Blacksmith Association (Accessed: gulfcoastblacksmith.com/discoveries-gallery/the-village-blacksmith-2/2/, 4 June 2019).

[93] Source unknown.

[94] M. E. Bond web site (Accessed: http://www.mebondbooks.com/2015/09/07/poetry-in-context-the-village-blacksmith/ 4 June 2019).

[95] Brigham, Willard I. Tyler. *The Tyler Genealogy: The Descendants of Job Tyler of Andover, Massachusetts, 1619–1700.* (Publishers: Cornelius B. Tyler of Plainsfield, New Jersey, and Bollin U. Tyler of Tylerville, Connecticut, 1912) 72, 73.

96 Ibid. 73.

97 Hildreth, M. D., S. P. *Biographical and Historical Memoirs of the Early Pioneer Settlers of Ohio, with Narratives of Incidents and Occurrences in 1775* (Cincinnati, Ohio: H. W. Derby & Co., Publishers, 1852) 398.

98 Andrews, Martin A. (Editor). *History of Marietta and Washington County, Ohio and Representative Citizens* (Chicago: Biographical Publishing Company, 1902) 504.

99 Charles R., and Norma L., and Norman R. Tyler. *The Descendants of Job Tyler Since 1619* (Zephyrhills, Florida: Self-published, 1985) 12-15.

100 Frederick William Coburn. *History of Lowell and Its People, Volume 1* (New York: Lewis Historical Publishing Company, 1920) 144, from Alan Seaburg. *Life on the Middlesex Canal* (Billerica, Massachusetts: Ann Miniver Press, 2009).

101 Bill Gerber. "Scofflaws on the Canal." *Towpath Topics*, Volume 48, No. 3. (Billerica, Massachusetts: Middlesex Canal Association, April 2010).

102 *History of St. Joseph County, Mihigan, with Illustrations Descriptive of Its Scenery, Palatial Residences, Public Buildings, Fine Blocks, and Important Manufactures.* (Philadelphia: L. H. Everrts & Co., 1877) 166.

103 From *History of St. Joseph County, Michigan*, with Illustrations Descriptive of Its Scenery, Palatial Residences, Public Buildings, Fine Blocks, and Important Manufactories. (Philadelphia: L. H. Everts & Co., 1877) 166.

104 Sergeant Daniel Tyler. *A Concise History of the Mormon Battalion in the Mexican War: 1846-1847* (Published by author, 1881).

105 Milo Milton Zuaife, ed., *The Diary of James K. Polk during His Presidency, 1845 to 1849*, 4 volumes (Chicago: A. C. McClurg & Co., 1910.

106 "Tyler, Daniel, [Autobiographical sketch], in Autographical accounts by Beaver residents [ca. 1897], 51-52. (Accessed: https://history.churchofjesuschrist.org/overlandtravel/sources/36958960623302380000-eng/tyler-daniel-autobiographical-sketch-in-autobiographical-accounts-by-beaver-residents-ca-1879-51-52?firstName=Daniel&surname=Tyler, 2 July 2019).

107 Elde Lance B. Wickman, "From Iowa to Immortality: A Tribute to the Mormon Battalion" (Accessed: https://www.lds.org/ensign/2007/07/from-iowa-to-immortality-a-tribute-to-the-mormon-battalion?lang=eng, 17 December 2018).

108 Daniel Tyler, A Concise History of the Mormon Battalion in the Mexican War (Glorieta, New Mexico: Rio Grande Press, 1881), 146.

109 From "Aunt Roma's Family History" (Accessed: http://www.auntroma.com/daniel-and-ruth-welton-tyler.html, 2 July 2019).

110 Charles R., Norma L., and Norman R. Tyler. *The Descendants of Job Tyler Since 1619.* (Ann Arbor, Michigan: Self-published, 1985) 67-69.

111 "Charles Marion Tyler." Find-A-Grave.com (Accessed 3 July 2019.)

112 William K. Goolrick and the Editors of Time-Life Books. *Rebels Resurgent: Fredericksburg to Chancellorsville.* (Alexandria, VA: Time-Life Books, 1985) 92-93.

113 Larry Tagg. *The Generals of Gettysburg: The Leaders of America's Greatest Battle* (Cambridge, Massachusetts: Da Capo Press, 1998) 190.

114 *Memoir of Brevet Major-General Robert Ogden Tyler, U. S. Army, Together with His Journal of Two Months' Travel in British and Farther India* (Philadelphia: J. B. Lippincott & Co., 1878) 15.

115 *Memoir of Brevet Major-General Robert Ogden Tyler, U. S. Army, Together with His Journal of Two Months' Travel in British and Farther India* (Philadelphia: J. B. Lippincott & Co., 1878) 19-20.

116 Frederic Rosengarten, Jr., *Freebooters Must Die: The Life and Death of William Walker, The Most Notorious Soldier of Fortune of the Nineteenth Century* (Haverford, Pennsylvania: Haverford Press, 1976).

117 From listverse.com, "10 Filibusters and Military Adventurers from History" (Accessed: https://listverse.com/2015/10/11/10-filibusters-and-military-adventurers-from-history/, 17 April 2019).

[118] According to some historians, after the Civil War the Knights of the Golden Table went underground and became a secret society. They claim that the Knight's new mission was to support a second, former confederate, uprising against the United States Federal Government.

[119] Stuart W. Sanders. "Robert Charles Tyler: Last American Civil War Confederae General Slain in Combat (Accessed: https://www.historynet.com/robert-charles-tyler-last-american-civil-war-confederate-general-slain-in-combat.htm, 9 April 2019).

[120] From video of Bill Corminy, 2 March 2018 (Accessed: https://www.youtube.com/watch?v=BO90GGZVMfs, 11 October 2109).

[121] Thomas Edgar Casady and Howard Mumford Jones. *The Life of Moses Coit Tyler* (Ann Arbor, Michigan: University of Michigan Dissertation, 1933) 21-22.

[122] Ibid. 52-53.

[123] Ibid. 55.

[124] Ibid. 74.

[125] Ibid. 78-79.

[126] Ibid. 153-4.

[127] Ibid. 109.

[128] Ibid. 153-4.

[129] Brian Hale, Amazon review, 5 April, 2015.

[130] Thomas Edgar Casady and Howard Mumford Jones. *The Life of Moses Coit Tyler* (Ann Arbor, Michigan: University of Michigan Dissertation, 1933) 220.

[131] Moses Coit Tyler. *Patrick Henry* (Cambridge, Massachusetts: The Riverside Press, 1887) 709-10.

[132] Israel Smith Clare. *The World's History, Illuminated* (St. Louis: Western Newspaper Syndicate, 1897), Introduction.

[133] Thomas Edgar Casady and Howard Mumford Jones. *The Life of Moses Coit Tyler* (Ann Arbor, Michigan: University of Michigan Dissertation, 1933) 269.

[134] Charles Mellen Tyler. *Bases of Religious Belief Historic and Ideal: An Outline of Religious Study* (New York: G. P. Putnam's Sons, 1897) v. (note: Text available online)

[135] W. Douglas Mackenzie, Reviewer. *The American Journal of Theology*, Vol. 2, No. 2 (April 1898) 398.

[136] Morris Bishop. *A History of Cornell* (Ithaca, New York: Cornell University Press, 2014).

[137] Source: Records, p. 1043, February 12, 1919, Cornell University Faculty Memorial Statement, 15 May 1918 (Accessed: http://ecommons.library.cornell.edu/handle/1813/17813, 12 April 2019).

[138] Brigham, Willard I. Tyler. *The Tyler Genealogy: The Descendants of Job Tyler of Andover, Massachusetts, 1619–1700.* (Publishers: Cornelius B. Tyler of Plainsfield, New Jersey, and Bollin U. Tyler of Tylerville, Connecticut, 1912) 461-2.

[139] *The Villisca Review.* 27 July 1905, p. 4.

[140] *Boot and Shoe Recorder.* 11 May 1898.

[141] From a circuit court case protecting the Tyler Hinged Last patent.

[142] Michael Preston Worley. "Franklin Tyler Wood." AskART (Accessed: http://www.askart.com/artist_bio/Franklin_Tyler_Wood/65266/Franklin_Tyler_Wood.aspx, 18 October 2019).

[143] This description of the life of Franklin Tyler Wood is taken from an article written by Michael James Thomas in 1996 as part of a show of Wood's work at the R.H. Love Galleries in Chicago.

[144] National Register Nomination Form, George F. Tyler Mansion, Bucks County

[145] The biographical information on Chaplin Tyler is blended from a number of articles submitted by Marion Lee Tyler Solokov.

[146] Karen Feldscher. "From One Centarian . . . To Another" (Accessed 20 March 2019, www.northeastern.edu/magazine/9809/chaplin.html).

[147] UD Daily Archive. "In Memoriam: Chaplin Tyler." 3 March 2004.

[148] Mrs. Theodore Roosevelt and Kermit Roosevelt. *The Story of Gertrude Tyler and Her Family, 1660–1860* (New York: Charles Scribner's Sons, 1928).

[149] Ibid. 3-7.

[150] Photo from JudyH, FindAGrave (Accessed: https://www.findagrave.com/memorial/141827797/gertrude-elizabeth-carow, 20 October 2019).

[151] Brady-Handy Collection, Library of Congress, Reproduction ID cph.3a26697.

[152] The letter is from the Theodore Roosevelt Center at Dickinson State University (Accessed: https://www.theodorerooseveltcenter.org/Research/Digital-Library/Record?libID=o283516, 17 December 2018).

[153] Library of Congress, ID LC-DIG-ppmsca-37316.

[154] Dr. Jeremiah Spofford. *A Genealogical Record, Including Two Generations in Female Lines of Families Spelling Their Name Spofford, Spafford, Spafard,and Spaford, Descendants of John Spofford and Elizabeth Scott, Who Emigratedd, in 1638, from Yorkshire, England, and Settled at Rowley, Essex County, Mass.* (Boston: Alfred Mudge & Son, 1888) 46.

[155] Much of the information on the life of Ann Drusilla (Tyler) Holmes is taken from the biography of Harry Truman, by Jonathan Daniels. *The Man of Independence* (Columbia, Missouri: University of Missouri Press, 1998) 31-33.

[156] From *The Inter Ocean* (Chicago, Illinois) 9 September 1898, page 8.

[157] From *The Evening Times* (Washington, D. C.) 11 September 1899.

[158] From the *Richmond Dispatch* (Richmond, Virginia) 14 September 1899.

[159] From *The Junction City Weekly Union* (Junction City, Kansas), 3 November 1899, page 5.

[160] From the *New York Tribune*, 14 September 1900, page 8.

[161] From *The Times* (Washington, D. C.) 3 September 1900. page 3.

[162] From *The Evening Star* (Independence, Kansas) 26 January 1904.

[163] From *The Tacoma Times* (Tacoma, Washington) 22 January 1904, page 2.

[164] Marvin Tyler, personal records.

[165] "Tyler Family DNA Pro" (Accessed: https://www.familytreedna.com/groups/tyler/about/results, 29 March 2019).

[166] "Archives" (Accessed: https://www.archives.com/genealogy/family-history-tyler.html, 29 March 2019).

[167] *Genealogies of Virginia Families: From Tyler's Quarterly Historical and Genealogical Magazine.* Introduction by John Frederick Dorman (Baltimore, Maryland: Genealogical Publishing Company, Inc., 1981) 771.

[168] Houseofnames.com. "Tillieres History, Family Crest & Coats of Arms (Accessed: https://www.houseofnames.com/tillieres-family-crest, 12 October 2019).

[169] Matthew Hale. *The Norman People and Their Existing Descendants in the British Dominions and the United States of America* (London: Henry S. King & Co., 1874) 437.

[170] Maps derived from https://www.ancestry.com/name-origin?surname=tyler.

[171] www.meaning-of-names.com/english-names/tyler.asp

[172] "Behind the Name," based on 1990 United States Census (Accessed: https://surnames.behindthename.com/names/list, 25 March 2019)

[173] Based on data from the United States Government Social Security Administration.

[174] *Heraldic Journal*, Volume III, 83.

[175] Source unknown.

[176] Bill Castanier. "1920s Michigan: Klan country?" *Citypulse* (Lansing, Michigan) (Accessed: https://lansingcitypulse.com/print-article-5626-permanent.html, 14 December 2018).

[177] Drawing by Larry Tyler.

[178] (Accessed: https://wc.rootsweb.com/cgi-bin/igm.cgi?op=GET&db=james_s_mills_jr&id=1650, 14 December 2018)

[179] John G. Metcalf, M. D., *Annals of the Town of Mendon from 1659 to 1880* (Providence, Rhode Island: E. L. Freeman & Co., 1880) 43.

[180] Thomas Gage and James Bradford. The History of Rowley: Anciently Including Bradford, Boxford, and Georgetown, from the Year 1639 to the Present Time (published before 1923 and now in the public domain) 177-178.

[181] Arthur Myers. *The Ghostly Register: Haunted Dwellings—Active Spirits; A Journey to America's Strangest Landmarks* (Chicago: Contemporary Books, Inc., 1986) 30. (Accessed: https://archive.org/search.php?query=creator%3A%22Arthur+Myers%22, 18 October 2019).

[182] Note: Access to worldconnect.genealogy.rootsweb.com is no longer available online. Info from Rebecca Tyler Allen -- Rebalexa@aol.com

[183] See http://boards.ancestry.com/surnames.tyler/1856/mb.ashx.

[184] Biography of Henry Tyler, geni.com, Kevin Lawrence Hanit, site manger (Accessed: https://www.geni.com/people/Henry-Tyler/6000000002979903448, 10 July 2019). See also "Tyler Family History, accessed: http://freepages.genealogy.rootsweb.ancestry.com/~nfurbish/tylerregister.htm, 10 July 2019).

Bibliography

Books/articles with photos and/or information on the Job Tyler family lineage

Anderson, Robert Charles. *The Great Migration Begins: Immigrants to New England, 1620-1633* (3 volumes, Boston 1995).

Banks, Charles Edward. *Topographical Dictionary of 2,285 English Emigrants to New England, 1620-1650* (Baltimore, 1957).

Brigham, Willard I. Tyler. *The Tyler Genealogy: The Decendants of Job Tyler of Andover, Massachusetts, 1619–1700*. Cornelius B. Tyler of Plainsfield, New Jersey, and Bollin U. Tyler of Tylerville, Connecticut (Publishers), 1912. (The major genealogical source for Job Tyler line)

Chalkin, Christopher W. *Seventeenth-Century Kent* (London, 1965).

"Founders of New England." *The New England Historical and Genealogical Register.* 14:316 (1860).

Hotten, John C. *the Original Lists of Persons of Quality ... 1600-1700* (Baltimore, 1980) reprinted from 1874.

Jones, Howard Mumford. *The Life of Moses Coit Tyler: Based upon an unpublished dissertation from original sources by Thomas Edgar Casady*, Ann Arbor, Michigan: The University of Michigan Press, 1933.

Lewis, James E., Jr. *The Burr Conspiracy: Uncovering the Story of an Early American Crisis*. Princeton, New Jersey: Princeton University Press, 2017.

Pearl, Elizabeth Sanborn. *Memories of West Boxford*. North Andover, Massachusetts: Eagle-Tribune Printing, 1978. (Stories of Tylers and others)

Perley, Sidney. *The Dwellings of Boxford: Essex County, Massachusetts*. Salem, Massachusetts: The Essex Institute, 1893. (Descriptions of Tyler houses and properties)

Perley, Sidney. *The History of Boxford, Essex County, Massachusetts, from the Earliest Settlement Known to the Present Time: A Period of About Two Hundred and Thirty Years* (Boxford, Massachusetts: Published by the author, 1880).

Roosevelt, Mrs. Theodore and Kermit Roosevelt. *The Story of Gertrude Tyler and Her Family, 1660–1860*. New York: Charles Scribner's Sons, 1928. (Personal reminiscences of Daniel Tyler family)

Savage, James. *A Genealogical Dictionary of the First Settlers of New England, Showing Three Generations of Those Who Came before May, 1692, on the Basis of Farmer's Register*. Boston: Little, Brown and Company, 1860.

Tyler, Charles and Norma Tyler. *The Descendants of Job Tyler Since 1619*. Zephyrhills, Florida: Self-published, 1985. (A follow-up to the Brigham genealogy)

Tyler, Laurence. "Abstract of a Will." NEHGR, 115:75 (1961).

Tyler, O. Z. *Sweet Land of Liberty*. Pompano Beach, Florida: Exposition Press, 1987. (fictionalized narrative history of early Job Tyler families)

Winthrop, John. *The History of New England from 1630 to 1649*, with notes by James Savage (2 volumes, Boston, 1825).

Index

Manufactured by Amazon.ca
Bolton, ON

10594094R00109